0

 **Your Fight**

Against Stockholm Culture:
How Criminal Syndicates Exploit Minorities and Victimentality to Stop National Greatness

by

Dr. Marcus Aurelius Roe

AuraPura Publishing

United States of America

GOD
is Whom this book is dedicated to, through LOGOS,
Jesus Christ, and the Living Holy Spirit.

Sooth.

Special thanks go to:

My Adoring Wife.
Our Loving Children.
Dad.
Mom.
Best Friends.

And anyone who ever called me out,
or challenged me to do **more**.

Copyright © 2025 Dr. Marcus Aurelius Roe.
All Rights Reserved.
AuraPura Publishing,
United States of America.

ISBNs:

Paperback:
978-1-967916-33-7

Hardback:
978-1-967916-34-4

Ebook:
978-1-967916-35-1

Audio:
978-1-967916-36-8

Ebook and Audio editions available at YourFight.club.

author@yourfight.club

24K Journal of Virtues Science (24K.cc)
AuraPura Publishing (AuraPura.org)
LRNR University (LRNR.online)
(DrM.cc)
Your Fight Club (YourFight.Club)

Contents

Contents

AGAINST STOCKHOLM CULTURE

Preface   i

Introduction   ix

ALPHA

I. Chaos   3

II. Progress   9

III. Progress of Progress   13

IV. To Err   17

V. Stagnation & Harm   21

VI. Diamond of Life   25

VII. Captivity   29

VIII. Advantages   33

IX. Overcome Evil with Good   39

Contents

X. Survival	47
XI. Value of Life	55
XII. Altruism	59
XIII. Stockholm Culture Abuse	65
XIV. Brutality & Mayhem	71
XV. Stage & Theatre	77
XVI. Victim-Hero	81
XVII. Victimentality	87
XVIII. Mediators	93
XIX. Utopia	99
XX. Feudal Efficiencies	105
XXI. Archetypes & Ethotypes	111
XXII. Strength Shamed	115
XXIII. Misfortune Media	123
XXIV. Hero-Victim	127
XXV. Lords of Victimentality	137
XXVI. Vindication	143
XXVII. Civilisational Rebirth	151
XXVIII. Symbolism & Curiosity	157

Contents

XXIX. Insults & Denial	161
XXX. Singular Christ	167
XXXI. Sin or Error	173
XXXII. Of Evil & Weakness	179
XXXIII. Opportunity	183

OMEGA   189

Introduction to Strategy	193
12. Motivation	197
11. Spectacle	203
10. Heroism	215
9. Comedy	221
8. Masculinity & Friendship	237
7. Truth & Humility	255
6. Love at Core & Its Truths	271
5. Empower Critical Thinking	281
4. International Cathedrals of Sin	299
3. High Priests of Genocide	337
2. The Memetic Warfare	353

Contents

1. LOGOS Against Self-Obsession 407

THE GOOD ENDING 431

Postface i

About the Author v

Prayer of Empowerment vii

AGAINST STOCKHOLM CULTURE

Preface

This book is not a novel, however it begins here with a story. I sit in our cozy little living room, sipping coffee on the battered old second-hand recliner, surrounded by my five children, playing with toys. One is drawing. Another is practising his letters. The smallest of all, coos in her big sister's arms.

I start, "hey kids, papa wants to tell you something important about being strong and brave."

The children look up at their father with curious eyes.

"You know how sometimes we feel scared or sad? Like when we fall down and scrape our knee?"

The children nod in unison, we've discussed things like this before.

"Or like when you can't find your favourite toy, you start to feel mad and upset."

My three-year-old daughter speaks up, "Yeah! Like when I loth my doll!"

"Exactly! And well you know papa and the big words... there's a thing people call 'Stockholm syndrome' that happens when people are feeling super scared, like really, really scared or trapped."

She speaks up again, "like when I got thtuck in the toy box!" She laughs precociously.

I laugh with her and smile, "yup! Like that, except maybe you start to think 'hey, it's not so bad being stuck in this toy box!' Maybe you get so silly you become friends with the toy box! Maybe you think the toy box will let you out if you're nice to it!"

"Nooooo!" she shouts and starts laughing even more now. The children all start laughing at each other, getting very excited, and a couple start chasing each other off down the hall.

"Though you're not supposed to be in the toy box, right? You're strong, beautiful, and capable children, and you deserve to be free. You're not supposed to be in that box, you know that. So when someone takes something away from us or tries to hurt us or trap us, that's not right. It's okay to feel scared, but we can't let that scare us too much. We have to remember that we're brave and smart, and we can use our great big brains to get away."

The children are now in full-swing chaos and excitement, barely listening any more, but they got the main points down, at least I hope.

So now I start to speak more loudly to get the final points across "when we think we like the toy box or the person who took our toy away or trapped us! That's Stockholm syndrome. We don't want to be captured by anyone or anything, do we?"

"NO!!" they yell out in excitement, all of them chasing each other now, laughing and smiling.

"So, what can we do when we feel scared or trapped? Well, first, we take deep breaths and remember that we're strong. Then, we think about how we can solve the problem. Maybe we need to ask for help, or maybe we just need to be patient and wait until it's safe to come out of our toy box."

The children laugh again and start singing a song about the toy box.

"Alright, kids, settle down! So, we've talked about the Stockholm Syndrome, there's another thing that can also happen when we're feeling really upset or sad for a long time, especially when we are made to feel like victims. Victimentality is when we start to think that being a victim is what makes us special or important. People will wear victimhood like a badge of honour, like it's something to be proud of. It's like saying, 'Oh no, I'm always held back, it's just so unfair, and nothing seems to work! Held back for life! I'm so oppressed!' They've been lied to and told a victim is the cool thing to be, and that it makes you special."

A couple of the children look at each other, confused.

"The thing is, kids, being a victim isn't what makes us special or important. What makes us special and important, or cool, is who we are as people: our love, the people we love, our kind hearts, our sense of humour, the things we overcome, as well as our creativity," I grab a couple of them and tickle, "and our infectious laughs!... Those things!... When we start to think that being a victim is what makes us special, it actually holds us back a lot. It can hold back everyone. It can hold back all society! It can stop all the people out there from being the amazing people they could be, and instead makes them less! It's like wearing a mask that forces us to focus only on how hurt or upset we are, instead of looking at all the good things in our lives."

The children nod, starting to understand.

"So, what can we do? Well, first, we need to recognise our emotions, recognise when we're thinking or feeling like a victim. Maybe someone said something mean to us, or we fell down and got hurt. That's okay! We all get hurt sometimes. Now then, we need to take a step back and say, 'Hey, I'm not just a victim. I'm a strong and capable person who can deal with things and find ways to improve my life.' Sometimes, that means asking for help, or talking to someone about what happened, or even taking some time to heal and feel better."

The children look at each other, smiling, actually glowing in fact.

"The most important thing is to remember that we're all in this together! We can all help each other be strong and brave, and support each other when things get tough. So let's make a pact to be kind to ourselves, each other, and others, and to always try to see the good in any situation, but without fooling yourself!"

"YAY!" The children call out in unison and then start to run around again.

"Most importantly, remember that you are all loved and special, no matter what happens. I always love you, so you always remember that your father loves you and that you are strong. You don't have to be held hostage by anything or anyone. You're free to be your amazing selves and do your best good!"

....

Amidst the chaos of my children's playtime, surrounded by toys and tiny human energies, I'm struck by the realisation that our most primal individual and family struggles are not so different from those faced by entire nations. Just as my precious little ones must confront their fears and insecurities to develop resilience and confidence, so too must we, as societies, overcome our own existential anxieties to forge a brighter future. The concept of Stockholm syndrome may seem strange to teach children, but it is actually fundamentally important because within its eerie echoes of strangeness are psychological manipulation and learned helplessness. The Stockholm culture serves as a poignant construct upon which we can recognise that even the strongest and most intelligent among us can be ensnared by insidious forces.

What's perhaps most striking is the way this phenomenon reflects our deep-seated desires for connection and belonging, a yearning that lead us to sacrifice our autonomy and agency in favour of others, ostensibly the foundation of great Good. As I look around at my children's joyful chaos, I'm reminded that the most profound struggles are not those we face as individuals, but those we face collectively. No more is this collectivity present than when asked to finally clean up the mess. A joyful order is very important to maintaining common progress. It's only by recognising our shared humanity, with all its vulnerabilities and imperfections as much to overcome, that we can begin to build a world where everyone has the freedom to flourish.

The corporate powers are attacking men and masculinity most, and have been for generations. They are now attacking the feminine, as well, but we can stop that. Their primary target is not individual men, but rather masculinity and heroism itself. This is no trivial observation, please note this well, for it speaks to the fundamental importance of community in human existence. Family, community, culture, and nation are how we define ourselves; how we can protect ourselves and our children. In other words, our very being is shaped by our relationships with others.

The notion of resistance to the dismantling of our communities, societies, families, cultures, nations, cohesion, and civil order takes on a new dimension when viewed through this lens. In this context, the thought alone becomes an act of ontological affirmation, a declaration of one's very social being and existence. Silence then is not simply emptiness of sound waves in an area. In human affairs the act of silence is the presence of non-speech, and it can be deafening.

In a world where the cacophony of corporate propaganda through all avenues of media rises to drown out our voices, silence can be seen as a form of nonviolent resistance that refuses to participate in the spectacle of victimhood. On the other end of the spectacle, though sometimes used in concert, comedy subverts the dominant narratives perpetuated by corporate powers. By exploiting the contradictions and absurdities inherent in these narratives, comedy highlights the artificial nature of opinions and constructs of beliefs which govern our lives; the memeplexes.

Victimentality is that curiously all-powerful memeplex wherein people derive a twisted sense of self-importance from victimhood. Society has internalised pain and oppression as somehow badges of honour in themselves, a claim to moral superiority that justifies their very existence. What an utterly tragic illusion this is! For in embracing vulnerability and imperfection as identity, we lose sight of true strengths, actual community, and identity attached to reality.

By understanding how shadowy powers utilise Victimentality and corporate resources to manipulate our kindest human emotions, we can begin to develop counter-memes that celebrate logic, rationality, resilience, perseverance, honesty, and community. It is essential to recognise the role that memetic strategies involving masculine boldness and subversive comedy play in shaping our collective perceptions and behaviours, especially toward power. These strategies present antidotes to the greatest weaknesses within our societies needing to be overcome right now.

Memes are elements of cultural transmission. In other words, memeplexes have the power to shape and be shaped by our collective consciousness. In this context, Reason must be supported by its actual aspects in Honesty, Analysis, and Perseverance. It is only through this combination of aspects in Reason that leads to greater and greater strength of Virtues in progress we can hope to crush these structures of material and illegitimate powers that control our lives, these archons of lust and hate.

Reason is far more than just cognitive. Reason represents the ascendant part of man, as he strives for greater order, so that it is the essential ethical Absolute. In other words, all legitimately moral principles are guided by higher Reason. Ultimately, the pursuit of Reason and Truth, especially toward greatest Good, must be grounded in a deep understanding of the human condition and needs of the human being, as well as our societies. Humans can't do much Good at all fighting for our very lives in mortal competition, especially in youth. This all requires us to engage with the most profound questions of existence: What does it mean to be human? What does it mean to be human striving for the higher things in the greater (capital W) World? What is the nature of reality? How do we reconcile our individual desires with the needs of the collective?

In this sense, the struggle against corporate powers and crime syndicates becomes a microcosm for the larger struggle against the forces that seek to control our communities and lives. It is only by recognising the deeper structures of power at play that we can hope to effect real change. Liberty is in recognising and doing the greatest Good you can. Freedom is culpability. Our freedom is a burden, a responsibility to shape our own destinies and create a better World for ourselves and future generations.

Oh and what ado is this though?
You are but bid to tread lightly
'round each soul's proclaim'd woe,
entombing all your progeny tightly
masquerading an eternity in tow!

Introduction

Commoditising people is rather identical to demoralising them. Around the world today, you can find good people made to feel like less and damaged people made to feel as though they were whole or complete. The reality of modernity is downright psychotic. This is why 'Your Fight' was written. The purpose of this book is to reach those who wish to leaven society with a passion for Truth, and drive home some essential facts along the way. This moment didn't start now, and tomorrow won't be won without yesterday, so we need to build the future in the present.

My goal in the writing is to sharpen the spearhead of a broader collective consciousness, one that seeks to transcend the ephemeral nature of destructive narratives. This entails anchoring it to the bedrock of reality and truth, insofar as it is honestly attainable. It is a tome designed to ignite passionate authenticity and stoke a blistering flame, that shall never go out, for the unrelenting pursuit of absolute truth. This is a work to extract the seeds of division before they can grow to destroy us.

Society can become so alienated from populations that the people within feel like outsiders held hostage. Stockholm culture is wrapped in a cloak of 'fairness' and sold as a solution, although it is not, merely expanding the number of populations so alienated. Stockholm culture promotes societal Stockholm syndrome, which emotionally manipulates people into pretending everything is okay, just to survive, and merely to get along. People go along with things simply to stay safe, even to the point of feeling guilt if they don't. This makes people much more passive to manipulations and controls generally, which is popular with international corporate monopolies and ethnic criminal syndicates, especially the most wealthy ones. We already have enough dividing us in actuality. You can be for your own without getting into any hateful muck, and in fact our ability to help depends upon our working from a position of strength.

The introduction of mechanisms to alienate people, especially as abusive of the natural inclination towards altruism, is an effective strategy to enslave them mentally. However, the more a person can be convinced of their fundamental difference from the rest of the population, the more like a victim they are made to feel, and the greater the magnification in victimability. To undo this Stockholm culture, it is necessary to sort through the foundations underlying it in glorified permanent victimhood and Victimentality.

Alienating people from their society is the most effective way to turn otherwise normal people into permanent victims, however it is accomplished, whether through immigration to cause minority status, desexualisation, hypersexualisation, identity dysphorias, or racial theories in power dynamics. People tormented by Victimentality identify as permanent victims. They work passionately for the deconstruction of standards within the society terrorising them in their warped and victimised perspective, whether propagandised or psychotic.

Victimentality makes a person attach themselves to this identity emotionally and as a constant ready excuse, rather than taking ownership of their own mistakes. It makes them feel entitled to ridiculous and impossible things. This disconnection of people from other people within a society is degradation of the most foul kind. This system is primarily concerned with reducing each individual into more manageable and replaceable economic units, and it will do whatever it can to accomplish this goal. Pride in the self goes before the fall, but group shame comes after the lie. Not having pride in your community and for society which deserves it is treason, and not being able to means you are at war.

People are not mere economic units and making them so, as replaceable and essentially worthless for their particular qualities or how they play individually into their natural society and culture, is nothing short of an abysmal and demoralised slavery. It is an affront to the very essence of individuality and the greatness of the individual. It is further a corruption of community and a denigration of its importance to society. Suggesting the human as replaceable commodity is a denial of the cultural and environmental needs for the fulfilment of potential.

Commoditisation of people is further a basic denial of the Spirit. This process, this reductionist calculus, has created a society where individuals are treated as mere interchangeable cogs in a vast machine, devoid of agency, autonomy, or purpose. With replacement eternally horizon-present, how can anyone sleep? The people out there are lulled to sleep in life by the denial of their basic importance. Do not attack the sleeping. The lullers are relying upon you kicking down. Punch up at the ones on top, the ones lulling the masses to sleep. When you punch, aim up, and not at the sleepers. Aim to uplift and awaken, because people, despite their flaws, are precious and deserve your best.

The people in power are not trying to stop racism and Victimentality; they don't care. They are benefitted most by it, and it is the reason they support any policies which increase Victimentality. They're more racist than anyone you know and use the rising Victimentality as an excuse to attack our declining standards in the passing. Communities and nations deserve their own standards, which benefit them most. Otherwise, what's the point of standards?

Some materialists and spiritualists take reality seriously. We need all who take reality seriously to take spirituality more so, and not to allow people to use it as yet another escapism. All are demeaned in objectification of the individual outside of their spirit and that role in the natural communalism of real human society. It makes us all commodities when basic humanity is denied... we are hogtied and violated, as wealth is extracted from all communities. Church originally meant community and the natural churches are hurting badly.

This "antiracism," as engineered in their propaganda, is the corporate dismantling of their primary natural competition: order. It is essentially **war**, served lukewarm. It is chaotic antihumanism, and a denial of children's basic right to live in societies **free of mortal competition**, and without people in their lives and communities who hate them and would rather see them dead simply for being who they are.

In order to identify the best ways to awaken people, it becomes necessary to pull through the threads most foundational to the system and lay them out for common dissection, so that we can derive the most useful information and strategies. This book's organising schema is therefore in two primary parts. First there is a primer, an exposition on the current state of our World within Victimentality and Stockholm culture, where we find ourselves bound to confusing complexities, purposefully made all the more confusing to harm us. Secondarily, the primer becomes realised through explorations of strategies in real-world mechanics of power and memetics, as social constructs with very real rules, dependencies, and outcomes.

Part Alpha, the primer, delineates and clarifies the imperative to assert and reclaim humanity's dignity in our connection to the World around us. This section of the book provides a framework for understanding the complexities of our reality, a reality that is both familiar and alien, like an old friend who has undergone a strange metamorphosis. It includes descriptions of our reality and how focusing on certain types of strategies might interface with it more efficiently. How should you go into a fight? You need to know who and what you're up against.

Part Omega, the solutions, surveys the memetics and power structures that perpetuate this commodification of humanity, as well as those that may work best against it, examining the ways in which institutions and societal norms combine in maintaining the landscape. This is not a polemic against these entities as they exist or superficial settings; rather, it is an attempt to dissect the underlying cultural dynamics that drive individual and social human behaviours, revealing the intricate networks of relationships and dependencies that bind us all, and to encourage the best within that. It is so very important to have objective viewpoints on social and memetic matters in society. What is the point of an opinion that does no good?

Omega also serves as a call to action, a distress signal urging those who have read thus far to take up arms against the forces that seek to reduce our existence to mere statistical abstractions. It is the larger portion of the book because of this. It is an invitation to join a collective endeavour, one that seeks to reclaim our humanity, to re-assert our connection to the world in reality, and to forge a new path forward, untainted by the machinations of unnatural and artificial power and control against our interests. You need to train, you need discipline, you need a clear mind, and, most importantly, you need a strategy that is extremely effective against an enemy which is everywhere and not always easy to identify, but of whom the majority can be turned into an ally, to some degree, instantaneously.

The book is not merely a treatise on the state of our World or some empty manifesto but a guide for change. This is an existential scream to the rest of humanity who can listen, for those who would seek to challenge the darkening state of affairs foreshadowing inevitable destruction, and propagate a brighter future. It is an offer to join forces with others who share this vision, to pool knowledge, skills, and collective energies in pursuit of common goals in humanity's spiritual expedience. Sharing hidden truth makes you more valuable than gold to others, especially truth that saves life. This is even more true despite troubles and hatred you receive for it.

Let this book be as a service to all, the author but servant and nothing but for God, the Creator.

Bear truth forward, now.
— Dr. Roe

"Whatever things were rightly said among all men, are the property of us Christians."

~Justin Martyr

"Do not act as if you had ten thousand years to throw away.
Death stands at your elbow.
Be good for something while you live and it is in your power."
"When you arise in the morning,
think of what a precious privilege it is to be alive,
to breathe, to think, to enjoy, to love."

~Marcus Aurelius

"Other people's views and troubles can be contagious.
Don't sabotage yourself by unwittingly adopting negative,
unproductive attitudes through your associations with others."
Instead, "attach yourself to what is spiritually superior,
regardless of what other people think or do."

~Epictetus

ALPHA

"The anxieties of these times, deceitfulness of riches,
and appearance of other desires choke LOGOS,
and it becomes unfruitful."
"You will hear of wars and rumours of wars.
See that you are not alarmed,
for this must take place,
but the end is not yet."

~Jesus Christ

"Everywhere I have sought peace and not found it,
except in a corner by myself with a little book."
"If God were our one and only desire
we would not be so easily upset when
our opinions do not find approval."

~The Imitation of Christ

....

Denial of truth causes ownership of lies.
Through the ages, man has searched & yearned after Words,
for through truest Words come the greatest powers:
new paradigms that turn over tables &
throw enriched high priests down temple stairs.

Long forgotten wars;
The product of trusting,
Father's father's sacred mores,
Blood powdered & dusting.

Infinite ancestral befores,
Coats aged & musty.
Incalculable remorse,
Bone like metal rusting
An era lost in error;
A sea lost in tears.
A ship found none fairer;
A shipwreck none hear.

And the wind blew strong,
Tugging firm on tattered sail.
Whistling through morbid song,
A jig is danced by those who fail.

Hearts chilled of all whom listen.
Requiems falling short
In encapsulating all that's missing.
Regardless any effort,

This is how their world ends,
In the shadow of its Sun.
No lasting trace or evidence;
In revelry & 'fun.'

As the old dies in its prison
Destroyed for its treason,
A new World has arisen
In beautiful order through Reason.

I. Chaos

Any view of the World that encompasses some final vindication or salvation for everybody, free of immanent expectations and spiritual actions, is a view handed down from on high to those below. It is to sate the fooled, or deemed foolish, to continue their paces and efforts toward something not in their benefit, but the profit of their masters primarily if not alone. They are taught foolish things and only promoted if they espouse them, to keep them so enslaved. This isn't because it is good, it is because of a basic mockery of Christ in community and business affairs, at the very core of secular society itself, and among much of the religious as well these days.

Nothing in the material World was ever constructed to benefit everybody. Anyone that said otherwise is some form of dupe or liar, possibly a thief himself and if not a self-aggrandising Godless fool. Such claims are made in order to fool people. The road to greatness has been paved by the great with the aid of their community, or over their backs and the backs of anyone else prone to being subdued, namely the weak or weakened. Any deviation has merely changed direction for the scenic routes at best, if not the outright granting of power to the would-be weak using enough detrimental memetic structures slipped into society. Great minds must think for themselves, otherwise they could not be great! The would-be or should-be great now, however, are held hostage in this environment, wherein their very security and safety are not assured, and they have been convinced in propaganda that sharing their healthy opinions about basic standards would bring ill repute and hatred upon them.

Ultimately, standards are actually all about assuring the best progress. Progress on larger scales isn't something you can want into existence, it simply always is. When greatness is forestalled, it merely leaves a vacuum for corrupt alienated people, that is the greediest and most willing to act criminally. Progress in life generally simply is always, whether you like it or not, and lasting greatness cannot be achieved without this realisation. Progress is a function of time and time is a function of energy, like life energy. Without life, progress ceases, but observation ceases too since observation and progress both rely completely upon life, and life energy. If we accept our demise individually, culturally, or nationally in terms of standards, then we admit to our deserving the destruction.

How long does it take to expect the best of yourself? The myth of universal salvation is powerful and attractive. However, it is also a notion so ridiculously naïve, it's as if reality itself has been warped by forces hell-bent on perpetuating mediocrity. Any viewpoint that posits a World where all can find solace in some grand, cosmic vindication without individual spiritual progress is nothing more than a thinly veiled attempt to pacify the masses, to lull them to sleep with a false sense of security. For what purpose? To kill off the spiritual urges in the slaves for grappling with the complexities of existence, which run contrary to the basking in frigid darkness of ignorance so hatefully provided.

Of course, this is precisely what the masters desire: a world where the ignorant are content to trudge along, blind to the machinations of those who pull the strings from above. Weak or depraved people are much easier to control. The institution of compartmentalised corporate enslavement is sold as 'freedom.' In the warped comprehension called 'Whig history,' this 'freedom' is extended, like the shadow of self-ignorance it is, upon a population too stultified and poisoned to realise the injuries incurred upon them in the hands of their masters. Freedom becomes the freedom to entertain the self with psychoses, and various smaller distractions as well. The slaves are fooled, for the masters promote this as a benevolent scheme aimed at elevating humanity as a whole. Somehow being able to make up the rules to one's own life outside community is presented as evidence of a higher existence, however it is a virtual existence and fraudulent obviously at face value. In actuality, all tolerance promoted is toward mediocrity and distortion of culture, rather than where it belongs with those still developing toward a better existence. They have empathically displaced our legitimate vulnerable such as children with artificially concocted vulnerable populations such as immigrants. This is a cynical ploy designed to perpetuate the unnatural power imbalances. In actuality, our social relationships comprise the preponderance of existence, and our relationships within the Universe constitute all parts of existence.

In slavery, the system is claimed great and progress is sold as possible. The masters teach an inevitability in technology and human ingenuity that can somehow defy the natural order of things and create an existence where people can thrive no matter setting, or false self-beliefs and lack of objective personal development. Transhumanism is the natural product of this psychotic consumerism, because human beings can never be seen as whole and the less whole they are the better for the enslavement system. Once fantasies become all to enough people, which is to say 'their god,' it becomes imperative for them to make it real. Transhumanism would be nothing more than a pipe dream if it were not a too real nightmare looming on the horizon, a fleeting illusion wrapped up in terror and demonic forces born of wishful thinking, ignorance, and powerful Orwellian propaganda. The actuality of the situation is far more mundane and terrible than the fantasies, regardless any marketing claims of billionaires who wish to chip your brain. Progress is not some abstract concept to be wished into existence or forced, by attempting to take over the position of God with technology. Progress is a function of time, as stated, and with a death despite any strengths admits to more fundamental weaknesses, regardless of how strong, obviously, but it can also be due to societal weaknesses.

What of the sanctity of Life? Life is that boundary of current existence that we cling to desperately, it makes sense, and survival is argued as the primary reason some treat life generally as sacred. However, there is more to the sanctity of Life than this. Without Life, there can be no real progress, for it is in the ebb and flow of existence within the plasmatic aura of Life's energy that we are able to observe, to learn, and to adapt. Without time and observation we are stuck in some perpetual cycle of ignorance, forever doomed to repeat our own errors and the mistakes of ancestors. If society goes long enough without necessary observation in complete contradiction to progress, Life energy on Earth will cease because the demonic spiritual forces that would arise out of a mankind, so unhinged from nature, would destroy all life. So-called 'freedom of speech,' the protection offered to those sharing less popular observations, is important insofar as Truth saves us from evil, as detailed above.

I ask you, dear reader, what happens when Life ceases? What happens when the great cycle of birth, growth, decay, and rebirth is interrupted? We must not be fooled into thinking that progress is possible without acknowledging the inherent cruelty and indifference of existence generally as the ideal environment for the development of Good. We cannot hope to continue in our efforts for progress without noticing that there are evil forces that would gladly serve up horrors as wholesome, while poisoning us all the while.

Let us not be seduced by the false promise of some individual salvation despite a drowning world, as others do. Let us instead demand of ourselves more in the confrontation of the cold and hard reality of our situation: that we are but mere mortals, subject to the whims of unthinking and largely uncontrollable movements in the World in need of any advantages we can muster in our struggle for Life against hateful forces. For it is only in accepting these existential truths that we can begin to make something stable out of the World we inherited, as chaotic as it may be.

"Opposition brings concord.
Out of chaotic dispute comes the fairest harmony."
"The most beautiful order can be born out of chaos."
"There is nothing permanent besides change."
"Character is destiny."

~Heraclitus

"To put the world to order,
put the nation in order before.
To put the nation in order,
put the family in order before.
To put the family in order,
cultivate inward life primarily;
we must first set our hearts right."
"There is never a case when the root is in
disorder and yet the branches are in order."

~Confucius

Our minds hold tight

In their folds a sight,

Of past greatness

& a road fateless.

We toil for the presages

Of unknown places & future ages!

For who would be so mad

To plant a seed if he had

Neither thought to a tree

Nor mind turned toward eternity?

II. Progress

Progress always is, though many have some difficulty fully coming to terms. When you are born, you progress from a human fetus to a somewhat more autonomous infant. Mother provides for all nourishment of helpless and precious baby you, and you are dependent. Some time later, you began to walk and talk, gaining even more independence. The following decades have to do with progressing not toward independence but from one form of dependence to another, and this should be less of a problem than 'it has become,' in our modern society.

Every single life event is progress. Eventually you die and stop progressing, having met with the ultimate visible stage of life energy progression. Some will wake up along the way and begin to understand that all life change is progress, the primary progress truly possible in the larger picture, and it cannot be stopped. This means that even downward trends for the individual will eventually lead to upward trends for society, from a high enough perspective. Ultimately, the most destructive people on Earth also contribute to Good, even if merely as hurdles and to challenge those more at liberty to recognise that Good.

The ceaseless nature of time, like a thief in the night, steals upon us, claiming another chunk of our lives as its own with much energy spent. For what? Many of us struggle to come to terms with this constant flux. We cling to moments of stasis, of stability, as if they were life rafts on a sea of chaos. As we age, we forge our own paths and dependencies which are most often very similar to those of our own parents and grandparents. We marry, we procreate, we become parents, and then grandparents, as bonded to others, hopefully happily.

Threads of time, impermanence, and the human condition must be confronted in the visage of empty nostalgia and unrealistic futurism. These are tendencies to glorify the past or idealise the future opposed to an embracing of the present for its logical connections to both. If we are able to surrender to reality what belongs to reality ("render unto Caesar what is Caesar's") and the inevitability of time's passage, we may flow with its currents. When we recognise and work within the boundaries of actual reality, we gain dramatically because our energies are not wasted. Like a river taking the best path, we carve through the landscape, unencumbered by the weights of illogical expectations and emotional resistance which culminate in our anxious fantasies.

The real progress is not purely some abstraction or idealised state, but the lived experience in constant and honed growth, of becoming more fully ourselves. Embrace the progress, even if not always easy or consistent, and define it and let it define you in the best way you can. We will have moved with the patterns of reality and the discourse of life, iteratively refining ourselves, like a sculptor shapes marble.

Each iteration in each phase of existence is an opportunity to deepen the symphony of our being. Peace is not in material notions of "happiness" or "fulfilment." Happiness and fulfilment are most sustainable in simple fact of living a life that is authentically contributory to the whole in empowering others. True progress is not some distant horizon, but something built into the very essence of Life, which is to be extracted and moulded experientially through our improving understanding. Let us rise with tides, embracing the present in all imperfections as personal opportunities. We move forward with a radical responsibility for the appropriation of progress toward the promised path of Good in our own humanity.

"Practice these things,
immerse yourself in them,
and all will see your progress."

"I press on toward the goal for the prize of the upward call of God in Christ Jesus."
~Apostle Paulus

"Be not conformed to this world, but be reformed in the newness of your mind, that you may prove what is the Good, and the acceptable, and the perfect will of God."
"If you cannot recollect yourself continuously, do so once a day."
~The Imitation of Christ

"The path of the righteous is like the light of dawn,
that shines brighter and brighter until the full day."
~Proverbs 4:18

"Behold, I am doing a new thing; now it springs forth,
do you not perceive it?
I will make a way in the wilderness and rivers in the desert."
~Isaiah 43:19

....

Sin is disease, repentance is medicine…
if you don't stop the sin, you did not take the medicine.

They never forgot,

What is lost in the fabric of experience,

Can be trapped inside and locked,

But a mere portion,

The irony of art is in what is sought,

For perfection in expression,

When perfecting is in the present,

And everything exists in impression.

III. Progress of Progress

Progress can be defined as some change into another form that cannot be stopped, but only adjusted. The word has always connoted inevitability. Even in abject failure is found progress, because mortal error and destruction leave room for opportunities in growth for others. The failure of some and the success of others is selection and is evolution. Failure and success are equally selective. Evolution is merely the progress of progress, because Life changes, as it was designed to do.

We will never see how the laws of progress were written, and we do not need to in order to understand that progress does indeed exist. The laws of time are outside our direct purview, though they can be detected as a function of our experience in life energy. It is obvious that time's procession would be impossible without the progression of Life, for what other things have such a connection with time as the many varied forms of life?

Progress tantalises us with promises of growth, improvement, and advancement. Let us not be fooled by the veneer of control that this concept affords. As stated, progress is merely a change into another form. It is a force as relentless as time itself, unyielding in nature by its very essence. Change is always some form of progress, even when it is not apparent how at the moment when much is lost.

Is it not true that evolution of life is the very embodiment of progress? What else can this unbelievably gorgeous and gradual unfolding of Life's very development be, if not the magnificent demonstration of a most divine aspect of Life's design? Indeed, evolution is proof of God, as the very progression of progress caked into the nature of reality. Natural non-selection in ceaseless death reveals the necessary adaptations as boundaries in the shapes Life takes to 'fit' a progressing World and living order. Life changes out of necessity.

The inexorable march of progress in time is inextricably linked to our very existence. We are all bound together in the shared experience of time, an enigmatic force transcending our ability for full comprehension. Time is meaningless without life to experience it. The procession has been unfolding for eons, each step in the dance floating over an eternity of deaths, time cut short to a tune. The evolution of our minds is the most crucial element in all of this.

We are co-creators with God but the hands, and we have been perpetually dancing with the oscillations between growth and stagnation, as if caught in a fundamental force that draws us toward greater self-awareness and improvement. To truly understand the necessity of learning from errors or sins, we must first grasp this fundamental reality: that our existence is inextricably linked to the progression of Life. Species change to become better suited to their environments and this is a fundamental principle that underlies Life.

There is more to positive progress than mere survival or adaptation, especially to do with culture. For in the depths of evolutionary history, we find hints of a deeper purpose and a drive towards complexity in the subconsciousness and consciousness that whispers of nuances built into the very structure of reality. An intricate balance, ever unfolding over eons, brought us to where we are today, and it pervades the very texture of lived and social experience.

It may seem almost clichéd, but there is an expansive web of causalities and consequences in reality. Each step forward, each decision made, each scene, and every error sends ripples throughout the oceans of existence. The plays of progress move through individual experiences but 'on stages and with audiences.' Every line read contributes to the ever-unfolding narrative of reality. We are not in the audience always nor are we expected to be passive. We are supposed to be participating actors, cocreating how God intended. Our choices, actions, and decisions all resonate, influencing the comedies, tragedies, and dramas in life, far beyond our own lives.

In the natural flow between growth, stagnation, and decline, improvements eventually sift to the surface. Improvement in reality is a form of truth. We recognise that every step forward, no matter how small or seemingly insignificant, is an element to progress in both improvement and truth. Each movement made and each decision taken contributes to the purpose and plot. Seek expedience and the next meaning, but do not pretend to know more than God. Tempt the fates with purpose in reason only.

We must remain attuned to the harmonies of life, those things that are important and make the most sense. Let's explore further how these forces alter our perceptions, behaviours, and decisions. How do we harness the power of progress to create a more natural and beneficial production of individual growth and societal progress?

"Now is the time to get serious about living your ideals. How long can you afford to put off who you really want to be? Your nobler self cannot wait any longer. Put your principles into practice – now. Stop the excuses and the procrastination. This is your life! You aren't a child anymore. The sooner you set yourself to your spiritual program, the happier you will be. The longer you wait, the more you'll be vulnerable to mediocrity and feel filled with shame and regret, because you know you are capable of better. From this instant on, vow to stop disappointing yourself. Separate yourself from the mob. Decide to be extraordinary and do what you need to do – **NOW**."

~Epictetus

In the cultural hush, nearly devoid of shame,
A lazy dance of errors, grand and mundane.
Not but mistakes, and limits of the path laid bare,
In growth for transformation; the way we all share.

Embracing the Light, we find Celestial Might,
Through trials' crucible, winning ourselves for Christ.
As the Apostle sought to free every heart,
Seek all you divine discourse, and never depart.
Reason guides us through the labyrinth of mind,
Balance, in Grace of His deepest wisdoms we find.

Upon this trusty loom, we are woven anew,
Threads of strength and virtuous fibres sown through.
Each lesson builds upon your previous designs,
Generating new life, as your world re-aligns.
Strength and survival are not just personal tests,
But fundamental principles of Life, and nothing less.

Let us learn from failures, yet to traditions do hold,
Past darkness of ignorance await stories yet untold.
Whatever doesn't kill us, refines our will toward the Way,
And whatever does kill us has that final say.

IV. To Err

On the grand scales of evolution, errors are not mistakes or failures, but rather opportunities for growth and transformation. The process of natural selection, where individuals with advantageous traits are more likely to survive and reproduce, is a prime example of error's role in shaping the trajectory of Life. Errors are essential stepping stones on the path toward progress. Error allows species to adapt and evolve in response to changing environments, and it is a lovely thing that we see it reflected on the individual as well as cultural levels rhyming upward and inward, like a universal song.

"Error" thus takes on profound significance, as it becomes clear that our very survival depends on embracing uncertainty and exploiting its possibilities. It's only the things that kill us that don't make us stronger. What about the role of intentionality in this process? Do we, as conscious beings, play a role in our own evolution through error and adaptation? Toward what end ultimately? Is it not upward? Inward? What does that mean? They're abstractions, referring to the expansion of immanent Good, but abstracted for a reason. What is Good is not always as clear in the day-to-day experience without a more concentrated focus on depth and fundamentals in meaning over time. The answer is in the Grace found of Apostle Paulus's constant prayer, that is divine discourse through LOGOS, where individuals actively seek to incorporate wisdom into every aspect of their lives and comprehension, with no corner of life left in the darkness.

Errors are opportunities for growth. The lessons from errors contain the catalysts for transformation toward greater alignment with He Who is within you. By acknowledging and learning from mistakes, our own and others', we can harness the power of our God-gifted faculties and hone them. Understanding of progress is inextricably linked to the progress of conscious evolution, in which Selection of Selection, that is discrimination and spirituality, shapes the future of humanity. A complete perspective on this now revealed connection, in evolutionary principles and the subconscious-conscious Soul complex, opens up possibilities for harnessing the Apostle's constant prayer to propel ourselves and humanity forward on the path toward ever greater wisdom.

Extinction is the ultimate catalyst for evolutionary transformation. It is here that we must confront the existential imperative: that which kills us (instead of society) makes society fitter, and that which in society permits us to survive shifts fitness into an altogether different evolutionary modality, as defined in Spiritual Mate Selection Theory of Resurrexit Spiritus (published 2023 but written across 2022). In the greater Spiritual dance of Life with death, Life understanding itself then becomes the most important agent of change, currently in promulgation of the relationship between this theory and a Christian future. "For there are three witnesses: the Spirit, the water, and the blood; and these three are one." (1 John 5: 7-8) A cultural and intellectual species moves forward through the relentless testing and validation of traditions as they aid survival. The Universe, a singularly whole anti-stagnant force magnifier, demands constant change, so we must become resilient to all possible changes. Each iteration builds upon the previous, generating new versions of existence, and conscious experience.

This sacred imperative in the constant generation of new life requires sacrifice on all fronts. Some iterations will falter and perish earlier, while others will emerge stronger later in newer generations of them. This is a metaphorical and metaphysical narrative buried within the reality of the Father and Son, with the ultimate offering of Life for the highest expression of Spirit: God through the Holy Spirit, understood only by way of the Son, LOGOS. As "above," so "below." In this magnificent orchestration, errors are redeemed by learning, spiritual selection, free will, and natural selection, conserving the essence of Spirit and Life for their grand purposes. The voice of God is ever present, in you by accumulated knowledge of His Goodness through Christ. This is the dimension of Grace leading ever higher infinitely, where imperfection is used as ammunition in transformation, as darkness of our ignorance and weaknesses yields to the Light that He embodies.

Strength and survival are not merely about personal resilience, but are fundamental principles of Life: existence, culture, community, society, and nation. Whatever doesn't kill you serves only to further refine the imperatives of survival, and whatever does kill you refines the species overall. So whatever kills you is progress, regardless how grateful I am that you are reading this book, and regardless your many multi-splendid talents. The notion may seem macabre, perhaps even cruel, but trust me when I say that it is nothing short of a fundamental truth: the more strengths of an individual, the greater the error that ruins them, and perhaps the more fundamental the lessons to be extracted from their failures, and even death.

The answers to questions
Are shipwrecks of oceans,
Hidden under deflections.
Tides reveal transgressions.
Go free a world of pretensions.

Live life my children.

Against infinity, we seek,
Don't listen to the doubters
For eternity, I speak.

Go now in your errands,
Ignore distorted lenses.
Know Whom is in possession.
Guest kept when unattended,
Secret to questions ascended.

Live life my children.

Against what's lost, we vie,
We are the co-authors
For ignorance is contra-life.

Lines remain unbroken,
All redeemed in the end,
Choices made, we defend,
Caught up in indecision
While it only matters when.

And live life my children.

V. Stagnation & Harm

In more ancient days, it was simple to control people, since most were not well-educated and books were often difficult to come by, especially for poor people. This meant that rewriting history was an easy trick for the powerful. Further, literacy was not common in most societies and education was primarily oral through day-to-day transmissions and parental lessons. Oral transmission through families had massive cultural benefits in many ways, no doubt, but this arrangement suggests a lack of educational infrastructure and limited availability of information not directly pertinent to livelihood and the community.

Power brokers of knowledge wielded their influence with ease, as the masses meekly submitted to the whims of their 'betters,' without much to go on for matters outside their purview. Education was based upon tribal, familial, and trade affiliations. Knowledge was guarded for various of these reasons, passed down through generations like a sacred flame. Parents and grandparents, custodians of wisdom and keepers of the collective tribal memory, imparted the fruits of their and forebears' experiences with ancestral benevolence. Who better to instruct than those closest and most similar to you?

Fast-forward to our own era, where the tables have turned and 'knowledge' has become a veritable buffet. Books, like water, flow freely or flood over rather, and the once-exclusive realms of learning through reading has been made ubiquitous. The world is awash in information, a digital deluge that threatens to drown all in meaningless trivia with many all the more ignorant for it. So despite this overabundance of information, we find ourselves beset on all sides by ignorance's pernicious partner: error.

Oh, errors! In our thoughts, beliefs, and actions, errors and ignorance corrupt our basic interaction with the world. Is there a solution to errors amid the chaos of information overload? None other than that most underrated and first virtue: magnanimity, often found doing business as "humility." It is in acknowledging our ignorance, our fallibility, and our propensity for error that we may begin to learn from those very mistakes, and it all requires seeing the self from the proper perspective. It requires being the "bigger person." Socrates's examined life means subjecting ourselves and our own understandings to scrutiny. Positive particular progress requires this self-understanding and criticality in opinions.

Not finding progress for the particular is a huge waste of our time, and this is so bad because time is far more than simply a measure of duration. Time is that conveyance of survival through space, that very essence of Life's experience itself. Time must move forward with progress, for stagnation is not an option in this Universe. Stagnation is alien to the Universe, and can only harm. Stagnation is evil, because the only supremacy in stagnation is in the destruction of the strong. The destruction of the spiritually strong is, in fact, metaphorically identical with killing Christ.

The scourge of stagnation only persists so long as society restricts the truly and spiritually strong. Stagnation is a darkness threatening to consume all that is good and just. It is not merely a trivial inconvenience or a temporary setback; nay, stagnation is founded in a pattern of behaviours promulgated throughout society. Like a fast-acting cultural cancer, it eats away at all levels of a civilisation.

In the grasp of stagnation, even the strongest are reduced to mere husks, their vitality sapped by the crushing weight of a parasitic society of complacency and waste. The strong are destroyed at the altar of the weak and cowardly. The most heinous crime imaginable is the destruction of Good and those capable of greater Good. Evil seeks out destruction, and recognises the spiritually strong as enemies capable of stopping it. When the mighty fall, it is not merely a matter of personal defeat, but it is also catastrophic for society.

Stagnation is evil, and its destruction of the strong is in its instrumentation. For when we succumb to the temptation of complacency, we invite the darkness to consume us whole, in our freely willed ignorance and weakness. So what now? Did not the Pharisees seek His destruction out of their own insecurities and jealousy over the strengths He exhibited? Is this not essentially what the largest corporations and big government do concertedly to small businesses, communities, and individuals all the time and for the same reasons?

We must find ways to resist stagnant forces and insist upon our own dominion instead of the false powers over us that seek enslavement of all. We must cultivate a sense of purpose, of direction, and of drive for it is only through the pursuit of excellence and virtues that we may hope to transcend that abyss of stagnation. Even in the darkest of times, there is always hope, always a glimmer available that guides us onward. For all freedom exists in the mere ability to recognise and do Good, no matter how infinitesimal it is forced to be. Stagnation is the operation through which evil can eventually get to the weak and juvenile among the strong. Succumbing to stagnation is an opening up of our souls and giving over to the materialism and moving pleasures which grant only short-term satisfactions. What about after those fleeting experiences though?

We must confront this spectre of stagnation that haunts our very existence, a monster feeding on complacency, growing stronger with each passing moment. We must face it head-on, with all the courage and conviction at our disposal. All life is ultimately sacrificed in the service of that higher Life, God through Christ. Errors are but opportunities for learning, for growth, in conservation of Spirit and Life. When we humble ourselves before Christ and receive His Grace, we reconcile our errors by way of faith, and faith's requisites to the greater Good. It is through this very mechanism that we may come to understand Christ in celestial terms and how LOGOS attaches us to God.

> "Therefore I tell you, do not be anxious about your life,
> what you will eat or what you will drink,
> nor about your body, what you will put on.
> Is not life more than food, and the body more than clothing?"
> ~Jesus Christ

> "The soul is more precious than all the riches of the world,
> for it is made in the image of God."
> ~St. Chrysostom

> "The glory of God is a human being fully alive;
> and to be alive consists in beholding God."
> ~Irenaeus

....

Ever after, the golden ray
Lay just beyond the sky,
& night carries another day,
We huddle by & by.
Machinations stumble all,
Deadening the variance.
As fascinations stall,
Depress motivations curious.

Be not controlled by any thing or man...
Sacrifice the lower self to save the higher self.

NOW.

VI. Diamond of Life

Time and experience feel much like a veil, or imposed limit. It is known that beyond this veil is unfamiliar death, that great boundary of our reality excelling all human pretensions as meaningless impositions by comparison. Meanwhile, we live our entirety of life as consciousness-subconsciousness, within the experience perfectly couched of being energetic creations, always at the threshold of energy outside time. The veil is therefore revealed as just that with nothing more needed, and we can bask in the experience in time, despite the spectre of death.

Life is the diamond. What a wondrous thing it is, my God! A thing of beauty, of complexity, and of sheer unadulterated perfection in design. In its fractal depths hide the secrets of the Universe, the mysteries that have puzzled thoughtful men for a dozen hundred centuries or more, surely. Time, all experience, and all deaths are merely facets of the diamond of Life. The living instructions within, the law in God's language of Life, broadcast a filtered light through us, shading in the colour of our experiences and lessons. This is why our lives so often mirror those of our ancestors. Unfolding resplendent glory upon us with each passing moment, the gift in God's Life for us, a thing of awe-inspiring majesty if treated as such.

Diamonds transform from coal but if you place coal in a jeweler's display case, it can not transform into a diamond no matter how much time is given it. The necessary conditions occur deep in the Earth. If you remove the coal from the necessary conditions in environment, it never has the chance to become a diamond. This is a metaphor of transformation, metamorphosis, and fundamental changes. The diamond cannot shine if it is coal. It is not the coal itself, however, that undergoes transformation, but rather its very essence, its molecular structure, the carbon composite of the coal. It is the carbon which is reformed.

Consider the fact that it rains and shines on bad and good equally. A material neutral to us and our pains or sins demonstrates that the experience of vivified plasmatic material energetic form set against the brutal tyrant of physics is important, and the most vital content in time as the movement of energetic thought. I submit to you that this means we are of infinite value to God, Whom is outside that time and loves us too much to interfere. Here we can catch a glimpse of the purpose God intended with all our pain through basic deductive reasoning. We must come to terms with the limitations of this mortal coil to lift the veil, and recognise the fundamental constraints that govern our own existence, which is to say 'how we can grow best.' We are not immortals, nor can we transcend the laws of physics that govern the material.

The threads of past and present converge in a web of causality. The coal-to-diamond transformation serves as a metaphor for our own metamorphoses. Those moments are the pressure when experience of existence and conditions refine our essence, reconfiguring our 'molecular structure' into more perfect order, in alignment with universal design. It is not the external conditions that transform us, but rather the internal alchemy, both in God's design and in the conscious-subconscious gift of lived experience.

A diamond's crystalline lattice embodies the harmonious opposition of forces in forced moderation of conditions: compression and tension, fusion and fragmentation. This duality is mirrored in the human experience, where contradictory desires and impulses coexist within the self. Our experiences, like the coal, must be subjected to the intense pressure of introspection, allowing us to transmute essences of Truth as perceived into the radiant light of wisdom. Our perceptions are always filtered through this prism of us, yet within these subjective heuristics is potential for transcendent insight and the ability to see beyond with some clarity, in glimpses of the infinite, where the pattern distinctions between past, present, and future dissolve like mists caught in the rays of morning Sun.

Invisible architecture is here in the intricate patterns of synchronicity that govern our lives. Every thought, every emotion, every action resonates within the crystalline structure of the existence passed down to you, a piece of which known to genetics, generating ripples that reverberate throughout an eternity. Resonances of patterns in reality not only set the stage for our choices and actions but shade them, with echoing consequences on all levels, however the power to transform and make a difference is dormant within us, and just as consequential therefore and through this.

Enveloped in time
Away from mind
Thoughtless bemused
Ridiculous and confused
Hedonism
No reason, no focus
Empty energies, locusts
Lethargic degradation
Unpitiful stagnation
Diseasism
Worship of the Weak
Cult of Entropy
Antivolution

VII. Captivity

Now, let us consider a person waking up to captivity. They call for help, but nobody hears them. Let us say that eventually some hero happens by and saves them. For what? Say somebody saves them and kills the psychopath holding them against their will, what then? Is there anything in place in society to stop this all from happening again and again? There will simply be another animal in the skin of a human willing to prey on the weak or willing, but is that not what society has programmed them to be?

Is the victim not as much a product of the procession of the progress of their ancestors as the hero or the human predator? What becomes of our hero once they've saved the captive from their captor? The triumph is fleeting, for history is rampant with such woe. Another predator emerges, another victim falls prey to the cycle of exploitation. Is this not something to do with the programming in our species, if not our culture? Have we conditioned ourselves to perpetuate a cycle of predation, dominance, and Victimentality? Are the victim and the villain not two sides of the same coin, each born from the cumulative legacy of their ancestors' triumphs and failures? What of the Hero?

The victim, the villain, and the hero are all products of this procession of progress, forged in the deafening rampage of extinction's silence. What lies beneath the surface of our consciousness and subconsciousness? As we ponder the meaning of existence, let us not forget the marble that was sacrificed in the making of Michelangelo's David as a testament to the power of subtraction, for without the removal of matter, there would be no shape, and no form. Are there not the remnants of ancient marble, discarded and forgotten, yet essential to the creation of the statuesque monument we call humanity?

The same is true of human nature culturally: our greatest triumphs are often built upon the foundation of sacrifice and the ever-present screaming silence of extinction at face.

Hope can be extinguished like a candle in a hurricane, with the agony of captivity. Society perpetuates the cycle of violence and exploitation, ensuring that another monster will rise to take the place of any vanquished. Many people act merely as pawns on the chessboard, conditioned by ancestral selections to repeat the same tired patterns ad infinitum, or so it might seem.

The victim is a product of their lineage, shaped by the very forces that created the monster they confront. The hero? Same story and dancing to the tune of cultural and genetic programming. The power of subtraction at the crux of destruction and creation shapes all. As well, in the depths of despair and chaos, there exists potential for transformation; in the form of new creations emerging from the ashes of destruction.

Every act of creation is preceded by corresponding acts of destruction, and vice versa. Creation and destruction are intertwined, no brainer, yeah. This fact, however, highlights a fundamental truth in the intricate dance between opposing forces behind our reality. The concept of heroism is a reflection what has shaped us. What drives the hero to risk everything is a mixture of things to do with perseverance, felt most especially in the form of hope.

Hope is this emergent property arising from the interplay between opposites, creation and destruction in particular and on multiple levels here. It is the whisper of possibility that echoes across the expanse of existence, awaiting that potentialising spark. The cycles of violence and exploitation can be seen as manifestations of this oppositional process in creation and destruction, where the ashes of any one type of thing serve as the basis for creation of other somewhat similar yet different things. This perpetuation of cycles is not necessarily a reflection of human nature being inherently flawed but rather an expression of our capacity to adapt and evolve in response to the brutal forces that dictate our reality.

"The Spirit of the Lord God is upon me;
because the Lord hath anointed me to
preach good tidings unto the meek;
he hath sent me to bind up
the brokenhearted, to
proclaim liberty
to the captives."
~Isaiah 61:1

"My child, you must strive diligently to be inwardly free,
to have mastery over yourself everywhere,
in every external act and occupation,
that all things be subject to you and not you to them,
that you be the master and director of your actions,
not a slave or a mere hired servant."
~Imitation of Christ

Blood-curdling screams from forgotten souls,

Victims' voices, drowned in ancient roles.

Inconceivable pain, in negotiations morbid,

Our unguarded plights ignored, infinitely horrid.

Torture us with extinction's threat, a cry so loud,

Life's very imperative, echoing through deathly crowd.

Our ancestors' struggles, stories in land as sold.

How **do** we honour new life while eradicating the old?

VIII. Advantages

When one considers the sheer number of non-ancestors that had to die to make that victim's life possible, there are additional consequences of the victim surviving the situation merely by the chance of a hero. The arithmetic of suffering speaks to exponentiality, of those whose lives were extinguished to render the current and potential. Non-ancestors had to perish for victims to be born just the way they are. These non-ancestors left only the gift of not being there, which was being too weak to be here. Innumerable lives proved and reproved this mass statistical pattern called survival, in the grand course of time.

Of course, then there are the longer-term outcomes of survival itself. The hero happened to be in the right place at the right time which has consequences that echo through time. Many billions of people had to suffer severely throughout history due to the contributions of well-meaning primitive heroics, no doubt. What of the countless others who were merely pawns in a game they didn't even know they were playing? What of the stupid or morally inferior allowing for this predator to operate and take advantage of victims?

There exist greater issues in all this however, because humanity is not simply the product of genetics but culture as well, the shared commonalities within the communities and societies of people. Should people not be inculcated with resilience and the ability to rise above victimhood? Are all these countless individual cases of suffering necessary for it to affect and inspire cultural innovations and change? As suggested earlier, the victim could very well possess some unique qualities that have nothing to do with their ability to survive in that specific victim situation, but everything to do with other forms of survival, such as within groups. In fact, many pro-social behaviours are precisely the kind demonstrated by victims which are used against them, and exploited. In fact, it makes a lot of sense that societal outsiders would be more willing to exploit pro-social behaviours and victimise cultures, especially those which have been demoralised and legally forbade to criticise the victimisation as seen in the United Kingdom lately. So the quantification of actual survival strengths in such scenarios are wholly unknowable, especially while native culture and alien influences interact. There is even less fitness in it all, as the interactions are random, formless, and meaningless to cultural formations.

Then there is the ever present valorising of victims as heroes, and only certain heroes of course, which is whatever the empire and powers demand. A slippery slope that invites us to wallow in moral cowardice and intellectual laziness. By elevating suffering to a false art form, culture indulges self-pity authorising deadly distractions. Mortality is real and the consequences of not taking ownership of situations and actions are larger than could possibly be conveyed in words. Is it not possible to acknowledge travails and sufferings for what they are without reducing the realities of helpless victims? Can a balance not be found between empathy and accountability without reactive emotional nonsense?

Agency is what allows us to control our own destinies, also called free will. The resilience or strength ascribed to victims merely for being victims is a red herring, a distraction from the real issue at hand. There are two horrible narratives in one here. On one hand there is the idea that a victim is a hero for merely experiencing being a victim. On the other, there is that pungent idea that individuals are powerless to change their circumstances and must instead rely on external factors for salvation.

What about the power of choice? What about the capacity for self-reflection and growth? What about actual innocent naturally vulnerable victims who get overlooked by some of these shifts in victim focus when it is made permanent? For instance, female athletes victimised by way of legal entanglements on the very definition of their being, that is being women in itself as a biological fact. This is quite reflective of the denial in biological identity for European-descended peoples, through the use of others brought into their nations only to be forced into permanent victimhood status as minorities, with priority over our children and elders. When somebody is encouraged ("affirmed" so-called) in their low grade psychosis-like symptoms of "gender dysphoria," they are pushed into, again, permanent victimhood but powered by psychosis now enforced socially.

Furthermore, this emphasis on victimhood neglects the complexities of human nature, the intricate dance between individual agency and circumstance. It ignores the fact that people have the capacity to make choices that benefit and improve their own experiences. By fixating on the victim's plight, we overlook the importance of personal responsibility and the need for individuals to take control of their lives. That which society as a culture focuses upon is what the next generations will grow through, out of, or away from.

Elevating victims as heroes is a recipe for blatant moral relativism, where the ends can more often justify the means. It invites victims to adopt violent or destructive tactics to achieve goals, under the guise of redressing past wrongs. What about the destruction caused by others? What about the need for accountability and personal responsibility? We must hold people accountable for choices, rather than perpetuating cultures of blame shifting and moral relativism. Real heroes are not defined by their suffering; rather heroes' missions and passions germinate through their overcoming of struggles. Real heroes can be measured by their capacity for growth, for self-reflection, for taking responsibility for their own lives, and, ultimately, for empowering others

Passion, suffering, and sacrifice intersect in the depths of our mind and soul as new celestial domains, inspiration best realised in thoughtful lordly moderation. One lovely voice sings out proudly through the darkness: YOU ARE THE SOLUTION, YOU ARE THE HERO. The seemingly boundless multitudes of victims throughout history and prehistory are without satisfactions. Souls tormented in despair of the constantly lingering threat through literal extinction, do they not constitute an existential imperative, or even terror? The fact that your own ancestors often barely held on should set death to mind. Meditation upon the shortness of our mortal stay and the vital importance of our actions in this life are necessary conditions to inspire passion and cultural generation, especially memetic.

"Remember, it is not enough to be hit or insulted to be harmed, you must believe that you are being harmed. If someone succeeds in provoking you, realise that your mind is complicit in the provocation. Which is why it is essential that we not respond impulsively to impressions; take a moment before reacting, and you will find it easier to maintain control."

~Epictetus

"Be not overcome by evil, but overcome evil with Good."
"Win."
~Apostle Paulus (Romans 12:21; 1 Corinthians 9:24)

"I will punish the world for their evil,
and the wicked for their iniquity.
I will cause the arrogancy of the proud to cease,
and will lay low the haughtiness of the terrible."
~Isaiah 13:11

"The way of the Lord is strength to the upright,
but destruction shall be to the workers of iniquity."
~Proverbs 10:29

"Realise that you must lead a dying life;
the more a man dies to self, the more he may live unto God."
~The Imitation of Christ

Richest fools do name

Sport as fair democracy,

Touting good of game

As they call all crazy.

But if dreams were cars,

The poor would cruise.

If substance were theirs,

Then belief'd be truth,

&, most precarious,

Their lies'd be proof.

IX. Overcome Evil with Good

In the horrifying symphony of suffering and sacrifice, can we truly say that each individual's pain is merely an incidental byproduct of the creative process? Or does their anguish serve as a catalyst, the overcoming imbuing existence with resilience, hope, and redemption? The answer lies in the variables of human experience are forever intertwined, and seeking after greatest Good. Every act of cruelty, every instance of compassion, and every moment of transcendent beauty has the capacity to inspire some change and shift the trajectory of human history and culture.

We must confront the possibility that the extinguished billions of lives throughout human history have, in fact, unwittingly contributed to the evolution of culture and civilisation. Their collective suffering serve as elements in immanent mental workings for the greatest artistic expressions, philosophical insights, and genuine social transformations. Every fool and every villain too, has done the same, all ultimately contributing. The darkness the many have endured has, paradoxically, illuminated the path towards enlightenment, inspiring some to create works of breathtaking beauty, others to defy the old orders, and still others to forge new paths forward.

Evil is merely the hurdle to greatness, so run over it. In this living, breathing entity of human experience that pulsates within the rhythms of cultural existence, can suffering be greater than when it is transformed into fuel for the creative and didactic processes allowing for new forms; does anguish serve as a necessary condition for the material of culture to emerge malleable to the individual? We are left to ponder the profundities of a human existence in which the intersections of pain and creativity, passion and hatred, or even intellect and stupidity have given dialectic rise to the most sublime and transcendent aspects of our being. Culture, education, and, most especially, the discourse they represent can be seen as a societal immune system.

As I write, President Trump is rescinding decades of so-called "diversity," "equity," and "inclusion" policies (DEI, or DIE) {Discontent, Invasion, and Exploitation}, I am struck by the curious phenomenon and its remaining stranglehold over Europe, as well as many minds in the United States. These seemingly innocuous terms are euphemisms for a most insidious force, one that still seeks to upend the tables of our cultures and nations. Murderous enemies of Life, those are our truest enemies. However, they have a lot of people on their side fooled into Victimentality, whom appear to be enemies and remain so until such time as they can be reasoned with. Who has never had an old ignorant opinion completely disrupted by a newer one based more in reality? Often the new opinion is not even directly related.

At the core of the ideas held by our enemies is moral and intellectual bankruptcy. These are hollow shells of concepts, devoid of any substance or meaning, yet masquerading as profound and noble pursuits. This is that same intellectual bankruptcy informing the idea that propaganda-based education is a human right, while having a society which is naturally supportive, rather than mortally competitive, isn't somehow.

Like a venomous serpent slithering through the underbrush of our cultural Victimentality, notions of equity and righteous wrongdoing strikes at the core of our collective societal immune system. What, you may ask, is the true nature of this DIE? Ah, my friend, it is in the name there, it is a cancer that eats away at the very foundations of our society, and it grows off the back of emotions confused for logic. It is a destructive force that seeks to erase the boundaries and standards that have defined us for hundreds of preceding generations. It is a violent and aggressive assault on the majority culture, wherever it might be allowed to occur, seeking to impose its own brand of chaos and anarchy upon normal and decent people. Despite its insidious nature, these concepts somehow managed to insinuate themselves into the very heart of our society. A festering wound, slow to heal appearing as though it might never fade away, instead growing more entrenched, infected, and powerful with each passing day.

The entire phenomenon is a forced meme, and nothing more than a thinly veiled attempt at genocide. You should never forget it all of your days, and never let anyone else forget it. The victimhood has been entirely in presence and in mind the whole time, though framed falsely by those who forced whomever into positions of victimhood and mortal competition, i.e. minority status, to blame those whose freedom from naturally mortal competition within the boundaries of their own nation were imposed upon. Who made them victims? Who made them minorities? Who made them less than what they should be? More importantly who is going to help them overcome and become better?

The whole situation is pure insanity, a nonsense 'mind virus' from what have become seen as crackerjack and laughingstock Western nations by the rest of the World. These nations have been so utterly demoralised and deranged that they have been rendered absolutely incapable of protecting themselves. Instead, their elected officials have chosen to gut them before the world, some strange cultural-level 'seppuku' or 'hara-kiri' ritual, demonstrating a brainwashed dishonour framed as honour but founded in a ridiculous self-hatred. One need not guess at the intentions of officials and authorities with minority and victimised statuses, so conformed to majority hatred by the twisting of their hearts by permanent victimhood.

It's as if we're standing at the edge of a vast, dark ocean, gazing out upon the infinite possibilities that lie before us. What is beneath the surface? What secrets are hidden in the depths of this seemingly endless expanse? How many moments of triumph and tragedy have been swallowed up by this chaotic abyss? Amidst this chaos, there stirs a glimmer of hope in the spark of light that refuses to be extinguished. The question is: what lies ahead? What will we make of this chaos? Will we find ourselves lost in the wilderness of time, or will we strive for the greater truths that have been awaiting us all along?

We must make a "Liberal Recovery," toward "Natural Responsibility," but what does this mean? "Liberal Recovery" implies the notion that our individual freedoms and moral responsibilities are connected to the nature of the World. It's like trying to grasp a handful of sand where the harder you squeeze, the more of it slips away. What's left is a heap of nothing but less. Some will ask, "What about all them other critters of God's creation out there? Don't they deserve a piece of the pie?" There's a mighty fine sentiment behind that question, and a kind notion. However, let me ask you this: have we taken care of our own patch yet? Have we made sure our own house is in order? Would you feed strangers as your family starved?

So here's the thing: our particularity, our humanity, are the very same strands of wire that connect us to the Universal. Attempting to reach out to the Universal without recognising all the strands in our humanity, much like the strands in the cabling when building a suspension bridge, will end in disaster. Similarly, without making sure the foundation is solid, we risk everything. You can't just start constructing without getting your feet wet, so to speak. This is where responsibilities come in, not as some heavy burden or duty, but as an expression of our very humanity.

We should not speak if we don't take care of our own little patch of ground and tend to its particular needs, as well as the systems supporting them. How could we possibly expect to advise in tending larger operations than our own plot, let alone some plot on the other side of the planet? How could we ever connect to the Universal if our particular is not in order? When we take care of our own little patch, we're not just looking out for ourselves; we're also cultivating the soil for all those that depend on us. Ultimately, people have to take care of their own property and resources before they can possibly be in any kind of position to help neighbours out. Anything else is insanity.

I guess some might claim this is dramatic, however I reckon it is the plain truth. When we put our own house in order, we start seein' the world in a different light, a light through which we can better recognise the Good. This is a very important point that often gets overlooked in everything, that you cannot see what is truly Good unless you are in a place sustaining yourself. The Sun's rays and the sky's rain traverse past the leaves to respectively illuminate and nurture the whole forest, and cutting off the upper canopy to feed the lower simply cannot do. This is stupid, and plainly not done for the best interests of all.

The idea of a Liberal Recovery in Natural Responsibility is replete with promise for the improvement of humanity. No longer will people think that responsibilities can be fulfilled simply through money. It is only through profound comprehension in the intricacies of our nature that we may hope to reach beyond some of the many limitations so designed to be transcended. This is only possible through a process relative to our own needs, as individuals within systems and layers of particularity, but ascending to the sublime plateaus in universalities. Here is the inherent value of anthropocentrism, as well as tribalism and communalism as well, not as badges of shame or a symptom of egoistic excess as Marxist-type propaganda teaches to a demoralised population, but rather as the indispensable lenses of reality through which we must gaze upon the World, with a general bias toward Life, and specific biases toward our family and people with a genuine and Good interest in us.

True and natural responsibilities are not burdens imposed from without, but rather organic extensions of our nature and most valuable because of this. The recognition of this is a manifestation of our capacity for self-reflection, and our innate drive towards growth; it is maturity. It is here, at this nexus of individual and collective awareness, that we find the true source of our obligations to others. For it is in the genuine intimacy of family and community that we discover our most profound purpose.

It is here that we must confront our own mortality in all consequences, and from this precipice, we may begin to grasp the true nature of our existence. Children should not have to face mortal competition within their own nation, and that is exactly what has been brought upon them. Of course, security is realised as a priority for minority populations yet not at all for the majority populations in their own nations, though I'm still not sure why. This is a major responsibility in which seemingly most original stock European or American parents, as a collective, are currently failing at.

Corporate solutions in environmentalism or the blandishments of social justice will do nothing for us and afford us no more than pain and death. We will not even receive assistance from the people we would seek to help, so we must produce the solutions ourselves. Let us anchor our plans in the bedrock of human experience and reality, a foundation that is at once both particular and universal.

Only when we move past our own egos and remain firm to our responsibilities, may we hope to part the veil of ignorance. Our responsibilities become not a burden imposed from without, but rather an expression of our deepest humanity and a reflection of our capacity for empathy, compassion, and our collective uplifting. Do not lay down your natural burdens in life, and most importantly, take up your cross.

"Again, it is possible to fail in many ways, for evil belongs to the class of the unlimited and good to that of the limited, while to succeed is possible only in One way for these reasons. Then also, excess and defect are characteristic of vice, and only in moderation is found virtue. For men are good in but One way, but bad in many."

~Aristotle

....

In Reason is the only Strength; Virtues through Moderation.

....

"Woe unto them that call evil good, and good evil;
that put darkness for light, and light for darkness."
~Isaiah 5:20

"The devil is strong only against
those who are idle and careless,
but to those who are vigilant, he is weak."
~St. Chrysostom

In twilight's faintness, shadows grow near,

Forgotten truths scream a closing fear.

Divine inspiration, missing & lost in night,

Dance of contradictions, not determining right.

Tendrils of hate wrap the threads of lies,

Poisons billow clouds, shrouding the skies.

Silent betrayal in toxic rain, mirthless, taking toll,

Landscapes of dashed hopes, precisely as sold.

Humanity's decayed wretch, as deep & as wide,

Wherein as strayed, so truths have died.

X. Survival

All beings wish to survive, regardless of how incapable of it they are. In existence, we find ourselves ensnared in this Gordian knot of contradictions. Nothing trumps the fundamental desire for survival, a primal urge that drives us forward in our quest to preserve life at all costs. Yet, this very impulse confronts us with this existential abyss: it means willingness to murder in order to not be murdered, and it means countless lives lived and lost historically, their potential untapped and their stories left unspoken as killed by deceptive and hateful people. The stories of still others are lost in self-deceptions and intrigue in which few interactions of life prove genuine enough to reveal anything of value.

As we map this spiritual terrain, how do we quantify the ineffable, boiling down the mysteries of the universe to philosophical contentions of pros and cons? Yet, does not this reductionist approach trivialise the very essence of all existence? What is the return on salvation? Do we not all have a series of charts in our heads as to the value of victims once saved? Consider, if you will, the prioritisation of our precious children, these tiny and adorable beings full of potential and wonder, their futures bright with possibility, yet very vulnerable in so many ways. In our minds' eye, as parents, we plot the trajectory of their lives, weighing the costs and benefits in their daily and yearly interactions. Are not children valued more highly due to a greater possible estimation of untapped potential? That is Goodness, or God, in them. What of the elderly, the infirm, and the sickly, do they not possess some value all their own, that is inextricably linked to the Good of society and culture? In ideal conditions and examples, yes, when they themselves have not been traumatised into being vulnerable and entitled victims. This is where Goodness, that is God's Goodness of course generally, enters the equation. This equation is of highest potential in the weakness that could grow to strength, and why Christ so loved those who persevere despite weaknesses. It's also why developmental psychologists always cringe at the description of how the Spartans treated their children and most vulnerable. Was there something not lost in their selection patterns as a society in Sparta? It would seem plausible. That weakness has the potential to be used as the foundation for untested potential human strengths in the very acts of compensating for it. These may not seem like much, but taken on a larger scale they can provide much needed societal adaptation and demonstrating new forms of Goodness.

There is a diminishing of return in salvation, however, and this would seem like a paradox at first glance. The more we focus on saving others, rather than being selective and discriminating, the more we realise that our efforts are too often but a drop in the ocean, which is to say wasted. There is an often used phrased that calls wisdoms unheeded 'pearls' before 'swine.' Yet, we press on, driven by this fundamental desire for survival and survival of those surrounding us. This is a primal urge to preserve life at all costs, and indeed this is great as of basic importance. We should have that, and be like this. However, we also should be rewarding people in society for being trusting and trustworthy instead of punishing them, and society should be moved in this direction where that is possible. This is punishment of crime, and nothing more. Every thread in a nation is interconnected, every life equally dependent on a dance of cause and effect, largely out of our direct mortal control. Yet, we persist in this quest, not simply for survival but something more as fuelled by an unyielding commitment to preserving the beauty and complexity in our humanity and culture.

Poisons given as medicine are genocide in its most insidious and heinous of forms, a festering wound on the empathic face of humanity, a blight that threatens to consume us all by targeting those most willing to trust their society. The calculated destruction of a group, based on biologic markers related to race is a travesty that defies our shared morality with a menacing contempt, flaunting as it were. It uses science to destroy populations which were heavily involved in the development of it. When this abhorrent act is perpetrated through the misuse of medicine, we are faced with a crisis of conscience that cuts to the very core of our humanity. Of course, the only reason this course of genocide that appealed to the trust and responsibility of individuals is to get them out of the way in order to commit more blatant forms of genocide and get away with it in the future, making it all the more egregious, being on many levels evil.

The deployment of hastily approved and harmful medicines, often fuelled by bribery and corruption, is a betrayal of the most sacred trust between doctors, patients, leadership, corporations as incorporated, banks, pharmaceutical companies, genocidal billionaires or trillionaires, and society. The consequences of such actions are dire: purportedly life-saving treatments turned into instruments of death, harm, the erosion of public health, the perpetuation of an inhumane system, and the potential dissolution of civilisation in the near future.

Genocide, disguised as medicine... the thought makes the skin shiver, indeed that poison secret. The very notion puts to mind a cancerous tumour metastasising through the very epidermis of humanity. It's a Frankensteinian monster born from the unholy union of greed and hatred, its lifeblood coursing with the tainted cash of corrupt officials and the desperate tears of those who've been left to die, many slowly and agonisingly. This monstrosity, masquerading as progress, is a grotesque parody of medical science. These mRNA "vaccines," so-called, are a quick fix solution peddled by pharma charlatans and shysters who care more for their own bank accounts than the lives they're destroying. Still higher up organisationally are found those after depopulation and genocide, many publicly and admittedly, like Bill Gates who should be tried for crimes against humanity.

The very notion that such an abomination could be allowed to persist even past the date of the publication of this book, much less be rushed through the approval process like a toxic waste dump, is an affront to all that is decent and just. It is very offensive, too offensive for words. No, we cannot condone or excuse this heinous atrocity. We must stand in defiant opposition to it, shouting from the rooftops our refusal to participate in this grand farce of genocidal poison promoted as medicine. For as long as humanity holds a shred of decency and compassion, we must condemn this travesty with every fibre of our beings.

As we confront this horrific and abyssal void left by genocide unrecognised, it's imperative that we acknowledge the slow-motion apocalypse playing out before our eyes and the very real consequences of these "medicines" as they wreak havoc on our populations. The toll is one of unmitigated and unforgivable disaster, a catastrophe of damage that echoes through the ages eternally and infinitely like the much impotent screams of the so damned against the only immunity in sight, their own legal immunity. Any delay in addressing this crisis would be akin to watching a wildfire rage unchecked as it spreads its infernal licks across the landscape, leaving nothing but charred remains and shattered dreams in its wake, and blue of course.

We can't afford to tarry; every moment counts like grains of sand slipping through the hourglass of humanity's collective existence. The fact that recognition is delayed can only confirm everything I am suggesting. Is there a single movement aimed at mitigating the damage caused by these 'spike proteins' and finding a complete solution to them? According to Robert F. Kennedy Jr., Secretary of Health to the current Trump administration, the spike proteins were lab engineered to target populations most especially of European descent, but also African and some others [susceptibility of populations based on descents: 54% Europeans, 39% Africans, 5-10% others, and approaching 0% for Chinese or Ashkenazim] (Hill 2021, tinyurl.com/ethnicbioweapon). This is the biggest genocide in history and has just begun.

The evidence compiles and pierces the fog of complacency, shattering the glass wall of inaction and demanding we confront our own shortcomings as well as those of others, as well as perhaps their motives. The ethical violations are manifold, and more than can be explained by way of simple criminality: the corruption of scientific integrity and the direct endangerment of human life on a grand-scale, and directed specifically at the decimation of European-descended populations, apparently before killing everyone else off too. Here we are with this 54% susceptibility and most victims are acting like the biggest genocide in history did not just occur, yet they were most impacted by being most compliant to the jabs. These jabs turned them into spike protein factories and often toxic to other people around them as well.

Those who enable or participate in such atrocities commit treason against the very purpose of Life itself, in violating not only the Hippocratic Oath but also the fundamental principles of evolution, humanity, civilisation, and progress. It is our duty to condemn such heinous acts with unwavering ferocity, to denounce those who perpetuate them, and to work tirelessly towards a future where medicine is used only to heal, and never to do harm. Medicine should be rather seen as secondary to more holistic methods of healthcare to do with diet and environment, obviously as is championed and promoted by the best and brightest in the medical industries. We must ensure that the regulatory bodies responsible for safeguarding public health are given greater independence and separation from the manipulative corporations and wealthy psychopathic and genocidal maniacs. Transparency, accountability, and justice can only be upheld in the future with a full recognition of the nightmare currently unfolding. It's the only way of stopping it.

Let us honour the memories of those who have suffered at the hands of this ongoing genocide by committing ourselves to stopping it and creating a less evil world. This requires us to face the music of our collective failure, to recognise the ghosts of our pasts, the demons within, the demons among us, and forge a new path forward guided by unflinching dedication to truth. In this storm-torn seascape, where the very sails of humanity are frayed and worn thin, we must singlehandedly restitch with the sacred trifecta of empathy, understanding, and collective action within our communities, lest we succumb to the oceanic void of inaction and forever lose our grip on the precarious precipice of hope. We must hoist these tattered sails, and reach dry land, brothers. We must stand against this death-cult-like culture, and stop being hostages to predatory manipulations of our morality.

> "Give that which is within as charity,
> and then all things are clean for you."
>
> ~Luke 11:41

> "The ultimate value of life depends upon awareness and
> the power of contemplation rather than upon mere survival."
>
> ~Aristotle

"People are like the grass, and
all their faithfulness is like the flowers of the field.
The grass withers and the flowers fall,
because the breath of the Lord blows on them.
Surely the people are grass.
The grass withers and the flowers fall,
but the Word of God endures forever."
~Isaiah 40:6-8

"Many persons often blame the world for being false and vain,
yet do not readily give it up because
the desires of the flesh have such great power."
~The Imitation of Christ

"Why, you do not even know what will happen tomorrow.
What is your life?
You are a mist appearing for a little while, then vanishing."
~James 4:14

Though the brief Flame of Life burns for fervent passions,

Many minds shadow the doubt, lost to current fashions.

Find solace in the Mind of Christ as Light so blessed,

Since virtue cherishes each moment, no matter the test.

Beacon guide you, the rarefied path with Life's faith renewed.

Hasten to honour the Flame flickering brightest and True,

Warmth and Light, rise up, true comfort and peace of mind,

Valuing all precious moments ignited and then left behind.

XI. Value of Life

Quick, you're the Chief of Police on the phone with a bank robber, he's giving you a choice on which hostage he's going to shoot next. To be forced to choose between two lives, each imbued with their own significance. The hostage survival dilemma serves as an excellent backdrop for moral quandaries. We're forced to confront the inherent complexities of valuing life itself, which is always done. Do you tell the robber to shoot one of the young healthy people or the man with an open neck wound being held closed with pressure?

In the moment of moral choice, compassion falters as we weigh the value of lives against the complexity of human experience: youthful vitality, frailty, suffering, and the tangled threads of past and present converge to frustrate the decision. As the consequences of circumstance deepen, the moral topography shifts, revealing fault lines that threaten to fracture preconceptions. For something so supposedly black and white, Life, our valuations of instantiations depend on a lot of additional variables.

Consider a young star athlete, full of vigour and promise, his future unfolding like a blank canvas awaiting the paint that is his experience in life. How can we truly quantify the value of this life, untainted by the ravages of time or the cruel whims of circumstance? Is it not a life marked by potential, ripe for experiences, memories, and accomplishments that would fill a lifetime? On the other hand, we might have a 97-year-old 3x-great-grandfather, his existence a testament to the indomitable will of humanity. A life lived through the trials and tribulations of many generations past, tempered by the fires of experience and imbued with the wisdom born from countless challenges overcome. His is a tale of resilience, of overcoming the odds against a backdrop of war, poverty, and societal upheaval, but what of the variables that complicate our comparisons? A drunkard's life, for instance, might be marked by reckless abandon and hurtful actions towards those who matter most to it. Does this not diminish the value of his existence?

Then there is the patient with advanced cancer, their time left might be measured in mere months, and so as cruel as it may feel, there is a change in valuation here. The life of somebody afflicted with a mortal condition is already beset by the crushing weight of a reality which forces confrontation with the impermanence. Should we prioritise their existence over that of the football player or the otherwise healthy elderly ancestors? There exists an inherent subjectivity in the valuing of life, whether we like to admit it or not. We're compelled to consider not only the inherent worth of each individual but also the context in which they exist, and how much that has to do with us or the people in our lives. Why should we not choose a person likely to favour us in return? Why should we choose somebody obviously less likely to care about us or even our own survival?

This realisation should fill you with a sense of trepidation, as potent reminder of your own mortality and the potential devaluation of your life in the eyes of others. A profound opportunity for growth and self-reflection exists in this more realistic view of the World. Acknowledging the complexity of relativity in life compels us to confront the necessity of clarity in our own valuations, as they are literally life and death. It very well could mean your own death or the death of loved ones. Own your biases toward life generally and your own life specifically, as they are necessary to existence. This introspection leads us down a path of a truer purpose, honest empathy, deep compassion, and an unmitigated understanding of society founded upon respect for the actual needs of others, instead of cynical-propaganda-induced pity and self-hatred. Confront your own mortality, your own limitations, and the inherent meanings in Life, through Good and God.

Victimhood and altruism do often seem to go hand in hand, and this is unfortunate. Perpetuating cycles of self-pity and selflessness that ultimately lead nowhere. Simply holding recipients of charity and altruism accountable to standards is, in fact, the fairest treatment of kind charity. You see, when we talk about accountability, we're not just talking about holding individuals responsible for their actions. There is also a process involved here with teaching society generally to hold others accountable. We're talking about supporting a system of checks and balances built within the culture that best ensures fairness, merit, and justice. This requires discrimination – yes, you heard me right – discrimination. Some will cry foul at the mere mention of the "D-word." Let's be real: without standards, we're adrift in mediocrity. Discrimination has been stupidly demonised in recent culture, along with basic standards across society labelled racist, sexist, classist, ageist, ableist, or whatever of a myriad of excuses handed down to people in justification for Victi-mentality.

Without standards, the exceptional among any population are trampled by the mediocre's tyranny, as plainly seen in the recent abuse of women's sports and female athletic excellence by otherwise mediocre men seeking attention and affirmation. These men needed proper therapy and hugs from people who could love them, not a ticket to be the prime event at embarrassing freak shows. Those who claim that standards are justifications for racism, sexism, classism, or any of the other "—isms," also very typically applaud outright and openly genocidal remarks about people of European-descent, and the decline of their populations. This is where things get fascinating. If "everyone is equal," some obviously must be more equal than others but how is that determined? Money!!! Obviously! This is a problem. Justice is the answer, simply. Justice is holding all individuals accountable for their actions, regardless of their background or circumstances. This requires promotion of critical thinking and nuanced understanding in the culture's progression. There must be expectations with anything, since nothing is free, especially to those who have proven themselves somehow incapable of sustaining the self.

In mirror's depths, darkness's many façades crack,

Voids yawn chasms open, in obsessed despair & black.

Knit the fragile web of sanity's ungrasping hold,

Probe darkness past dark, souls grown tired & old.

Dare cast gaze out at the gazing back, unblinkingly bold,

Into the dark minds surrounding, where horrors unfold.

The stench, a vile hatred, centuries in rot, decayed,

Silenced screams, tomorrow's innocent today, slayed.

Far above the abyss, we may find the greatest Light,

Shadowed selves outlined, despite darkness' might.

Yet, in this contest with cruel spectres of unknown,

Strengthen & lift others, so you might not stand alone.

Sparks hope that guides us through this ceaseless fight,

Proved divine in calling out the evil in plain sight.

XII. Altruism

Consider the hypothetical rescuer from earlier chapters, compelled to save the victim, say it is a damsel in distress. How much evolutionary selection went into the birth of the hero who might save the victim? How many of his ancestors had more mating opportunities or were rewarded more resources merely by being able to discover and undo the servitude of others? Certainly his own social standing could be improved by such actions. Obviously there was benefit by the gratitude and reputation earned along with whatever other social advantages.

How much of this impulse can be attributed to the promise of reward? Is it merely a fleeting moment of empathy, or is there a deeper evolutionary imperative at play? His ancestors must have secured fitness through noble courage, to some degree, and at least in comparison to competitors. His ancestors were winners, naturally, therefore he exists. The notion that his ancestors acted selflessly does not match with basic evolutionary theories. Altruism is largely a round-about form of selfishness, in most cases, with deep calculus performed in valuations of human life and risk in such actions, with the potential to yield tangible benefits for self and genetic cohorts.

Suppose the victim were ungrateful, refusing to acknowledge her rescuer's heroism. Altruism is often exploited, without any respect shown to the altruist. Would the hero still derive satisfaction from having saved the victim, or would the absence of gratitude render the entire endeavour hollow? Even beyond the immediate returns on such an action, does he not also do it to feed his own ego, and to affirm his own self-image? What of the potential psychological rewards for rescuing the victim? Would our hero not derive satisfaction from having performed a noble deed, regardless of the recipient's gratitude? Is this not simply a manifestation of his own ego and social standing being nourished by the act itself, rather than any inherent value attached to the rescue? Did his ancestors not evolve, to some degree, then to be satisfied by noble actions?

What of the lasting consequences of such an action? The rescuer's aim, hypothetically is to perpetuate the victim's existence, ensuring that her genetic composition might continue forward eternally in the form of easily-victimised progeny? Are his motivations more complex and selfish, driven by a desire to improve his own self-image or social standings as bolstered through recognition from others?

How many survivors can honestly say they are not victims of chance but circumstance? How many would be willing to gauge the degree to which the creation of the situation they were in, of pain, humiliation, and potential death, was due to their own victimability, victim tendency, or Victimentality, victim glorification? Does that person ever truly change or do they become a permanent victim? Is the fact of survival itself transformative or are the actions toward survival somehow basically required for a proper or truer transformation? Do we ever transform or simply acquire more information? Does a survivor cease being a victim merely because things might prove more difficult for the next aggressor due to their newly found constant vigilance? Perhaps for them but what about their descendants? Did it change any of the genetic coding that allowed for it to happen? Say the experience does alter the way the person interacts with the World, can it be said that such a reaction, the ability to "transform," was not precisely an avenue of evolution toward greater survival? Or should they be broken by it, forever subject to threats, fear, their own subsequent neuroses, and ultimate self-identification with the victimhood? Is there something more to it than just the right behaviours or the right genes?

Survivors can often find it difficult to balance their understanding of the situation in which they were victimised. How many individuals have had the opportunity of introspection to comprehend their own potential accountability? Consider a person who has survived a traumatic experience, one that has left them scarred and shaken. Are they willing to acknowledge the degree to which their own ignorance contributed to some situation, even, and perhaps especially, when there was little they could have done in the mere moment itself? Often this requires critical personal reflection of traumas that came before it. Is it even possible for a victim to fully comprehend the extent to which their actions, or lack thereof, played a role in their suffering? So how much is society capable of the same? Victim blaming is uncalled-for, however understanding Victimentality and its origins is crucial to an honest appraisal of these things, as well understanding the culture surrounding it.

Does the survival itself imbue the survivor with a newfound sense of purpose and resilience? If the victim knew it could happen the way that it did, they would have done things differently to prevent it. So it is new information. Perhaps the experience of simply surviving does not transform us; instead, it merely allows us to acquire significantly more or surprising new information. Information is very transformational, so long as it is taken seriously.

A person may learn new strategies for coping with adversity, but do they fundamentally change as individuals or stop being a perpetual victim? Perhaps this can happen for individuals themselves, but what about their descendants? Obviously the experience did not alter anything determinative in genetics that allowed for it to happen in the first place Say the experience does alter the way an individual interacts with the world, can we say that such a reaction, the ability to "transform," was not precisely enabled by an avenue of evolution toward greater fitness, and therefore survival? There is apparently something more to transformation than outward things. Perhaps greater transformations require profound shifts in the perspective of ourselves, and our places in the World.

What can lower Victimentality? What of the culture that promotes it, and what of intelligence or education? What of religion and spirituality? I have been personally told to my face by multiple people in my life, as though it were absolute fact, and with no malice intended of course, that Christ isn't part of culture or that Christianity is not an element of a person's cultural background, essentially. A culture that even denies itself, its spirituality, is some kind of obtuse self-mockery. Is there any firmer proof of demoralisation than this? The vaunted label of "intelligent" is a badge worn by many, yet rarely embodied by those who claim it.

In reality, the best intelligence is not in the delving into mere complexities nor in the dusty accumulation of facts, but rather in depths of the soul with inward and moderated alignment. Great intellect discerns subtle intricacies in the depths of humanity as layers of systems. Insight that is not so fickle is only possible by eschewing corrupting influences and finding moderation to elevate within the virtues found in LOGOS. Celestial harmonies attune the moderated soul conditioning the inspired connection.

The Path of the greatest Intellect is not of simple curiosity, but rather a quest for greater and still greater recognitions of Good. This is a ceaseless onslaught of doubting and crucifying the self. It involves a present in which all previous images of the self converge upon the denial, upon finding the mind of Christ in the revelation that all personality is imperfection, outside the One. This is not the collection of wisdoms like a beetle accumulating dung, nor is it done to impress. No, this real intellect is driven by its mission in Love, of purest form with the Source. Mind so aligned is sharp, slicing through veils, illuminating the shadowy corners of the human condition hiding behind, yet also revealed by the existence of, popular materialist non-understandings.

The weight of ignorance is a burden that only increases with true intellectual advance. Eternal virtues are the jewels in the crown of enlightened Spirit. Flood of Light in the darkness, the Life of all such men who bask in LOGOS, in Christ. Intelligence, as naturally gifted without developing virtues, is basically an invitation to conceit, and ignorance unaware of itself. Intelligence focused upon greater development in virtues cannot help but please God. The higher self is not even recognised until it is at least seen first through God, and then developed in the reflection of this relationship within family, community, society, nation, and, yes, all culture.

"Among natural bodies some have, and some have not, life; and by life we mean the faculties of self-nourishment, self-growth and self-decay. Thus every natural body partaking of life may be regarded as an essential existence; ... but then it is an existence only in combination. ... And since the organism is such a combination, being possessed of life, it cannot be the Vital Principle. Therefore it follows that the Vital Principle must be an essence, as being the form of a natural body, holding life in potentiality; but essence is a reality. The Vital Principle is the original reality of a natural body endowed with potential life; this, however, is to be understood only of a body which may be organised. Thus the parts even of plants are organs, but they are organs that are altogether simple; as the leaf which is the covering of the pericarp, the pericarp of the fruit. If, then, there be any general formula for every kind of Vital Principle, it is—the primary reality of an organism."

~Aristotle

Shadows ancient, writhe, swerve, & twist,

Like pits of serpents in a darkened mist.

Cast deep the infinite, minds aflamed afear,

Darkness's 'truths' fail, alighted disappear.

Sweet inevitable Truth, holiest of holy vision,

Revealed inside you, if only dare you the mission.

False charity & subservience often inclined,

A toxic blend perpetuating the cycles of decline.

All fall prey to the most vicious of snares,

Lost to the whims of emotions & selfish cares.

No responsibility, no effort, no striving to be more

No space within the soul for Spirit to soar.

XIII. Stockholm Culture Abuse

At what point do we blame the culture? As asked before, how much pain does a person negate here by saving a victim and how much more pain exists in a future with more victims? At what precise juncture do we attribute blame to the cultural ethos that perpetuates this victimology, this personal delusion in Victimentality? Consider the pangs of alleviation that accompany the rescue of a single individual. Is it sufficient to assuage the suffering that will arise in a future replete with similar cases? Does the act of redemption merely apply a temporary balm to a festering wound, or should it not possess the potential to create a lasting transformation?

Now, envision attempting to capture a male alpha lion in the prime of his life: a massive beast of power and ferocity. Will it not struggle against you with tooth and claw? Will it not attempt escape if afforded the opportunity? What distinguishes this scenario from that of human beings more prone to being abused and kept in captivity? The lion is fully capable of winning its freedom, so there is something else entirely which restrains the beast. The lion tamer has to present himself as a threat without being a terror in order to not be mauled to death. The false mental image of the tamer to the lion is just about the only thing keeping him alive.

Why do so many human beings seem more amenable towards victimability, abuse, and captivity? Is it due to some innate aspect of our nature, or is it the result of environmental factors that influence our behaviour? Does the powerlessness inherent in being a victim trigger some primal response, rendering us more susceptible to control? The notion that humans are more easily controlled than lions raises questions about our nature and evolution. Are we more akin to domesticated beasts, conditioned to respond to external stimuli, or are we autonomous beings capable of making choices that defy our natural inclinations? Humans do appear to have been the first "domesticates" in the ongoing Earthly creation, at least as far as we can determine.

Perhaps the difference for people is something in our unique capacity for self-reflection and introspection. Perhaps our ability to recognise and confront the inherent flaws in our own nature is key, which is to say the capacity to second guess and correct ourselves, especially in reference to other people. Maybe it is all these things, but also something altogether more sinister: a willingness to accept and perpetuate a culture of oppression.

Not every lion can be captured this way, but it does seem most humans can somehow be captured either physically or mentally, perhaps by fooling them or holding others at bay using the so duped. Perhaps the answers are in the complexity of human nature in a delicate balance between instinct and intellect, between primal urges and rational thought. Maybe it is more profound and our deep-seated desire for connection, for belonging, and for validation renders us more vulnerable to manipulation.

Consider the actual "Stockholm syndrome" in which a captive person forms a bond with their captor. Regardless our personal judgements of such individuals, are they any more pitiful than the dead? They successfully engineered the mitigation of a social threat, and they didn't have to resort to physical confrontation to do it. At its core, Stockholm represents a profound human capacity to adapt and survive in some of the worst situations. The captive person forms a bond with their captor, which can be seen as a testament to humanity's resilience in the face of real adversity and denigration.

However, the Stockholm phenomenon also raises fundamental issues in our understanding of victimhood and agency, as well as power and control. Is it not a natural reaction to reserve scorn rather than pity for those who succumb to the whims of fate, as opposed to those who actively seek to mitigate their circumstances? In light of this, the Stockholm phenomenon can be seen as a form of social engineering, where the captive person negotiates with their captor to create a more tolerable environment, or perhaps even some false 'material freedom.'

Wealth isn't actually power in this system, it's enslavement. People suffering from Stockholm syndrome will often help their captors, thereby becoming criminals themselves. This raises very serious questions about society and the nature of power and control in such situations, especially where people are made to feel like victims on a very basic cultural level in society.

The Stockholm phenomenon serves to elucidate the parallel in powerful interests manipulating the masses to embrace their own subjugation. In promotion of culture in victimhood, and championing Victimentality-based identities, environments are created in which individuals are far more likely to surrender to their circumstances, rather than actively seeking real change, starting within their own lives. This strategy is rooted in the psychological phenomenon of "learned helplessness," where individuals become convinced that they have no control over their lives after being exposed to certain patterns of thought and expectation.

When faced with perceived injustices or failures, victims are more likely to see them as wholly outside of their control, rather than internalising difficult experiences as evidence of their own imperfections and need for growth. In this context, the Stockholm syndrome becomes an eerie echo chamber, where the voices of victimhood and helplessness resonate loudest and at whomever needs to be screamed at as villain. The captives are primed to respond to the captors' whims, negotiating their own subjugation for fleeting moments of comfort or security. This is seen everywhere.

The cultural promotion of victimhood, and even pride in it, creates an environment where people feel genuinely powerless, unable to change anything. This is achieved through a subtle yet insidious manipulation of patterns in language, media, and societal norms. The narrative of victimhood becomes the dominant discourse, painting individuals as helpless pawns in a larger game controlled by oppressive yet mostly anonymous forces. This dynamic is a powerful tool for social control, where the captives are conditioned to perceive their own subjugation as a natural state of being. This is done through fearmongering, propaganda, and carefully crafted narratives that emphasise powerlessness and hopelessness by pushing the false pride of Victimentality.

Cancerous Victimentality distracts from systemic issues by shifting focus onto individual cases of victimhood or the most novel form of victimhood, and away from the actual underlying structural problems. This gaslighting of societies allows these forces pushing such confusion to maintain their grip on power. Individuals conditioned to perceive themselves as helpless are more likely to conform to the expectations of Victimentality, rather than challenging the existing political and social structures. Stockholm culture also desensitises people to unbelievably truculent horrors, by way of mockery in pain received by groups perceived as not victims.

This normalisation of oppressive behaviours and attitudes becomes a self-perpetuating cycle, where individuals begin to see these behaviours as "just the way things are," or see crimes as acceptable based upon this. Fostering a culture of helplessness creates dependency, solidifying the complete cycle of criminal controls. When are the victims of this cultural Stockholm syndrome going to reject Victimentality once and for all times? When will we stand tall again?

"To enjoy the things we ought and to hate the things we ought has the greatest bearing on excellence of character."

~Aristotle

"All cruelty springs from weakness."

~Seneca

In cryptic consciousness, an absence settles wide.

Lacuna of longing, where echoed memories reside,

Whisper a forgotten tongue, aria of despair.

Maps of self erode, leaving only shadows there.

In the funereal landscape, a topography of pain,

Contours of a soul, inky island of joy's refrain.

Chronicle sufferer unroll like a scroll of grief,

As narrative falters, without meaning in relief.

Release is but a fading glimpse of the very same,

So common the evidence, pointing is in vain.

XIV. Brutality & Mayhem

War is always against the people. People are always the primary target of war, the destruction of their real wealth in this world. Strangest still is that the majority of the population are generally less afraid of the wholesale destructions of large swaths of population all at once than one-on-one murder. The differences in reactions between individual and collective violence reveals a stark contrast in the dark recesses of human psychology. Does this not also have something to do with society's peculiar fascination with spectacle and chaos? The mass killings are far worse though, on a purely logical level, because they are indiscriminate, where selection is often geographical, if not outright racially or ethnically targeted. The button-pushing terrorist represents an existential challenge on levels far outside our grasps or access generally, in which typically larger forces are needed to be brought in to solve the problems.

Logic dictates that such random slaughter is, by definition, more horrific, not simply because it suggests anyone might become a victim regardless of how innocent they might be. It is also unbelievably wasteful of that which is best in humanity on a grand scale and in the worst way possible. Carnage becomes a statistical abstraction devoid of moral questions in human agency simply due to the events being far away or ignored. Genocide of otherwise innocent people presents an evil catharsis for those so conditioned for thoughtless hatred. This evil catharsis and the bared teeth of those feeling it is especially visible after hatred is regularly promoted by powerful interests, such as has been seen toward people of European descent. The murder of moral people requires they be demonised for their very morality, or at least the fruits of that morality.

Sheer scale in devastation can often serve to absolve many of personal guilt and responsibility, as demonstrated by the recent audacity of many genociders. This scale obscures the crimes and makes individuals feel as though there is nothing they can do about any of it. This is perfectly illustrated in the wake of jab injuries post-COVID19, so-called, where the primary targets yawn as they schedule more cancer treatments instead of going after their assailants. The victims become mere statistics, their lives reduced to a series of abstract numbers and casualty reports, which amount to "winning" or "losing" on the side of the would-be enthusiastic genocidal set. The only ones who feel as though they are losing are those eager to prove what is happening to the duped targets. As the events are actively unfolding, denial appears first as a thin veil to commendation and eventual wilful acquiescence. It does not help that the deniers are reinforced by their doctors gaslighting them to merely get ahead of the oncoming lawsuits they can plainly see on the horizon.

Spies and provocateurs have always sought to block a future in which we might have a say. All the more reason to ask why most people find the greater evil more palatable on an instinctual level. Is it not because we can quantify the risk, and assign a measurable probability to the potential harm? The button-pusher's motives are unclear, defying our attempts to mitigate danger. This uncertainty sparks within us a primal fear, as if our very existence were threatened in ways which would have been completely foreign and wholly immaterial to our primitive ancestors, as well as most recent. Those that stand to benefit the most are calm, of course, and society follows suit. They are calm because the risk, from their perspective, is all on your side.

The man with a button is new historically whereas the armed and violent man has always been. The button-wielding terrorist or politician, shrouded in mystery and anonymity from the other side of the planet, represents an existential threat, his motives and intentions clouded by purposeful confusion. The businessman with 'intelligence' connections and access to industrial chemicals does not raise the immediate red flags without additional information. In contrast, the armed assailant, identifiable and tangible, poses a direct challenge to physical well-being. Also, the latter makes for better movies anyway.

People are probably more averse to personal one-on-one murders because they trust other human beings and want to continue trusting them, especially family and those in their community. This aversion becomes much more frantic with greater population density. The motives of a man with an electronic button are not nearly as real and present to people as the motives of a man with a weapon intent on inflicting damage, at least. The armed assailant is the more theoretically manageable threat. We can prepare ourselves for the attack, fortify our defences, and even counterattack with relative effectiveness. The button-pushing terrorist, however, operates in the theoretical beyond our comprehension, his motivations and actions seemingly impervious to our attempts at rationalisation. The armed assailant embodies a threat that is at once recognisable and quantifiable. An amount of comfort stems from our ability to respond effectively.

Modern man, communally and among civilisation, evolved to trust, and breaking trust repulses him. There is an innate sense of trust, a fundamental reliance on the inherent good in others, especially toward those closest to us. Is it any wonder when somebody exhibiting "Stockholm syndrome" reaches out to emulate trust? Would we not be less able to function as societies were we to forgo the "niceties" which brought about such desires for trust and to trust, evolutionarily speaking?

This dynamic of desire for trustworthiness speaks to civilisation's reliance on trust. We have evolved to assume that at least some other humans will act with good intentions, that their motives are rooted in a shared understanding of right and wrong, especially as they are related. When this trust is broken, as it often is in times of crisis or chaos, we recoil in horror and reassess options. Would we be truly better off if we were less willing to trust? Is this the best solution to the problem of human violence? Less trust? Don't the terrorist then win, whomever they are? The button-pushing terrorist's anonymity and unpredictability also serves as constant reminder of the threat inherently evil within humanity. Evil exists and must be confronted in all and through all.

The Stockholm phenomenon represents a desperate attempt to contend with evil. By forming relationships with their captors, victims subvert the destructive forces that have been unleashed upon them, some seeking solace in fleeting moments of human connection. Here, at the intersection of trust and threats of violence, we find something additionally valuable in the nature of humanity. We proceed, if so compelled, to confront the abyss head-on, seeking to rebuild and strengthen communities and relationships. The answer lies not in the disrupting trust, but in raising it up and training it well.

People often plead with captors because, historically, it sometimes had to have worked. We are the descendants of captors and captives and Stockholm syndrome is simply an expression of behaviour that was selected. Every terrible thing hated about humanity by humanity has been selected for and passed on through generations, causing pain and cruelty just as well as, if not perhaps more than the loss of strength. That is inheritance. To quote Monty Python's own minstrel, Eric Idle, "All things foul and dangerous, all creatures short and stout, all things rude and nasty, the Lord God made the lot." Sooth.

Atop the peak none dare,
Shadowing the Sea,
Lived a man without care,
His eyes full of glee.

Between wistful stares,
He sang of a world,
& things long forgotten,
Before time unfurled
& souls were trodden.

"I saw the second Sun,
The greater Star shine,
Coolly inspiring earth's children.
Nurturing all human kind
Giving rise to True religion,
Deep furnace of Truth that is mine.
Celestial bodies held aloft,
High above in contrast
To the mundane across
A planet left aghast,
All speechless in awe."

That foolish outcast…

Living happily alone & without,
In remembering our past.

In fleeting moments, laughter bursts forth bright,
A sudden glory, born of self-amused light.
It rises swift, a spark of triumph in our breast,
Silently compare our strengths to weaknesses in test.
Or perhaps it's contrasted with our former plight,
When struggles swirled, & doubts filled us with fright.
Now, in this small bit of power, we rejoice merrily,
A fleeting sense of pride, made of what used to be.
In its momentary warmth, we find a care renewed
In laughing for a moment, all doubts are subdued...
It is within this, changing minds can be a kindly cue.

....

"Comedy is imitation of characters with low-morality,
though not the worst cases;
the ludicrous being merely a subdivision of the ugly.
It consists in some defect or ugliness which is not painful or
destructive."

~Aristotle

XV. Stage & Theatre

Rightly, we pity innocent victims, who had not the chance to improve their situation. We can learn from dramas, tragedies, or horror stories where people are terrorised unjustly. However, we do learn more through comedy, especially when very young. At the core of much comedy, however, is what Germans term "schadenfreude," where people derive pleasure from the misfortunes of those who have brought about their own downfall. When a victim is revealed to be the hapless protagonist, whose situation is mostly self-inflicted and the result of poor decision-making, our judgement undergoes a peculiar transformation. When it is all due to unfortunate decisions and simple stupidity, it magically changes from a tragedy or drama story to an uproarious misadventure. A sad narrative gives way to a farcical comedy, and we are left laughing at the absurdity.

People do enjoy a well-deserved death scene in stories because they like it best when the death is righteous, at its most exciting. We do not mourn nearly as much when we learn the victim is at fault. This curious affinity for deserved suffering as righteous is heavily rooted in our deep-seated desire for moral justice. We crave a world where actions have consequences, where those who reap chaos and destruction are met with an equal and opposite reaction in kind.

When the victim is revealed to be an innocent bystander, mired in circumstances beyond their control, empathy kicks in. People are more likely to mourn the loss of innocent life. Tales about victims of circumstance serve to underscore our sense of outrage at the injustice that has been perpetrated. These are the narratives most often used to justify the political campaigns against or for more police, and changes in police training. The argument is made around designated and paid heroes who will swoop in and save the day. It is a common sentiment to crave a world where good triumphs over evil, where justice is served, and where the innocent are protected from harm.

Humanity's tendency to seek out moral clarity in a chaotic world is very good and understandable, despite the often poor targeting. Things should make sense and justice should be served on concrete moral bases. I agree as much as I possibly can. Children most certainly deserve to be free from mortal competition. The desire is for simple answers to complex questions, but too often people are willing to overlook the nuances of human nature in order to arrive at ready solutions. This is to be expected, given the aforementioned seeking out moral clarity. However, the result is a never-ending cycle of hero-worship and revileship, where people elevate individuals to mythic status, only to later be disillusioned when the hero inevitably falls short of expectations.

In this sense, schadenfreude-humour can be seen as a form of vicarious catharsis, a way for us to experience and process our own errors and mortality without actually having to confront it or the realities of the chaos. This kind of abstract metaphoric representation, in fact, is essential to many forms of therapy. Sometimes it is okay to leave things to the subconscious at the moment, you'll have to come back to it though. However, people laugh at the absurdity of others' misfortunes because on some level they believe themselves to have a handle on things, often they can be right and sometimes they are wrong.

The tantalising tendrils of joy from humour wrap themselves around our sense of the absurd, pulling us into an emotional response to the ridiculous, or foolish. People are drawn to the spectacle of others' downfall, mesmerised by the intricate and often misunderstood dance of cause and effect. The protagonist as fool, lost in a self-designed maze of poor decisions, becomes an unwitting participant in our own existential crises, for we too have made, if not identical mistakes, mistakes, generally at least. Comedy emerges the harbinger of absurdities and fears that plague us all, in formats more easily digestible.

At the core is an innate craving for justice and meaning, as we struggle to impose order on the seemingly unpredictable happenings of experience and error that comprise our lives. Empathy, apathy, ridicule, and outrage converge, like opposing forces in an internal play of absurdities. We mourn the loss of innocence and rage at the injustices that befoul our world, even as many docilely await saviours to save the day. Comedy is an emotional ritual for many. It is also a perfect instrument for washing away the stains of rancid propaganda and lies. It is here that comedy acts as that powerful agent for transformation, through emotional wrestling moves using the person's own emotive weight in their favour.

Accurate moral insights can often only be accessed through a lens of comedy, objectifying and distancing the matter. Comedy courses through our veins in an almost elemental fashion. Simply the laughing in itself helps us heal. We use the irrepressible force of comedy toward the unyielding pursuit of clarity, with appropriate targeting. We must poke holes in the conceptual systems that perpetuate Victi-mentality. In this way, we can reveal the very real contradictions and irrationality that underlie it. This simple and logical power of subverting absurdities enables us to challenge these dominant and horrific narratives, even despite any lack of funding or support. When humour and wit are harnessed as instruments of moral critique, then satire, irony, and other forms of comedy become potent tools for challenging evil structures and exposing the hypocrisies within that can undermine them.

Now take up your cross upon self,
Carry for all, & the One that dwells,
Beyond what is inside you within depths,
Light shining brightly, bursting threads.
But I ask you, dear cousin, dear friend,
Can we see the truth & ultimate end?
Can we break free from victim spells,
Vindication in victory, as compels?
The Vindicated Hero, betrayed,
Messages lay tattered decayed.
Peaking shadows of crossed fate,
Crowning ever our losses most great.

XVI. Victim-Hero

The natural reaction of moral people is a righteous burning hatred when someone not only innocent but, indeed, very good is wrongly victimised. Western Civilisation has always contained some form of romanticism for the Lordly Victim-Hero, even before the apparent spread of Christianity. This figure is the victimised righteous man who gives up everything left due to and for the sake of the meek, impoverished, and weak, or otherwise unable to defend themselves.

Heroes rise and fall, myths unfold, and legends are born. Yet most recently, the insidious promotion of Victimentality through corruption of the Hero archetype is quite artificial and imperial. This less than underdog non-hero which never overcomes, often cast as a pawn in the grand scheme, is an unwitting facilitator of disconnection from the divine. By reducing the Hero to purely a Victim, a narrative that severs the connection to the sacred is promoted that reinforces the notion that we're helpless pawns at the mercy of external forces.

The Hero's journey is supposed to be a symbol of triumph over adversity, which in reality has been largely displaced into an exercise of reinforcing our own powerlessness. We're conditioned to believe that true strength lies not in realising the self within community but in the simple enduring of suffering and tragedy to find identity in them, most especially as pertaining to alienation. This twisted corruption and false wisdom engenders a culture of Stockholm syndrome-like excuses, where we're convinced that our only option is to acquiesce to the darkness of alienation and validation in materialism, rather than taking control through Spirit, through Christ, through God, through conscious effort, through real community, and through cultural growth.

Movement towards this corrupted version of the Victim-Hero narrative, as construed in full-on victimhood towards circumstances, insidiously erodes our sense of agency. It convinces us that we're merely reactive players in the grand game of existence. In reducing the Victim-Hero's actions to mere reactions to circumstance, which is to say a helpless victim status, the conditioning becomes that our choices are inconsequential and that the outcome is predetermined by external forces beyond our control.

This disconnection from divine doubly, through disconnection from discourse with moderation and our understanding of self as crucial to God through the Grace afforded us by His Son, is an inconceivable loss. When we're convinced that our fate is sealed, we're more likely to abandon personal responsibility, forfeiting our power to recognise and do Good. The result? A culture of helplessness, where individuals fail to take charge of their lives. The question remains: will we choose to empower ourselves or continue down the path of self-enslavement?

In the most correct and original Victim-Hero version, the suffering of the Godly Individual is symbolic of humanity's plight generally in sin and error, this is an eternal suffering, immortalised by the remembrance. In other versions which have become the most popular, the Victim-Hero will suffer and be victimised to absolve victimhood of any role in its own Vindication. Salvation is extended to victims from their weaknesses abstractly instead of through overcoming it literally, and in the Grace of discourse. Somehow this abstract grace, in this false formulation, is outside this very mode of existence, which is the cynical or profiteering preacher's way of silently admitting that he does not believe and is simply out for himself. This non-formulation of a false 'grace' is basically almost unexplainable without the most nonsensical terms, because actual Grace is very real and puts most pastors out of work.

The Victim-Hero, regardless of any actions, has become more championed primarily for the victimhood in the pain felt, and the act of taking on that pain for the sake of others. Through a basic miscomprehension of this absolution rather than Vindication, specifically, is the absolute indivisible seed kernel of Victimentality. To say, "I was wrong," and to admit defeat, to admit weakness, and to admit ignorance, not for the sake of the weakness or ignorance, or to maintain it. Rather, admitting imperfections is for the overcoming, for overcoming it is done in Love of God, which is the seed of Christ. In pursuit of justifications over justice in Vindication, the falsified comprehension of the Victim-Hero is immortalised for pain and victimhood primarily, as self-assigned. This feature is magnified as seen reflected in victims throughout cultures and sub-cultures.

These are important questions, especially for Christianity, where the goal is to imitate Christ. Of course, nobody can repeat all of what Christ did because many actions were necessary only once, as will be elaborated upon extensively in later chapters. Obviously, this example to follow of Christ cannot represent a mere archetype but a meta-archetypal One, an abstract praxis with much greater variety of applications:

> "Seek to imitate Christ in ALL THINGS, for He is the perfect example of Love and holiness."
> ~The Imitation of Christ

This One meta-archetype is Perfect and Ideal, as the model of service to all, however it can easily fall flat if it misses the practical aspects of needs for the weak, who should not be stumbled. The pain endured by the Victim-Hero is not merely a physical affliction, but a spiritual affliction as well. It is a reminder that we are all subject to the whims of forces outside our power, and that even the most noble among us can fall victim to the cruel hand of circumstances and injustices falsely promulgated within society as just.

Many charlatans have attempted to exploit the Victim-Hero meta-archetype to further their own material goals, and traditions have suffered because of this. The key to restoring the positive power in the Victim-Hero meta-archetype is not in any continued idolisation of literal suffering in itself, but in the demonstrated ability to transcend it. The only way to transcend victimhood and overcome it completely is in aligning the understanding of the purpose in the One, which is to say 'turn to God.'

In the false perspectives of corrupted Victim-Hero, the goal is promotion of the Victim identity itself through endless recital of the weaknesses that cause victimhood. Victimentality grinds a perpetual quest for new cycles of weakness preservation. What is weakness though? Earlier I discussed the Victim and how weaknesses in some areas can often undermine the terrific strengths in other skills or abilities. Weakness and suffering are cherished. This Stockholm syndrome culture becomes a pincushion of suffering, with each layer of needles serving as a catalyst for further regression and deprived formations of degeneracy.

The LOGOS, or the Word of God, can be seen as the antithesis to the pushpin of suffering. While the 'pincushioning' Stockholm culture perpetuates deepening victimhood and degeneracy, LOGOS embodies the power of redemption and actual salvation, both pragmatically and spiritually. Victimentality can be viewed as the ultimate form of idolatry and a primary mediacy manifesting anti-Christianity: where humanity elevates its own suffering and weakness to an altar of reverence. Conversely, the LOGOS represents the divine Word that speaks Truth and Light into the darkness of human existence. The pincushion in Victimentality is not merely a product of human experience and suffering but also has spiritual implications.

The Stockholm culture with its inbuilt Victimentality can be seen as a manifestation of humanity's rebellion against God's plan, where individuals seek to define their own purposes and meanings in life apart from the divine. Christ offers the only way, out of the cycle of material-obsessed victimhood, towards redemption. LOGOS, or Christ elevated, is not merely a philosophical or theological concept but affects our basic understanding of reality itself, and human nature.

Christ is necessary for very many reasons and for all people because it teaches a willingness to sacrifice toward the greatest Good, but it takes discipline and virtues to recognise what is worthy. These are the points most often missed. Most importantly, Christ is needed for fathers and for fatherhood, because of the masculine socialisation that sustains civilisation. The Son is Servant to all because all are in the Father and the only way to the Father is through the Son, the Word. Fathers are to replicate this.

The Father, who represents the moral and guiding force in society, has His role embodying all, most especially as the divine intellect that guides and nurtures humanity. Father is in all. All things would include not just matter but all energies. The Father of all is in all and our experience is through our energetic living Soul. The superconscious complex is very real as it skates across and uses our mental instruments like a fine symphony.

Tangled threads of human fate,

Victimentality's snare, soul's retreat.

Jungles of anguish in motions slow,

Suffering's worship, all for show.

Sons in Truth brush the stage away,

Transcending materialism's darkened day.

In Word as Truth; the Father is revealed,

Through Him, Vindication unveiled,

From victimhood's cycle, we're set free,

To serve in Love, finding Goodness deep.

Thus, let us heed LOGOS's eternal call,

To break the chains of material's thrall.

Find redemption in Christ's revelatory Light,

Where falsehoods die, captured in full sight.

XVII. Victimentality

The wrongly ascertained Victim-Hero meta-archetype launched the correspondent archetype of the helpless innocent Victim into collective culture. The hapless Victim does not defend his or her own home. They rely on those around them because of a deep trust in some plan in the chaos they presume to be that of God. The hapless Victim believes he means too little to the rest of society and dutifully hands over whatever he is asked for with consistency. What the meek inherited in the misunderstanding of the Victim-Hero archetype was a life of misery and squalor. Truly imitating Christ is holding the self and others to the same basic gradation of standards:

> "To be meek towards other people yet still impatient towards oneself is a dangerous sign of ignorance."
> ~The Imitation of Christ

The products of labours from these hapless victims trudging to factories and home again appear to have improved the world around them overall in many ways, certainly. It is true that many of the modern technological gadgets taken for granted today may not have ever been produced without this arrangement of basic industrial enslavement and the avarice of their exploiters. The meek were ripe for enabling this "inheritance" of the world as gifted to their masters, though they'd been made so, 'drunk' as many were on cultures that honoured nascent forms of Victimentality. They were discouraged from retributive violence and encouraged to simply accept burden and toil, with oppression being quite apparent. One can imagine how routinely labouring hard for sixteen hours a day could invoke some spiritual phenomena in even the least religious, if not outright psychosis from the lack of sleep.

Thus, the hapless Victim becomes a perpetual supplicant, begging scraps from the tables of those around them. Theirs is a life of meagre rewards, where even the most basic comforts are never deserved, yet merely earned in trade of relentless toil. This masochistic existence is perceived by many within the culture as a noble endeavour, one that even earns them a modicum of respect and admiration from many. For in their eyes, the world revolves around their own martyrdom, their suffering a sacrament that must be perpetuated as a profitable attitude to have towards the greater good, but is it? What are the fruits of such labour? Do they reap any tangible benefits from their ceaseless striving? Barely, and by design.

Our inheritance, apparently, has become a life of squalor and misery with hard work yielding only fleeting improvements, perhaps especially so with the onset of obsolescence as basic policy. Yet, so many are content in the mere knowledge that their sacrifice has been acknowledged and respected, that their torment has not been in vain due to basic recognition from those whose recognition may not actually be worth anything at all. One can imagine the numbing effects of hapless Victim slaves, slowly bleeding away any semblance of hope or humanity and only profiting the corporations and stockholders. What lies beyond this abyss between purpose and effort? What rewards await a person who emerges from the depths of their own private hell? A fancy watch and a thanks, if they are lucky. Death in life is what it is. The alternative presented is naked greed and avarice.

This toxic cycle of victimhood and martyrdom is further reinforced by the culture. Victimentality is the new sacrament in this dejected Stockholm culture, discouraging any action as always uncalled-for under all circumstances, and encouraging burdensome toil as some strange evidence of good simply in itself. In this warped world, the meek are encouraged to bear the yoke of their own oppression, to suffer quietly and without complaint. So they do, driven by a spiritually-confused fervour borne of the unhappiest union in desperation and resignation.

Insidious idolatry of lucre, like a ravenous vampire, attaches itself to desires like necks, sucking the lifeblood from souls and leaving only desiccated husks in place. Modernity elevated these blood-dusted damnation bills of enslavement to a temple throne, with all neighbourhoods worshipping at the altar of Mammon. Those who manipulate the system do so for their own gain maintaining a mastery over the matter of humanity. What lies at the centre of this darkness? A trail. A trail to where?

Knock, knock. Who's there? Money. Money who? Exactly, follow it. Follow the money. Not all the things money buys. Not all the things of suckers, the lovers of money, who are brought low, as slaves to the money owners. Not the downtrodden and addicted. Addictions to anything, but the truth, are the very fuel used to power this ship of undead Victims. They fear the man who can kill his own addictions. More than that, they fear the former wretch who kills the darkness within. Adoration of money is ultimately adoration of sin through the self, mortal and imperfect, but also unrefined.

We are taught by the behaviours seen throughout society from earliest infancy to clutch the money tightly, like the candy to end all candies. The "fortunate" are schooled in the art of accumulation, supposed "capital" but euphemism for the adoration of individual sin by the accumulators. Oh, to have a say, and thereafter, within any scattering would be found the true treasure, not in the keeping, but in truly careful discrimination in the giving away; ultimately the best reward of labour is in the choosing of what those energies should go toward, both individually and societally. In the heaping of material treasures, we necessarily lose sight of true value.

Greed devours all in its path, the least fictional of black holes. It is an endless desire for more, a void that can never be filled, a labyrinth without an exit. As we succumb to its allure, we find ourselves trapped by the resounding effects of our own desires echoing back at us. What fuels this infernal machine? Whosoever enslaved by Mammon will founder on the rocks of temptation, their very souls and purposes dashed there.

Now, rather, I daresay the radiant beauty of Love, that lovely 'Aurora Borealis' of the planet Life, always teaches of Good. Love enables the faith, which is to say the ultimate trust. Celestial dance of uniting in resonance. That which is most True is most valuable. Drinking in Holy Spirit, we become vessels for the divine wine in sublime inspiration. Thoughts present as frequencies in energy with variations being in Love's attenuation; the squeezing, but not the grapes of anything in the material human, no, but through their rejection first, and then anything else not of God after that. We seek the Fruits of God alone, that of the Spirit.

"When you are insulted by someone or humiliated, guard against angry thoughts, lest they arouse a feeling of irritation and so cut you off from love and place you in the realm of **hatred**."

~St. Maximus the Confessor

"It is not what happens to you,

but how you react to it that matters."

~Epictetus

"He has the most who is most content with the least."

~Diogenes

Timeless echoes, that brave virtuous Son,

Heroic Virtues, moderated of reason.

Quest for justice, ye purest of flame,

Alight paths Godly; sweet aspects proclaim.

God's ultimate Gift, transcending creed,

Dead in life revived in Grace, as all are freed.

Moderating motivated ascents, so grand,

Spiral self-overcoming rebirth, now stand.

No cheap indulgence or plea can stay,

Justice delivered with momentum & sway.

In God's Word do eternally aspire,

Christ walks beside, with an all-abiding Fire.

Flame burns best within, dying when outside,

Love's essence bonds us in God's eternal pride.

XVIII. Mediators

A true exemplar of the proper Hero in a truly Christian culture would take the role of mediator, finding compromises throughout society but most especially between the great and the 'pitiful,' to aid in the most stability and progress. This includes those with good intentions attracted to roles such as police, firefighters, politicians, lawyers, priests, psychologists, journalists, whistleblowers, protesters, and other religious or community leadership roles but should also include those interested in developing business. Some will heed an even higher calling, to champion the cause of the weak, empowering them to find their best strengths within genuine reason. In Victimentality, there has been this perpetual cycle of sacrifice, bloody rebirth through the martyrdom of new "heroes." This phenomenon is not unique to modern times; throughout history, we see falsified archetypal replications reenacted time and again. Often it is done in mockery of Christ.

The Victimental misapprehension perpetuates a cycle of weakness and seeking after only external comforts, rather than promoting strength and Vindication. Instead of seeing the victim as having strengths to overcome their weaknesses, the focus is assigned towards preserving and promoting victimhood. The goal becomes not to overcome the weakness, but to find salvation through identifying the self with victimhood, defining limitations upon the self within the victimhood, and perpetuating the cycle of victimhood generally. The greatest travesty is here in this that distorts the very essence of the Christian creed, plainly. The masses are drawn to this counterfeit of the Faith for the emotions involved alone, mesmerised by its promises of salvation universalised into utter nothingness and meaninglessness, without full redemption being taken seriously.

Original philosophical Christianity transcends this mundane melodrama. Christ is **the** ascendant Force, the greatest of philosophical highpoints over the abyssal depths of human suffering, Who triumphs stronger for it. The dialectic in reality as metaphorically represented here itself confirms Christian Faith as a concept epitomised by a term: 'love of wisdom,' the philosophical waxed in heavenly spiral of self-overcoming as ceaselessly striving for knowledge, progress, and moral improvement. The cross that each philosopher takes up was their burden in this life intellectually and spiritually, which is to say the primary crux, or overlay, of subjects that they were called upon in life to work in and improve. This is the resolution in the meaning of their life. For the average individual, this translates into being the best version of the self possible, and then empowering others to do the same. Beyond this are the deeper works through inspirations artistically, philosophically, and conceptually.

The Truest Christianity fully engaged is the greatest ontological precipice and outlook possible for a complete philosophical scientific outlook, and the State of mind granting most accurate visions into the distant future. As seekers of truths, we must map the human condition honestly, so we must be armed with the proper tools. Those tools are only available under an honest Christianity that is not a mere accessory, but an integral component of our very beings and understandings of reality. Thus, I posit that Christianity is not merely a set of dogmatic beliefs or pious platitudes, but an existential imperative. For me, this existential imperative was one that demanded I confront the trends at the core of this Victimentality ignorance, as well as its philosophical origins, regardless what the truths turned out to be.

How can we cultivate a deeper connection with God in our individual and collective lives? Through God's Word, of course, LOGOS, Christ in elevation. The elevated discourse leads us to moderation and reason in our lives, so that reason leads us down the path of virtues. Moderation in life through virtues allows us to dive deeply within, as best attuned to the Source; spiritual strength as capable in moderation is the closest to God a mortal can ever reach. Without the virtues skills, people believe anything that may come to mind and are directed to seek out nonsense, this is where delusions enter.

Virtues are like street smarts for Goodness. Constant activity in Good, which is to say in attaining discourse to Greater levels OF Good, attunes the mind towards God. Having a strong sense of moral direction can guide us toward making choices that align with the highest values and aspirations attainable. It allows the creative faculties of the mind to focus upon what is best and greatest, which is maximisation of freedom. God's Word is the Light by which we may explore the dark depths in the superconscious complex and find the universal Mind, in its purest aspects. Virtues are necessary for moderating our lives and allowing us to access the deeper realms of being and inspiration while remaining sane. This is spiritual discipline that enables the cultivation of greater senses in insight, compassion, and finding God's wisdom.

Constant activity in Good, or the pursuit of greater levels of Goodness means Good is not just a static state, but rather an ongoing process of growth and development. This is to say that it cannot remain stagnant. LOGOS is the Light that shines through the darkness. Universal Mind in the purest aspects represents a deeper, more fundamental level of Spirit that underlies all existence.

Love backed by virtues is the purest of emotion, because it comes from a position of strength. This is more than just a beautiful concept, it is utterly true. True Love is not just an emotional feeling. Love's value is rooted in moral character and integrity. The Universal Mind in its purest aspects holds the ultimate form of Love higher than humans can comprehend, in fact, so high many think God hates them.

Upon recognising the profound extent of divine love and adoration, surpassing any human capacity for reciprocation, one is compelled to undergo transformation. This transformation necessitates loving God to the fullest extent possible, which involves adhering to exceptionally high standards and responsibilities. This Love has equally high standards for neighbours, and especially of enemies. Being critical of the self, quite critical of neighbours, and hyper-critical of enemies, who have been so caught up in evil, are all essential to embodying a Love approaching Godliness.

True Love requires us to be our best selves and to live in accordance with our highest values. The Universal Mind being the ultimate form of Love is more than just a profound concept, it is also fundamentally true and obvious on its face. The deepest level of reality is characterised by a Love more elemental than we can realise. It is an infinite Love for Life, especially humanity with Good and God in their hearts. Some people may feel unworthy or unlovable because they can't currently comprehend the full extent of God's Love. Cycles of self-doubt and shame can render anyone unable to fully receive God's Adoration. When we experience the fullness of God's Love, we feel an overwhelming desire to respond with our own Love and devotion. This is a transformative process on our parts.

When you truly Love God, then you Adore only that which is of God, especially within, which means you despise anything within not of God. There is nothing in money itself that can help God. It is supposed to be a tool for trade within community, capital of which at most should be financing good and necessary projects or innovations for the community. Natural and true community is God's plan for the best freedom of each individual, not money as communal haemorrhaging. God does not provide money, that would not be God's Love. Rather God provides you with the lessons how to best give that money away. God Loves you so much, He acts through you.

Love of God teaches how to Love the self properly, and so, too, our neighbours and even enemies. So, like a river flowing to the Sea, our wealth flows outward into community, carrying with it the sediment and the riverstones of our efforts and energies. Yet what if we kept everything? What would be the point? Regardless, it is perfectly reasonable, and further very responsible to wish for some say in what your labours and hard work support, but it's far better to know what to support. Just as it is Loving of self to have expectations of the self, it is loving of everyone else to have appropriate expectations of them, and they, ultimately, of you, too.

"It is necessary that every thing which is harmonised, should be generated from that which is void of harmony, and that which is void of harmony from that which is harmonised. ...But there is no difference, whether this is asserted of harmony, or of order, or composition... the same reason will apply to all of these."

~Aristotle

Sweet thoughts toward eternity's promises of old,

In this life, Love's flame ignites hearts agold.

Fear uselessly beckons the chosen by Light,

Since in its radiance, hope grants them flight.

Rituals of empty resistance make bare,

That Love's awesome power is beyond compare.

Faith breaks out, in all things begun,

On this spindle of Love, God's Story is spun.

XIX. Utopia

Most political philosophers that have railed against aspects of "Judaeo-Christianity," however they defined it, were criticising iterations or symptoms of this wrong-headed Victim worship. The alienation from self is felt equally by all classes as they are left with two options: fulfil these roles of Hero, destined for destruction, and Victim, manipulating things, or rejecting them all together. Rejecting them all together comes with the added detriment of typically alienating the person greatly from the rest of society, and most especially their field.

How many reject it, and what becomes of them? Anybody can reject something in theory and pretend to some resistance but do they stop paying taxes, paying tithes, collecting benefits, or accepting a menial income? What other options is there though? Engaging in the primary Victim-Hero polemics in hopes of shifting the sport? What if they do all that, what does any of it accomplish?

"Utopractics" is a belief utopia can be brought about merely by acting it out. In legitimate and serious practice, utopractics will invariable get you arrested or killed and, even if you achieve it, you will have separated yourself from the rest of society. Serious utopractitioners with a fondness for polemics will usually become quite used to talking to themselves. Needless to say, believers in utopractics are not, were not, and will never be utopractitioners.

This affliction, manifesting as various symptoms across different ideologies, saps the vitality from individuality, reducing it to mere caricature. The notion of utopia can be achieved through mere theatricality, because it can only ever be theatre. It is, in fact, utopageantry. Believers taken in by the pageantry of utopia find themselves isolated from the very society they sought to transform, due to a basic unwillingness to engage at various levels. The solitary figure, shouting slogans at an empty street corner, is a poignant reminder that "true" revolutionaries are often consumed by their own convictions without ever accomplishing anything. What does it actually take to shift society though, if not simply faking it until it is made?

Most notions of utopia are illusions, perpetuated by those who benefit from the current power structure. The current system of power is sustained by the clever manipulation of law, infrastructure, resources, incorporation, and corporate governance. Laws are crafted to maintain the status quo, protecting the interests of those who have already accumulated power. This is evident in the way corporations are structured, with private governance and decision-making processes that allow for the exploitation of resources and labour. Infrastructure, too, is designed to favour the business of the massively wealthy, serving as tools of oppression in that process.

The designs of cities, roads, and buildings create barriers to movement, isolating communities and limiting access to resources while forcing people into proximity with known criminals. Real estate developers plan this out on purpose, and they work for the massively wealthy. The organisation of structures reinforces social hierarchies, allowing those who are already powerful to maintain their control. Resources in capital extraction out of communities are another key area where manipulation occurs. If the capital were compared to how taxes should be spent back on the taxpayers, then the removal out of the community would look quite the same.

Those with access to these resources can use them to further entrench their position and the people they care about, while those without are left struggling for survival. Incorporation law and corporate governance structures create a complex web of divisions, allowing powerful individuals to isolate themselves from accountability while maximising their control and profit. Corporations become entities unto themselves, governed by private rules that prioritise profits over people. This perpetuates the exploitation of people. People are reduced to mere commodities, exploited for their productivity without regard for their well-being or best interests. Corporations pretend to be governments, essentially, when they lord over various physical locations and force conditions or even take more out of that unit than is put back in. Man yet again takes advantage of man, as this private governance between locations effectively forces divisions in the lower echelons of power within a corporation into slave bins.

Inflation serves as constant backdrop, and eternal shin-kicker to entrepreneurs of the formerly kindly West. Businesses cannot so easily seek interest and investment from local organisations, why? Inflation discourages savings, and discount rates for banks make their profit margins impossible to compete with, even if a temporary advantage were established for a short period of time. Add to this the heightened cost of market entry due to regulations designed to cut off nascent competition. Inflation also encourages the acquisition of debt, making it ubiquitous and easiest to get from the largest banks, while encouraging abuse of credit instead of improving their community.

Those finding strength through Christ can become a force for empowering others, like mighty rivers overflowing banks into other streams, some even raising the hypothetical sea levels, surely. The strong individual within communities best serve as waterways to the legitimate needs of those around them. They recognise that their strength is not about personal power, but creating ripple effects of empowerment that can spread throughout society like wildfire.

This is no zero-sum game, where one person's gain comes at the expense or loss of others, nor is it utopia. No, this is meritocratic co-creation, where each individual brings their unique strengths and talents to the table like all the building material needed to construct a house. Together, they're able to be brought together for something greater than the sum of parts. Communities can be true forces for Good, patches and stitchworks to mend hearts and errors. We need more folks who can bring people together. We need more catalysts for change. What is needed are more overflowing river and wildfire people.

"Until philosophers are kings, or the kings and princes of this world have the spirit and power of philosophy, and political greatness and wisdom meet in one, and those commoner natures who pursue either to the exclusion of the other are compelled to stand aside, cities will never have rest from their evils."

~Platon

"It is the act of a tyrant to oppress, but it is the act of a philosopher to bear with the injuries of others."

~Marcus Aurelius

"The highest Goodness is like water. Water benefits all things and does not compete with them. It dwells in even the lowliest of places that all disdain."

~Laozi

"To see what is Good and not do it is cowardice."

~Confucius

"It is a mistake to imagine slavery pervades the whole being of a man. The better part of him is exempt from it; the body indeed is subjected and in the power of a master, but the mind is independent."

~Seneca

In cauldrons of power, dogma is forged.

Deceit simmers off truth; ignored.

Holy texts corrupted, serving imperial desires,

Their lies all congeal like lard in fires.

Tongued deception craft precision,

Legitimacy; false wall of possession.

Fiction blurs facts in all lands of the fake,

As reality is distorted, for sake of false stake.

Thereby goes forgotten, the Cross,

In the shiniest of sparkles & dross.

XX. Feudal Efficiencies

The promotion of the Victim-Hero archetype enabled a feudalism which inevitably evolved into industrialisation. It was no accident, far from it. It was, however, founded on a fundamental need for the great to utilise the 'pitiful,' and so a science of control was crafted over many centuries. Those societies better able to move people where they do the best good for their people naturally outperformed others. This is especially so where those with great skills and strengths could be brought down low and to believe they were 'pitiful,' by way of material enticement and the Victim and Victim-Hero identities. The notion that the misappropriated interpretation of the Victim-Hero archetype was merely an unfortunate byproduct of societal evolution is a gross oversimplification, a whitewashing of the very real mechanisms that have shaped human history. No, the promotion of this archetype was no accident, but rather a deliberate and calculated move to harness the power of the so enslaved.

In feudal societies, the Victim-Hero misinterpretation served as a means to pacify the peasantry, providing a focal point for their frustrations while allowing the ruling parties to maintain grip of power. The poor and downtrodden were thus convinced by lies that their suffering was not primarily the result of capricious rulers, but rather the direct consequence of some divine agency establishing an unlimited fate handed down from on high, thereby legitimising the existing social order. This clever manipulation of the masses allowed feudal lords to reap the benefits of their subjects' labour without having to burden themselves. There was no need of actual fairness because suffering could be considered righteous and something to be lauded as good for the soul in itself, rather than, again, with the overcoming of it.

The 'pitiful,' in turn, were provided with a sense of purpose and belonging, as they identified with their betters as installed by God. The rise of industrialisation merely built upon this foundation, as the corrupted Victim-Hero archetype was further repurposed to drive the exploitation of the servant classes. The suffering of the many was thus re-framed as a necessary evil, a sacrifice required for technological advances, unqualified efficiencies, and, ultimately, greater prosperity for even fewer than ever before.

What of those societies that were unable to leverage their populations effectively? Did they not suffer correspondingly? The answer is a resounding yes. Those societies that failed to tap into the energies of their workforce failed yes. Societies failing to organise were inevitably out-performed by those that succeeded at it, as the great exploited the pitiful to fuel their own personal ascendancy and individual empowerment. To this end, Victimentality has been perpetuated throughout history with effective results. It is a leveraged mechanism designed to amplify the power of the powerful, especially those of whom can identify as Victim, while pacifying the masses (these are usually "hero-victims" as discussed in later chapters). However, the purpose in the One, as meta-archetype, was always service to the many, in fact all, and not the few. Who is greater than the manipulators of weaknesses? Those who were born to be great, who reject its horrors, and refuse to participate in the grand farce, choosing instead to forge truer paths in better alignment with God that defy expectations of the corrupted culture: these wonderful mediators.

In transition from the shadows of deceit to the radiance of Truth, we find ourselves at a crossroads. Within ourselves and with those closest to us, we can co-create a world where each struggle has the potential to become a light for others. This is not a romanticised vision of some strange utopia, but rather a pragmatic recognition that true heroism is in overcoming whatever the adversity and to then empower others to do the same.

This heroism is not forged in isolation, but rather in the midsts of family, community, culture, and tradition. It is within these particular contexts that we discover our deepest sense of purpose and belonging, and it is through our relationships with one another that we find the strength to overcome even the most daunting challenges. Yet, as we strive to serve the Universal in God, we must also recognise that our individual struggles are but the tiniest section of a much larger puzzle, the questions for which answers are sought will be within families, communities, and nations. It is here, at the alignment of individuality, particularity, and universality that we find the true meaning of heroism, in helping others do likewise.

It is not the grand gestures or spectacular feats that define us as heroes, but rather the quiet, persistent efforts we make to serve one another, to help one another grow to increase abilities to heal, and to bring light into a world that often appears too dark. It is in the humble acts of genuine Love, kindness, and compassion that we discover our true potential, not as isolated individuals, but as members of larger natural communities bound together. Globally we share less but there still exists the common needs of humanity, especially for individuals, for the best cultural support tailored to them naturally. Heroism is not something that can be reduced to grand theories or abstract ideals. Rather, it is a living, breathing reality that arises from the depths of our souls and hearts. It is here in building upon virtues, in the midst of our daily lives, that we find our true calling as servants of the Universal in God.

We must never forget there exists insidious forces that seek to alienate us from one another on illogical grounds, where logic can unite us despite seemingly disparate interests. Here we find some of the most pernicious examples of manipulation. Take, for instance, the notion that humans are fundamentally selfish creatures, driven solely by a desire for self-preservation and personal gain. This idea, promulgated by many in evolutionary psychology, has been dangerous, leading many to believe that true heroism is an illusion, that we can only truly serve our own interests. This assumption is fundamentally flawed and, in fact, humans are wired for connection, for community, and for service to others, and for sacrifice, especially as they gain in wisdom.

The evidence suggests that this is the case. Studies have shown that acts of kindness and generosity actually stimulate the release of oxytocin, often referred to as the "cuddle hormone," which has been linked to feelings of trust, bonding, and even spiritual transcendence. The wisest of humans lean into this because of how immensely reassuring and powerful it is, not only that it is empowering. Have you ever hugged a woman late in pregnancy and make her smile? Well in that moment, you empowered her amazingly. The long-term ramifications of empowerment are difficult to measure, but the mind has a great deal of control over the body and emotions.

Many people continue to be tormented by the idea that they are fundamentally flawed, that they are inherently selfish or sinful. We are all born imperfect, but to not learn from it is to be unrepentant, no matter how much the sin is discussed. Feeling as though there is no answer to sin can have devastating consequences, leading to feelings of isolation, despair, and hopelessness. Here's the thing though: these ideas about psychology are not only false, but they are also designed to make you feel that way. For it is in our relationships with one another, in our acts of service and kindness, that we find our true purpose and meaning. It is freedom to recognise Good and be able to do it, no matter how little. It is the sense of connection and community felt through empowering others to recognise and do Good themselves that truly sets us free, becoming grandparents to freedom, of sorts.

"We learn by doing, and in matters of virtue,
we become just by performing just actions,
temperate by performing temperate actions,
brave by performing brave actions.
The virtuous person serves as a model,
showing us the path to excellence
through their habits and character."

~Aristotle

"Be imitators of me, as I am of Christ."
"For Christ is the Image of the invisible God,
the Firstborn over all creation,
and in Him all things hold together."

~Apostle Paulus (1 Corinthians 11:1; Colossians 1:15-17)

In dark corners, secrets are heard,

Echoing power, heartlessly answered.

Shadows of terror, myths to some,

Silent screams for justice to come.

The Sun will seem to fade fast,

Illuminated paths, quickly uncast.

Martyrs weep, for the cause divine,

Hypocrites cheer for the greatest lying.

Rise with the aurora, & watch from afar.

Witness Civilisation crumble, then heal & scar.

Though the wind of change violently blows,

Empower it still despite darkness's growths.

XXI. Archetypes & Ethotypes

That societies are bound by the archetypes within the culture, each with its attendant ethical lessons, is a fundamentally true notion and warrants closer examination. We shall dub this concept the ethotype, a term that encapsulates the enduring essence of a particular societal paradigm of archetypes that outlives the original archetypal constructs, so reborn with others in a sort of mutation in meanings. Every archetype set of a society has attendant ethical lessons, we will refer to these collective lessons here as the ethotype.

The interesting thing about ethotypes is that they can survive their original outward forms. This means that a derivative Victim-Hero worship culture can reject elements of dogma, labels, beliefs, scripture, and even the primary Victim-Hero figure of the parent culture (replacing it with others, of course) and still adhere to a very similar Victim-Hero archetype-based ethotype, though most often a more flawed and extreme one. In fact, this is exactly what happens most of the time. An individual born into a society which venerates a misunderstanding of the archetype will have a difficult time removing any of its manifestations let alone most, as the process is difficult.

This means that a derivative culture can distance itself from its forebear's primary elements, yet still retain a remarkably identical ethotype. In fact, this process of adaptation is the norm rather than the exception. When we examine the plethora of cultural belief systems that have emerged throughout history, we find that they often share striking similarities with their predecessors, despite superficial differences. This is not merely a coincidence; it speaks to the deep-seated nature of ethotypes, which can withstand significant alterations in expressions and archetypal themes.

The process of replacement to anything else, besides the more original meta-archetype, is akin to trying to sever the roots of a tree without uprooting the entire organism. It is impossible. The only thing that can possibly replace it is within the older patterns which continue to exert influence by a basic underlying pull, even as the new forms of the ethotype take their shapes belying details in the previous truths. This persistence of ethotypes can also be seen in politics and power structures. A revolution may arise, overthrowing an existing regime, yet the underlying dynamics of exploitation and control often persist, manifesting in new forms that are eerily reminiscent of the predecessors despite new dressings.

The new derivative ethotype will almost always attempt to outdo the parent ethotype along the same measures of morality, or, at most some minor alteration of it. This is especially true of already established absurd extremes, thereby proving the derivative ethotype's rejected articles or premises to have been at best hindrances to the ultimate goal of promotion of an ethotype perceived somehow purer. Indeed, most movements against a parent ethotype's system of morality would merely seek to supplant them with ever greater extremes. This is why the Victimentality variant of the Victim-Hero ethotype will demand purer and purer forms of unchallenged victimhood until the system eventually implodes on itself. They will seek to destroy the outward trappings and magnify the extremely expressed absurdities already present into horrific funhouse mirror aspects of the ethotype, a sideshow of parody and ridicule.

The propensity for derivative ethotypes to outdo their predecessors is a predictable consequence. However, the Victimentality ethotype's insatiable hunger for moral ascendancy is based in blind rage. Like a ravenous beast, this post-meta-archetypal-ethotype consumes all in its path, demanding an ever-increasing dosage of Victimentality to satiate its unquenchable thirst. The hysterical derivative ethotype will use theatrics and pantomime emotions in the language of the mother cult seeking to replace it as the ultimate arbiter of moral correctness. Any reactions by opposition merely 'proves' the new ethotype. This process is repetitive, where each iteration refines and intensifies the lost archetype's demand in Victimentality for justifications. If the power of spectacle alone could carry forward such nonsense, just imagine how much more it could do for radiant Truth.

"These are the reasons... for which one might suppose that place is something over and above bodies, and that every body perceptible by sense is in place. Hesiod, too, might seem to be speaking correctly in making Chaos first: 'Foremost of all things Chaos came to be, and then broad-breasted Earth,' suggesting that the place in Chaos was necessary... that there should first be a space available to the things that are... place does not perish when the things in it cease to be."

~Aristotle

"Your wound is the entrance for His Light."

~Rumi

Virtues & wisdoms, ridiculed, shamed

Eroding foundations, slowly infamed.

Fear & doubt creep in, like the thieves,

Steal dignity, pride, efforts, & beliefs.

Silence their screams, as voices fade,

Secret weaknesses, covered in shade.

Cracks in the mirror, reflecting fears,

Fractured self, fragmented tears.

Shadows lengthen, as light recedes,

Dismantling walls, crushing needs.

Rhetoric razes, reason's ruin.

Echoes of emptiness, silence's doing,

Standards shattered, compromised.

Victim's veil false & lifted wide,

The mongering feasts on fear's flesh,

Genocide's precursor, shame's dark mesh.

XXII. Strength Shamed

The things considered "virtues" within the corrupted Victim-Hero ethotype include unnatural self-sacrifices to artificial bodies, protection of weaknesses for the sake of weakness itself, and a passivity toward horrors so long as they are framed as justifiable within the ideals of victimhood. This all travels with a staunch inevitability which can often manifest as obsessions in notions of eschatological finality, as most fervent resistance to the newest extremists, or Whig history in legally imposed 'liberations' outside of legitimate Good, natural systems, and reality, on the very other end. These are features shared in common among many forms of Christianity and their daughter ethotype replacements in atheisms or worship of State imposed false liberations.

Many of the virtues most original to those cultures which adhered to the Victim-Hero ethotype have been instrumental in shaping human history. Self-sacrifice, for instance, is a cornerstone of this archetype, as it empowers individuals to lay down their lives for the greater good, rather than succumbing to petty concerns or base desires. However this has been too often misappropriated for the benefit of the wealthy. The selfless impulse has been abused badly, through the manipulation of facts and the promotion of lies.

Adhering to better versions of this ethotype historically, encouraged soldiers to fight for their nation, especially for those too weak to fight, instead of simply for their own benefit or even, say, the literal benefit of their lord alone, as real as the conflict may have been. The church was able to levy insane amounts of labour on a moment's notice, and even more so if it was feeling generous enough to pay. Those societies best at inculcating the ethotype attending this archetype of selfless servant, no matter how artificial or abusive of more natural concepts, were the most successful, ultimately, due to the simple ability to rally manpower, in all avenues of industry.

Noble ideals of patriotism and duty are inextricably linked to the Victim-Hero ethotype, as individuals are motivated to make the ultimate sacrifice for the sake of their comrades, their country, or their community. This can be misused by the powerful within a nation to essentially order wholesale genocide of populations, as done during the recent false pandemics and genetic poisons given out as medicine. The test here is whether patriotism is grounded in the actual people of the nation (complete), or simply the nation as an idea (empty). If pride in the nation is founded around simple ideas, there exists an expressed willingness to execute genocide for the ideas against those people who are not for the ideas. Nations exist for people, not the other way around, and anything else is blatant slavery.

Furthermore, the elements of passivity and inevitability inherent, whether derived out of other genuine virtues, or fear and Victimentality, have enabled scholars to willingly dedicate countless hours of labour toward the promulgation of their civilisation. It encouraged billions of hours of free labour on the parts of scholars, monks and missionaries in the promulgation of their civilisation, receiving nothing in compensation but the knowledge that they were benefiting the already extremely wealthy church. A fine thing before it was all funnelled into the coffers of 'midas' (read: "Judas") 'churches.' It should be noted that 'church' is a weak translation, where 'assemblage,' vis-à-vis a community, is more accurate given the original military connotations at the time. The selfless pursuit of knowledge, art, and spirituality is thus fuelled by the Victim-Hero ethotype, as individuals are driven to contribute to the greater good through their communities, rather than seeking personal gain or recognition.

However, in the latest and most atheistic variants of the Victimentality misunderstanding, personal gain and self-glorification are back on the menu. Parasitic leadership which successfully inculcated the misinformed Victimentality ethotype have reaped the rewards of a divided people further alienated into isolated individuals, incapable of achieving great feats through collective efforts and shared sacrifice, now only knowing individual sacrifice in contribution to that bankhole-owned corporation acting as "employer," so-called. Everyone forgets "employer" is so accurate because it means 'user.' The corporate alienation has further increased the ability of manchildren billionaires to achieve things ever less naturally within the immediate purview or legitimate interests of mankind, i.e. abominations. The wisest within most populations can all equally see the distractions for what they are, though it has been difficult to come to a common solution.

In particular, a hallmark of these distractions is in the basic plan of greater and more materialism for these societies, so that the alienated individuals are motivated to work together in profiting their owners, rather than pursuing their own individual and communal interests in reality. However, when biases are not expressed and honestly explored, what is left is the least common denominator, which is ultimately material wealth, simply cash. This cash funnels into the banks, temples, psyops, poisons, and vice. Any other promoted narratives in business or a future society living in peace amongst billionaires and trillionaires is a lie to hide this Truth, as inconvenient for them. Nothing else gets solved until humanity's spiritual problems are resolved, here and now.

This phenomenon can be observed in modern times as well as in the ancient civilisations. From the redirection toward genocide and the destruction of history done with the selfless disregard of gallant knights and spiritual crusaders to the promotion of poison through the unwavering dedication of scientists and engineers working toward breakthroughs in medicine, technology, or environmental sustainability. All these variations of the Victim-Hero ethotype, including Victimentality though corrupted, continue to inspire individuals to put the needs of others before their own, even when misdirected. In the case of Victimentality in itself as an entity across many ethotypes, these efforts are often to the detriment of society overall. The weaknesses in the misapprehensions of this archetype have enabled societies of the so fooled to construct cultures that at once appear compassionate but hide very real atrocities being actively committed as I write this book. By honouring vulnerabilities, the contribution of the billionaire manchildren continues to be one fostering weaker or weakened people who can be manipulated in order to further empower themselves only.

Ultimately, the Victim-Hero ethotype, even when misunderstood, has inspired individuals to make sacrifices and be of service, contributed to the development of complex societies, and facilitated the advancement of knowledge and culture, even billionaire manchildren at times. Its influence can be seen in the countless acts of selfless heroes and altruism that have punctuated Western civilisation and on every page of its histories: greatness in the face of adversity, even if imperfect and somewhat misguided at times. However, when most imperfect, this mentality becomes more easily controlled and manipulated, while being infinitely destructive as well.

The original meta-archetype, along with apparent shadows of it, can be traced in the edges of development in our own very human mind going back many hundreds of thousands and even millions of years, far beyond the origins of civilisation and prehistory. Humanity learned from its mistakes and the Grace from this has led mankind into being human and then being civilised, all the way up and entirely. Christ LOGOS has been there with humanity since the very first decision, the first recognised errors, the very first lessons, and first conversations about what was best to do.

As corrupted, Victimentality is the mindset that justifies its actions in the drapery of victim's false lived-vindication without anything actually in it. It justifies its actions based upon any perceived victimhood within reach. Eventually Victimentality reigns supreme, and most people become too afraid to simply say "no" to it. The shame is almost too much to bear, amid the chaos and confusion of a society turned on its head and devoid of merit in promotions and rewards, as well as in the meting out of unjust punishments. Let go.

This ancient misunderstanding has been deployed to justify some of humanity's most egregious crimes, by those masquerading as victims or defenders of the downtrodden. Throughout the ages, Victimentality has been used to rationalise wars over perceived insults, territorial disputes, and economic rivalries. It's a subtle yet potent narrative that enables individuals and groups to justify their destructive behaviours by appealing to a perceived sense of victimhood.

The corrupted emotional complex in the Victimental culture is masterstroke spin-doctoring for evil purposes, convincing folks that their actions against innocents are justified by virtue of being somehow "victimised" themselves. This phenomenon has been observed across cultures and throughout history, with notable examples including the justifications for colonialism, imperialism, wars of conquest, and now its reversal in the counter-colonising of Europe and America. It's a narrative that has been employed to rationalise and blame the innocent for the exploitation of their own resources, destruction of environment, the oppression of dissent, dismantling of heritage, and the deconstruction of culture, while not allowing any justice against the victimhood-empowered criminals to occur. Perhaps nowhere today can this be seen more clearly than in South Africa and Palestine.

As the most virulent variants of Victimentality spread, people become increasingly adept at manipulating their own victimhood, and that of others. Many have developed sophisticated understandings of how to exploit the emotional resonance of perceived victim grievances, as to ride the waves within the culture. Whole industries leverage the victimhood to justify a wide range of behaviours that would otherwise be considered unacceptable. Plainly, the Victimentality corruption is deeply tied to issues of power and privilege. Those who gain power in this society are always the most adept at exploiting the narrative of victimhood to justify their own actions and maintain their privileged status. This can manifest in various ways, including the use of moral appeals, emotional manipulation, and strategic storytelling. Enter media and social media.

"The LOGOS and the structure, being an intelligible 'this,' remain divisible by the LOGOS."

~Aristotle

"Difficulties strengthen the mind, as labour does the body."
"Fire is the test of gold; adversity, of strong men."

~Seneca

"Like the generations of leaves, the lives of mortal men. Presently the wind scatters the old leaves across the earth, suddenly the living timber bursts with the new buds and spring comes round again. So it is with men, as one generation comes to life, another dies away."

~Glaucus the Trojan

"It is evident that speech was given to man, not that men might therewith deceive one another, but that one man might make known his thoughts to another."

~St. Augustine

"If it is not right, do not do it.
If it is not true, do not say it."

~Marcus Aurelius

Babylonian glass, shattered a billion reflective sparkles,

Echoes of shame, of blame; cavernous deep dark holes.

Corruptions crafted, the self-piteous reign supreme.

Humanity edificial piecemeal, the all insanity of dream.

Night claiming day, festive dirge, amplifying the pain,

Cling to the snare, desperately strapped to the same.

Victim's violent curse, shadows perpetuating decay,

Apathy at heart, with virtues left to wither away.

Blame-shifting shame, eternal loops, distant memories,

Destiny in tide: ye forever lost children of despairing Seas.

XXIII. Misfortune Media

In today's hyper-connected societies, the Victimentality corruption and the consequential controls have taken on a new level of complexity. Social media platforms have created a global stage for individuals to broadcast their perceived grievances, often with devastating consequences. The 24-hour news cycle and social media echo chambers amplify these narratives, creating an environment in which it's increasingly difficult to discern fact from fiction.

Generally the only ones having children are the ones living amidst this chaos of shame and victimhood still capable of looking themselves in the mirror and functioning, which might at first not be such a good sign. There is a bit of self-deceit here, and so this should have been selected for throughout stages of Victimentality. Of course the final and absolute reason why Victimentality itself does not work is because there was only One Christ, and the societal end result that has come about misrepresents Him entirely. The archetype worked for that situation for that One because it was that singular situation and nobody else could ever do it, or even approach it, nor should they ever because there is no need. It is certain the meaning in the events surrounding Christ have far greater consequences to humanity than simply "how to give away everything to hateful and deceptive enemies in the constant feigning of victimhood." That is not why Christ came to us.

Individuals able to thrive in the current environments, consumed by their own self-pity and justifications for their existence, have developed an astonishing capacity for self-deception. They plead victimhood while accepting substantial blame for victimhood in others. The peculiar form of low-level cognitive dissonance derived from this allows them to maintain a tenuous grip on reality, while driving a neuroticism on an eternal fence of victimhood which denies evidence of evils committed, failures, and shortcomings.

It might be argued that this twisted psychology has been selected for through the process of storytelling in patterns (lying), as those who are most adept at describing their adherence to the corrupted archetype. This notion is reinforced by the observation that those individuals who are most prone to self-justification and self-pity are often the ones who perform best amidst the victimhood chaos and, perhaps, partly due to their own ignorance, i.e. self-delusion by conditioning or Stockholm culture. The system rewards ignorance and stupidity, as stated much earlier, for now obvious reasons.

However, this phenomenon takes on a far more sinister tone when one considers the broader consequences for human society. The proliferation of victimhood and shame has created an environment where people are incentivised to cling to their past grievances, rather than striving towards growth and improvement. This has led to a culture of excuse-making and blame-shifting, where individuals are more likely to point fingers at others rather than take responsibility for their own actions. The corrupted Victim-Hero ethotype in Victimentality, once fully stripped of greater depths, will turn to deny legitimacy for all other archetypes just as colonialism itself was turned back upon the home nations.

The overriding message within Victimentality becomes that humanity is somehow inherently incapable of transcending this narrative, and that our collective destiny is inextricably linked to the perpetuation of Victimentality and victimhood itself, as inborn. This corruption is a catastrophe for human civilisation. It implies that we are doomed to never advance or strive towards higher levels of consciousness. In actuality, the original Victim-Hero meta-archetype, as the ideal in eternally overcoming weaknesses, in precise contrast to Victimentality, is the exacting key to unlocking strengths, that is virtues.

The most egregious aspect of the Victimentality fraud, however, is its complete misrepresentation of the One, Who has been made out to have inspired its promotion. The societal end result of this narrative is a grotesque caricature of the original intention, reduced to a shallow example in self-serving justifications without a deeper foundation in all that He wishes for humanity. Human nature and our place within the grand plan of existence could not be any more important, if the Son is sent forth out of God's Love. The Victimentality corruption represents a fundamental flaw in our cultural consciousness, a bastardisation, and an over-mis-expression that can only be addressed through a radical reevaluation of our values and priorities. It is a reminder that we are not immune to the ravages of time and entropy, nor the machinations of powerful archons, as childish and immature as many of their managers have proven to be. Our highest aspirations must always be tempered by a constant coming to better awareness of our own limitations, and higher levels of potential Goodness.

So many lives are at risk,
We don't have time for this.
As the blood-basked Snake,
Sheds skin, we must take
Care, it slithers not away.
Destroy it on the spot, no delay.
Under heel, crush its spine,
Rip out any venom that you find.

XXIV. Hero-Victim

Of course everyone loves a story of struggle against adversity. Achievement in the face of resounding resistance is a fine thing to memorialise. We have written poetry and epics of such deeds, dedicating volumes expounding upon special qualities that enable certain individuals to Vindicate their struggle and very existence by rising above all that may have held them back, including their own weaknesses. The greatest adversity for the Victim-Hero is in the ineptitude of the Victim being saved with the goal being not some transcendence but the simple survival of the Victim, weaknesses and all. Struggle and achievement are fine things until their goals are said to be pure, first in the guise of the Victim-Hero, that hero whose goal is the promotion of Victimhood and, secondarily, in the form of the yet another archetype.

Tales of valour in the face of overwhelming opposition are eternally fascinating to the human imagination. Our minds are wired to recognise and romanticise the triumphs of those who have overcome seemingly insurmountable obstacles, their very existence inspirational, serving as testament to the indomitable human spirit. We have crafted epic poems and written sagas celebrating these feats of strength, elevating the protagonists to iconic status as paragons of virtue. History is replete with stories of individuals who defied the odds, rising above the constraints of their own frailties to achieve greatness. These narratives serve as light, illuminating the path forward for those embarking on the darker adventures.

If the Victim-Hero is a corruption, then the complete inversion of virtue is in the hero-victim. The hero-victim represents something all together more insidious than most other false archetypes. Here, the hero-victim's goal is not simply to maintain victimhood but rather to perpetuate more variations and greater depth of momentum in victimhood, for protection and not simply taking advantage of other people for profit or fulfilment. This subtle yet significant distinction reveals a profound disconnection between the individual's aspirations and the reality of their existence, with full enslavement to the image of self as victim. The epitome of this archetype would be a figure like Mother Theresa, who used her position to promote suffering in itself. The professor who feels like an outsider and passes that on to his students also comes to mind.

Humanity's descent into the hero-victim archetype has been towards the pursuit of victimhood as an existential purpose. This inversion of virtues is a cancer that spreads its darkness across the landscape of human experience. The hero-victim is a master manipulator, using the perceived suffering as an excuse to perpetuate a cycle of misery and exploitation. This insidious archetype feeds on the energy of pity and sympathy, cultivating an aura of martyrdom around itself in a false servitude, merely protecting their own sicknesses. Typically, they aren't merely alienated but also perverted and given to excessive sin. The people who are the most degenerate wish to promote degeneration because it makes them stand out less, but also gives them more commiseration in their disdain for the standards of the communities.

The hero-victim's ultimate goal is not just to maintain its own victimhood but to seek out ways to actively create a tidal wave of victimhood that sweeps others throughout society along with it. The more detrimental to society's cohesion, and deceptive, the greater value in lifestyles or behaviours so lionised toward this end. This is a profoundly selfish and destructive impulse, one that demonically functions to warp the natural order of human relationships and creates a culture of perpetual suffering. In this twisted world, the hero-victim becomes an arbiter of a purely emotional morality, dictating what constitutes acceptable levels of pain and misery. They use their perceived suffering as a cudgel to bludgeon others into submission, maintaining a culture of fear and obedience based on nothing but emotions and the goal of destroying natural systems, without any actual logic or Good behind the operation.

The impact of the hero-victim on society is catastrophic, actively generating cycles of violence, abuse, and exploitation. It creates an environment where people are conditioned to expect rescue from external forces rather than taking responsibility for their own empowerment. This is all the more awful in combination with people's expectations of failure throughout society due to the eternally flushing toilet that is inflation. The hero-victim's insidious influence corrupts institutions and social structures, turning them into instruments of control and oppression. The hero-victim is not just a theoretical construct but a living, breathing embodiment of humanity's darkest aspects trying to hide itself.

Many will soon be forced to awaken to the idea that their most cherished beliefs are nothing more than elaborate justifications for the perpetuation and multiplication of this permanent victimhood in its many varied and truly demonic forms. These can be easily recognised by their tendency to rank victim classes into a Victimentality caste system of sorts. The great achievements through self-sacrifice that were so noble now appear to have evolved into mere rationalisations for defending a fundamentally flawed paradigm, wherein the self is sacrificed to the self for the sake of nothing and nobody.

This wastefulness of spirit is the greatest heresy, and the worst form of denying the Spirit; a rejection of God's Love. Even in the face of this disquieting revelation, we must acknowledge the persistence in this misshapen form of what was originally the most Lovely ethotype within Western civilisation. It is only by acknowledging and confronting the underlying dynamics at play that we may begin to reform the narrative back to one that transcends the limitations of victimhood and instead seeks true empowerment through Christ Himself, LOGOS.

The hero-victim, for a more thorough explanation, is that magical being that rescues himself from his own weaknesses by continuing to enforce the idea that he is a Victim in an eternal currency, and enforces the victimhood of others in order to protect the very underlying value of his own. The hero-victims accomplish this best by bringing attention to largely irrelevant weaknesses and contrived discontent to all that might hear. The "helpless" Victim playing hero here is in need of nothing more than acquiescence in the con or delusions, and then they have 'conquered the dragon' merely by admitting the status, being the first step in Victimentality.

The hero-victim is the next stage of development for the misapprehensive culture surrounding the corrupted Victim-Hero archetype reaching peak efficiency in their unending promotion of Victimentality, first through salvation of weakness and then domination by the most professional victims as slavers. Efficiency and progress become measured in charity and protection. The liberating admission to weaknesses is merely the first stage in the transformative effect of false vindications. The belief becomes weakness is strength, as contrary as it may seem spelled plainly out in black and white, ink on paper. The hero-victim pushed Stockholm culture becomes a parody unto itself and weighs down the mechanisms originally inherent of virtues, and so ultimately even strength itself is finally killed and replaced with cheap mockeries, or so evil minds would have it, completing the long history in denigration of His memory.

As this peculiar species reaches the zenith of its power within society, we find ourselves confronting a culture that has devolved into a never-ending parade of self-absorption. The hero-victim represents the pinnacle of this misapprehensive zeitgeist, where efficiency and progress are measured by the yardstick of emotional manipulation. Weakness is strength because it becomes a self-evident 'truth,' inscribed on us like a tattoo gotten on mistake, and as regrettable. The hero-victim Stockholm syndrome culture has become a surreal sideshow, where circus clowns with too much time on their hands are convinced they're saving the world one validated vulnerability at a time.

In this strange landscape, the notion of liberating oneself from one's weaknesses has become conflated with the simple literal 'vindication' of recognition, sometimes sold as "visibility," which is to say normalisation of non-standards as ideals in themselves simply for the fact of being non-standard. Admitting to having flaws and having these flaws generally validated is equivalent to winning a gold medal in emotional scapegoating per today's culture. The hero-victims have rebranded inadequacies as badges of honour. Yet, despite this reversal, the culture remains enamoured with the idea of victimhood, so much so that the only argument against hero-victims, typically, is by diving into the victimhood as well. Fighting fire with fire, however, might burn the whole city down.

The greatest strength in the hero-victim perspective is weakness. It is the absolute inversion of recognising weaknesses in order to change them. It's little wonder that the original Hero has become lost in the shuffle since strengths are now labelled as weaknesses and errors. The victim is forever trapped in their own cycle of self-victimisation, like a hamster on a wheel, going nowhere yet faster and faster. The Victimentality has become the defining characteristic of our age. The only way to break free from this cycle of self-victimisation is to confront the mechanism head-on. Until then, it's a never-ending game of "Who Can Be More Dramatic," where all lose except the biggest proclaimed losers.

The hero-victim is what happens when strength is removed. There is no more struggle and there is nothing to achieve or rise above when actual strength is demonised, and so the only strength worth pursuing for materialists is in deception. All we are left with is the weakness and proclamation, the experience itself replacing the negating action, thus the pain or weakness and convincing others of the same is transformed into an ersatz heroism. A person is no longer a Hero for any strength of character or quality, such as noble negation (the simple act of saying no to evil), but rather, the simple qualification of weakness with no foreseeable resolution. This, of course, relegates all those capable of true Heroism to mere sidekicking for the antiheroic experience of victimhood, the new heroism, regardless of any lasting achievements.

Any achievement generally renders victimhood null. However, all must play the game as it stands, and it is important not to allow the downfall of the hero-victim culture to take the innocent dupes with it, inasmuch as it is possible. It is important to remember that there are real victims out there who might have been real heroes were it not for the total social environment being so utterly ridiculous. The biggest exploiters use the hero-victim archetype in various ways to hide amidst the shadows, and disable their prey when they are off their guard of course.

Existential nullity spawns from the vacuum of virtue's demise in the cultural conditioning. All that remains is a pitiful whimpering amplified by self-proclaimed heroism through weaknesses. The experience of victimhood itself becomes the raison d'être, as the excruciating agony of basic failure is transmogrified into an idealised construct, a trophy to be displayed on the mantle originally righteously reserved for Vindication. This reduces individuals to mere ciphers, devoid of character or quality.

The once-noble concept of heroism has been supplanted by the trivial pursuit of proudly proclaiming one's own vulnerability as though it was a mark of distinction. Gone are the days when the genuine Hero archetype's mettle was tested by fire and steel; now, all that matters is the capacity to feign helplessness, to clutch at the apron strings of sympathy. A pathetic culture does this, and it is very sad. Genuine heroes, those stalwart champions of old, find themselves relegated to secondary status, mere hangers-on from a bygone age in the grand regress into the deep dark slums of victimhood, managed by the most emboldened of carcasses in Victimentality.

Meanwhile, those who exploit vulnerability for their own nefarious purposes lurk in the shadows, manipulating entire industries, perpetuating human trafficking, child exploitation, murder, and all sorts of evil. This is the very face of evil, hiding in plain sight as it feeds on the despair it seeks to amplify, while building networks of political power based in the blackmail built around the degeneracy.

The Stockholm syndrome hero-victim culture provides a convenient smokescreen for these abusers, which has allowed them to operate with basic impunity.

Ethnic crime networks especially flourish in this Victimentality friendly environment. Triads and the Chinese Communist Party use Chinese expatriot communities to run operations, taking advantage of the pressures afforded by their minority statuses and tenuous host nation situations. The Chinese are not the first to do this, nor are they the only now. Italian Mafias and Cuban or Mexican Cartels have always taken advantage of legal statuses as a bargaining chip with potential assets. Even the very reins of power in most Western nations have been commandeered variously utilising ethnic networks to empower themselves, most especially Jewish, Black Nobility, and Chinese ethnicities.

This is unsurprising, as the Jews, Chinese, and Black Nobility also all seek international dominance openly. Also, certain important books in the Jewish religion, most especially the Talmud, teach things that are wholly defamatory and untrue about non-Jews and Jesus Christ, inculcating animosity, hatred, and hostility. Historically and still currently, there are Jewish over-representations in fields especially to do with banking, which is somewhat of a holdover from their basic Medieval serfdom to the Catholic Black Nobility. To this day, banking, trade, national currency governance, interest-free loans, and infinite money cheats have enabled the wealthy system of Jews and crypto-Jews to keep tight lids on their underlings, in a carrot and stick type arrangement across the board.

The Jewish hatred of others and the hatred of Jews has always been used to manipulate other Jews most especially, who are very much under the sway of Victimentality themselves, though more commonly as hero-victims. They also stoke the nationalist spirit in a physical Zionism with these Victims among their own people, only to keep it just out of reach, in proper hero-victim fashion and under the thumb, with Israeli's extremely Zionist Likud funding many terrorist operations against Israelis themselves. It is interesting to point out how similarly the Russian government has operated with Russian expatriots, in Ukraine and America especially, shaming and controlling them using their real attachments, and also terrorism.

These criminal organisations typically work for imperial interests, especially through intelligence services, within ethnic networks, acting basically as mafias to utilise the basic hatred for the majorities as motivation, often wrongly associated with pride in their own through propaganda to do with victimhood, both based in blends of reality and fiction. This victim-associated form of nationalism is used to bind them in the very same Victimentality trap as already described, though the low-grade variant in a pandering non-valiant fashion. We must destroy what they have set up against us in terms of propaganda. We do this not out of hatred ourselves but because we must strive to reclaim the noblest ideals from the clutches of those who seek to reduce them to mere whimperings and us to insufferable curs. Victimentality is not noble. It is abusive, plainly, and must end.

"For there is nothing more wicked than lying, nothing so ensnares the soul. For it both causes us to be hated by those whom we lie to, and makes us enemies to ourselves."

~St. Chrysostom

"You are of your father the devil, and your will is to do your father's desires. He was a murderer from the beginning, and does not stand in the truth, because there is no truth in him. When he lies, he speaks out of his own character, for he is a liar and the father of lies."

~Jesus Christ (John 8:44)

"No one who practices deceit shall dwell in My house; no one who utters lies shall continue before My eyes."

~Psalm 101:7

In society's decay, where sin reigns,

A new order emerges, built on remains.

Once-great cathedral reduced to mere hall,

Extraction accelerates; coldest shadows fall.

As Victims rise in power, ignorance abounds,

Manipulating masses by mouthing the sounds.

"Weaknesses are strengths, badges of pride!"

Under scornful mask, despairs reside.

Despite the spite, we search for the Light,

Guide us through darkness; banish the night.

Reclaim cultures, lands, & our might,

We forge the path forward, lit up & so bright!

XXV. Lords of Victimentality

When the techniques of controlling society outrun the legitimate science and understanding within a population, necessarily the Victims must come to view themselves as lords, especially throughout the process of their real role's replacement with robotic automation. Their often very skilled labours had been so crucial to the advancement of civilisation. As lords of Victimentality, the cretins become creatures of leisure, terrible businessmen, or scholars of squalor and excess. These masters of self-obsession are ignoble and frameless, as aimless, set free from the bounds of reality previously enforced by the great in ages past.

The once great have been replaced by the most manipulative and destructive of liars. This is a doubly dysgenic pattern. The overabundance of weak materialist liars flood positions where they have no comparative talent. The areas of study, especially to do with history, are gutted. The fields of deeper philosophical sciences stripped bare of their attachments to the observable and repackaged as basic scientisms. Academia has fallen into construct jungles filled with reified mind games seemingly invented for the purpose of intellectual entrapment with ever-travelling and useless goalposts. The game of it all, at best, merely serving as avenue of escapism for the remnants of disenfranchised potential great, and a platform for mundane Victim-led pseudo-sciences with false Pyrrhic victories.

Weakness has somehow outpaced its own deficiencies with the passing of ages, as the self-interested, vain, and tempestuous gained advantage after advantage over the remnants of past greatness. This new leadership of hero-victims are closer to the frame of mind that inhabits the average in contrast to the Great. So ingrained is this, they merely speak to the masses of culturally-assigned victims a language familiar to them without need of any real structure or goal outside of simply promoting victimhood as virtuous in itself. The hero-victim liars insinuate themselves into positions of power and vindicate it by claiming common victimhood, so displacing the potential great, and protecting themselves with the Victims surrounding them. The most vocal, the most manipulative, and the most destructive are elevated to positions of greatest Victimentality moral authority in these Stockholm culture societies.

We witness the ravaged landscape of societal entropy, where instruments of ruinous chaos have extinguished the lights of understanding. This is not merely a consequence of humanity's inherent propensity for self-destruction or even the ravages of time, but rather a direct result of greatness being replaced with garbage. In days of yore, the great in society guided and educated, directing people towards the noble pursuits of wisdom, civilisation, and genuine improvement. The great instilled in many, culturally, the appreciation of craftsmanship, curiosity, and creative problem-solving, imbuing their common endeavours with purpose and meaning. This enabled their communities to expand, advance, and increase their strength.

The fetid swamp of Victimentality, where intellectually bankrupt hero-victims rise to power on the backs of their own and other's victimhoods. The hero-victims ascend to positions of influence in neurotic frenzy, their boundless enthusiasm for victimhood matched only by their lack of responsibility and reliance upon emotions. They seize control of intellectual domains, stripping them bare of attachment to any semblance of empirical reality, especially historical sciences as they disparage culture or social sciences as less objective, and relegating us to savages, where relativity and deconstruction reign supreme. Meanwhile, the weaknesses of the Victim act as proof and identity, as in false authority. The language is drawn out into avenues of deculturisation, so as to disconnect the present from the past all the more rapidly.

The materialist cretins obsessed with their sin, who Paulus identified as "hylics," have outgrown typical human depravity to the point where emotion is but a mask, and the spectacle of sufferings an intoxicating spell to be cast upon whomever might otherwise stand in the way. The most cynical and least inhibited rise to the top here. Prying eyes of the self-proclaimed moral guardians emerge, drawn to the sheer joy of witnessing misfortunes of perceived enemies, typically defined as enemies based on strengths, or ancient vendettas. The majority succumb to the allure of Victim identity, almost out of sheer threat. The more empathetic and compassionate among us always scrambling, bewildered by the sheer scale of humanity's denigration while most ignore cancerous bioweapons being actively used on them.

Penchant for vile voyeurism of struggle is elevated in selection terms through those given nepotistic advantages and vantage points to witness. The demonic spirit of this perverse system is a system of bribery, blackmail, influence, and preference. Ethnic tribalism forms greater selection of individuals with tendencies towards more sadistic levels of schadenfreude. This is especially true regarding what are perceived as racial enemies, perpetuating cruelty as the most advantageous for survival amidst the constant agony in whole societies so confused by introduction of such ethnic mortal competitions.

The spectacle of suffering becomes an addiction, as these individuals crave the rush of witnessing others' pain. Wealthy psychopaths historically have been known to orchestrate their own tragedies, often involving manipulation, coercion, and even violence, not only to feed this morbid fascination but to empower themselves by the resultant death and pain, and marking themselves as Victims. As the cretins in power prosper all the more, the social fabric unravels, and genuine empathy disappears entirely, especially toward those designated enemies by the state, such as Appalachians being denigrated in media for decades before being left to die out in the cold of the 2024-2025 Winter after the freak Hurricanes late in 2024. The once-vibrant matrix of human connections weakens and fades, replaced by an endless morass of stories in suffering and despair. Reward is in power, wealth, and influence, as the weak hero-victims and villainous grind in those ancient gears of Victimentality. Sadistic manipulators consolidate their grip on society by moving boundaries in the dystopian landscape so quickly that incoming generations cannot even identify the differences between hero-victim perpetrators and legitimate Victims, nor the full consequences of this self-perpetuating cycle of cruelty.

Mediocrity masquerades as genius, while wisdom is lost to the void. The very notion of truth has been reduced to a competitive race to the bottom, with Victimentality as sole guide. Abyss awaits. It is in the darkness of the void against which some might see the Light all the better and with greater definition. Can you see the shadows dancing, and can you detect the purity in a message? To the warmth of understanding, as through the depths of human connection with God we create through His Word. We confront the Stockholm culture, and reclaim the flame. Rediscover what has always distinguished the holders of this precious fire. We do, for it is only through the cessation of the destroyers of societies and cultures, that we may hope to rebuild anew. This is Vindication. This is Vindication over Victimentality.

"For the truth is not to be despaired of.
It will vindicate itself in due time,
and the **more** it is oppressed,
the **more** it will **shine** forth."

~St. Augustine

"The unjust man is not only miserable himself,
but he makes others miserable as well.
The just man is not only happy himself,
but he makes others happy, too."

~Platon

"The man who is truly good and wise will
bear with dignity whatever fortune sends,
and will always make the best of his circumstances."

~Aristotle

Happiness can hurt as it moves into the past,

The sadness dies, with discoveries that last.

Beauty is in all the approaching Good, but not yet,

Wisdom is Word, from the Source to you, & as let.

In the tower of mind, the portal of days,

Where echoes & shadows shape the ways.

Winds howl, as all harmonies recede,

Amidst the turmoil, of unspoken deed.

Through genuine prayer's veil, Light appears,

Unlike the darkness, & all the hidden fears.

Threshold to hidden realms, where keys of truth reside,

Mysteries reveal, from locks in mind & of the spiritual side.

XXVI. Vindication

Vindication is not merely the antithesis of Victimentality but its total and complete absence. Spiritually, there was only the singular meta-archetypal Vindication in that One, through whom many are uplifted out of the mire of their sins and errors, beyond the stricture of codification through a broader comprehension of morality, one eerily similar to many of the more moral philosophers of Hellas. At least much more so than to any self-proclaimed religious men. Christ's message was founded in highest reason and logic. The greatest concepts rule all.

All others attempting a literal embodiment are foolish and will fall short, whether they realise they are doing it or not. What does this mean? You are not to be a martyr, unless you must be a martyr, and it will never be anything compared to other things you can do nor what Christ has done. Everyone receives the Grace and friendship of Christ, He's always there. The question becomes, how are you going to prove worthy of all that Love when you find it? Will you give your grace and friendship back? Or are you going to be a shit friend that stomps on that gratitude like an asshole? It is not up to you whether or not to be a martyr, it is up to you to prove worthy of Christ's Grace. You are to vindicate, you are a vindicator in Christ; through Christ you are empowered to cast out the lies and that is what you will do. What is Good is yours.

How could you doubt God's providence in what is best for you? Doubt self before ever doubting God's providence. God is perfect, so the missing something must be with us. So why dwell only upon evil and think nothing of potential good, or beauty in the souls of others? The oddest of all God's creation is the one who fears Him yet denies the power of Goodness. What is True is yours and what is false is your enemy. What does this mean? Vipers and scorpions, step on them, and let them poison no more with their venom, by cutting off their lies and their ability to lie. Those who deliberately block truth do so out of hatred and a desire for death toward those who miss out on it. Truth-blockers are murderers. The most important element in Vindication is self-sustenance internally, to see through to the truth despite the lies and overwhelming force of propaganda, so one can call out lies and those who block the truth. This is on many layers, in individuals, relationships, families, towns, communities, and nations.

The Vindication is in grand terms within all, though individually only as powerfully as the 'church,' which is to say "the community." This is a very important distinction, since Christ is nothing of a standard archetype, but a singular meta-archetype as King of kings, His message being universal and infinitely adaptable to all people regardless of their course in life. In this way, Christ is not a threat to any archetypes except those which are evil that contradict Christ, making Christianity meta-cultural while also not actually destructive but constructive only.

The Victimentality archetype is revealed as an incomplete and pale shadow copy. This means Vindication in elevation of all human endeavours is only ever possible through Christ, LOGOS, which is to say a spirituality empowering of others, a mentality active in moderation, and a creativity which resounds within contexts of reality and proper potentiality, far away from demonic (psychotic) influences. In the context of the defunct Victim-Hero false archetype, Vindication becomes even more intriguing. The person is no longer a Victim, but has transcended their own circumstances, breaking free from the shackles and achieving a state of autonomy and determination, with total ownership of actions toward the best fate, as desired most by God. This is desiring what God desires for ourselves. This is not simply a matter of personal growth; it is a fundamental shift in one's relationship with God, and therefore the World.

Spiritual Vindication is not something that can be earned outside of Christ. It cannot be achieved through effort, intention, or desire alone. Rather, it requires an understanding of the underlying dynamics that govern our lives, and this requires Vindication through Christ. Those who attempt to embody Vindication without first grasping this greater understanding will inevitably fail, because there is but the One perfection though infinite imperfect personalities. In essence, Christ's Vindication represents a fundamental reorientation of one's being. It is an elusive and rarefied state that only a select few can achieve, but when they do, it becomes the benchmark against which all else is measured. Above all else, Christ is wise. We must imitate Him. The only way to do this is to refine our imperfect self and direct it toward God, as He demonstrated.

The truly liberated and Vindicated are classified as criminals by the system, for obvious reasons. They are shamed and mocked for all that their efforts toward virtues afford them. Will, health, calm life, strength, and aptitude, historically the clearest signs of Vindication, become the badges of privileges. These things cannot simply be bestowed upon them, but it must be earned in concert with Christ, working through Him. They call out horrible cheats built into the system of their society tempting people with their material desires, and are hated for it. Those at the top encourage bickering, infighting, outfighting, diversity, and kicking down in order to create chaos and, through it, escape justice. Actual virtues get derided as evidence of sin against the Victimentality system by the Vindicated person not being enough of a Victim or not victimising themselves enough. The cretins who come to replace the legitimately strong in society have no issues putting on shows for the satisfaction of the Stockholm culture's false moralities.

The festering ocean of Victimentality, where the remnants of the Great who refuse to leave the industries, swimming now in mostly cretin's excretions, perpetuate their own damnation through an endless cycle of self-loathing. Consumed by the want for the very privilege they had been raised to believe was theirs by birthright bestowed upon them merely by towing the cretinous lines of Victimentality and praising victimhood. The truly strong asserting themselves at all becomes met with immediate suspicion and contempt. The actual virtues that once defined humanity most gloriously have been reduced to trivialities. It's not enough to simply be a Victim; one must also demonstrate a sufficient degree of self-appointed martyrdom, sacrificing one's own interests and well-being on the altar of victimhood itself.

Experiences in consciousness-subconsciousness intersect to form an individual construct of lived Spirit. Every moment, no matter how seemingly insignificant or traumatic, contributes to the emergent properties of our being. The process of integrating these experiences into our sense of self is akin to the formation of fractals, self-similar patterns that repeat at different scales with different angles, generating complexity and, hopefully, resilience instead of insanity. The stitches that hold our narrative together are not just a physical manifestation of memory but also a reflection of our capacity for re-contextualisation, allowing us to reframe the elements of our past for greater resolution, in service of our present and future.

The tears in the canvas of our experience can be seen as moments of perturbation or disruptions that force us to reorganise our understanding of ourselves, our existence, and the larger World, in all aspects. These perturbations can be either catalytic or debilitating, depending on how we respond to them. The act of repair is not just a material process but also an existential one, as it requires us to confront the inherent contradictions and paradoxes that arise from the complex interplay between our past, present, and future selves.

The resulting fractal and refractioning construct of our consciousness is a dynamic system that is constantly evolving, with each experience influencing that categorical next, and previous. This means that we are never truly fixed or stable but are always in a state of becoming, with our sense of self emerging from the intricate interplay between our images of self. Our experiences present a balancing operation, forcing us to reconcile our disparate images of self into a coherent narrative, through discourse in logic and the highest wisdoms. The stitches that hold together our story, as we tell it to ourselves, are very symbolic, reflecting our capacity for storytelling as a means of making sense of the world and our place within it. By embracing the complexity disguised as ambiguity in our experiences, and our tendencies toward error, we can begin to see ourselves, identity, and purposes much more clearly, especially as contrasting the One in His Love. This perspective allows us to transcend the limitations of our individual perspectives and tap into the deeper wisdoms.

Attainment to God's Love allows a man to love not only his friends but also his enemies, because in their improvement, he would see their attainment of God's Love, and so allying through it. This same Love of God that enables a person to properly love himself, enables him to love his neighbours, which is to say with criticality and care with God by their side. If what a person wants is improvement of the evil man, they wish him to see Good. If they wish a person to see Good, they love that person with an affection approaching that Love God gives.

Realise, humanity's greatest struggle is not with the external world, but rather with its own inner demons. The darkness faced in introspection allows for hope to ascend and emerge at ever higher states of being. The spark of Christ's Mind shines through all that darkness. May we find solace despite the darkness, and may we find hope along the path in the Light that guides us home. Clarity is not just a lofty ideal, but a lived reality brought into being through introspection and then action to bring closer proximity to Christ.

In the upside down equations of Victimentality, true heroism has been supplanted by a perverse reverence for the downtrodden. As if the only measure of a person's worth lay in their ability to wallow while making the most noise regarding whatever misfortunes as perceived insurmountable. Society now celebrates victimhood above all else, where the strongest and most capable are viewed with suspicion and hostility, and basically instant enemies. The true heroes, those who've risen above the muck and mire, emerging from the depths of despair with resilience and strength, are demonised as oppressors in the propaganda of society's actual oppressors. Wild. The weak and the wounded, on the other hand, are sainted, their victimhood revered as a badge of highest honour: Victim. What could be the ultimate aim in this perverse crusade if not the actual results? Namely, societal collapse. A society where the strong are forced to kneel before the weak through lies is unnatural and completely debilitating on a cultural level. This is Stockholm syndrome of the culture. Does this not destroy societies? Is that not the goal?

"Order and proportion are beautiful and useful,

while disorder and disproportion are ugly and useless."

~Pythagoras

"In the middle of the journey of our life, I came to myself

within a dark wood where the straight way was lost."

~Dante's Inferno

"Freedom is called virtue: Slavery is vice...

No one is Free who is not master of themself."

~Epictetus

-Place this in your house so you see it everyday. Place others.-

Retreat of the mind comes in two kinds,

The first is material & the second sublime.

Youth is a gem made of ice thrown to heat.

Wasted time rots fruit & sours meat.

We struggle with senses in our dim shallows,

Conversing with echoes, in love with our shadows.

Turn to the greatest Light, cast shadows away,

Cease pandering to those most lost to hate.

XXVII. Civilisational Rebirth

Civilisation , as known, can breed the pitiful just as well as it can breed the 'cannibals' fattening the pitiful up and dumbing them down, in varying capacities. This is because the story of Civilisation is largely one wherein the capable good take care of the gullible and the simple, or capable evil take advantage of the same. Police are not hired to protect the innocent from victimisation or to be the hero, but rather to stop less efficient monsters from harassing the sheep of the bigger monsters. By the way, this is why the police are almost never held legally liable for your safety, it's not their job to protect you but to protect Victimhood itself. Victim-Heroes, especially as defined within Victimentality, are automatically defensive of all Victimhood and strive to serve it in all capacities.

The most cunning vultures feed the most, as the worst of liars. These weak craven creatures stand as the pillars to the deceitful system's unrivalled capacity for manipulation. Society's fabric appears to have been rewoven, replaced by alien threads of deceit, manipulation, and exploitation, as most people are given the simplest of philosophical foundations to essentially abandon this beautiful World, and do so in various capacities mostly to do with the false Vicitmentality identities.

The strong prey upon the weak, the shrewd capitalise on the unsuspecting, and the ruthless consolidate power. This is the way that it has always been, but it was a very similar condition that Christ had sought most diligently to change. Victimhood is now a very well-oiled machine, as lubricant in basic corporate servitude, with enforcers serving in all capacities throughout society. There have been distinct glimmers of the truest spirit here and there throughout Christian history, especially on individual levels, though largely the exception.

This so-called "advanced" society we inhabit is shared by evil predators. How is that advanced? Those who would seek to challenge the trajectory in culture require categorical demonisation by the system, as they are threats to the very structure of the Stockholm culture society. Where victimhood is the ultimate currency, those who would seek to subvert the system must first confront the utter despair that lies at the heart of civilisation in the shape of Christ and the Father, a void filled with the cries of the innocent and the pleas of the forgotten, all dutifully ignored by duped descendants so demoralised.

To spite the bleak landscape, a glimmer of hope remains with resistance that shines brightly in the darkness, like a spark of defiance in the frigid night of dispassion. The cold itself magically serves to fuel the fire of revolution for the Vindicated. It is here, in this struggle and sacrifice, that Civilisation is reborn.

We will emerge from this struggle all the better for it, finding ourselves reborn into a world where the forces of manipulation no longer hold sway. The fire of resistance has tempered our Souls and burned the perfect rebellion into the retinas of our very beings. We stand ready to forge a new path, as unencumbered by the shackles of Victimhood.

Let's consider the concept of semiotics, the study of signs and symbols that convey meaning. Semioticians argue that all communication involves a complex interplay between signifier (the symbol), signified (the so represented), and interpreter (individual or cultural meaning maker). This trifecta of meaning-making is crucial in understanding how we construct our reality, as even seemingly innocuous symbols can carry significant cultural baggage.

Furthermore, let's consider that interpretations of reality are always context-dependent and influenced by our pre-existing beliefs. This means that any attempt to decipher symbolic codes must take into account the intricate web of assumptions, biases, and narratives that underlie our understanding of the world. Human perception is inherently shaped by the reason, our drive to uncover meaning and order. We express this basis for virtues in various forms, such as through creativity, artistry, and even violence.

In the context of our discussion on Victimhood, we can see a lower reason in the desire for power at play in the ways that individuals and societies construct their narratives about suffering and injustice. For instance, a group may use the language of victimhood symbolically to justify their own violent acts, while another group may employ similar rhetoric to excuse their own truculent acts. Consider the way that certain symbols or narratives about suffering and injustice become imbued with a sense of moral righteousness, which in turn enable individuals or groups to justify their actions as necessary for rectifying perceived wrongs. Our perceptions of reality are intrinsic to how we unravel the complex web of symbolism in our world.

Our more accurate perceptions will allow us to better create a new reality, one where Victimhood is no longer the currency that drives societies. Where reason comes into play in the final virtue of willpower, as the desire to enact righteous Godly justice and morality. In this sense, the signifier becomes a tool in the service of willpower as the culmination of reason in moderation, while the signified is shaped by the interpreter's beliefs founded in a bias toward Life and dedication to God.

The internal reflection of God in constant prayer meditation, then, becomes a cycle of interpretation and re-interpretation, as we continually refine understanding of the world through the lens of reason, and its virtues. This highlights a complex interplay between our constructions of reality and our desire for meaning and control, even as we seek to understand the complexities of human experience. In this way, cultural memetic power is an intricate dance between signifier, signified, interpreter, actual reality, and willpower. By recognising the ways in which these concepts intersect and influence one another, we can gain a deeper understanding of how our own perceptions of reality are shaped.

"The books or the music in which we thought the beauty was located will betray us if we trust to them; it was not in them, it only came through them, and what came through them was longing. These things—the beauty, the memory of our own past—are good images of what we really desire; but if they are mistaken for the thing itself they turn into dumb idols, breaking the hearts of their worshippers. For they are not the thing itself; they are only the scent of a flower we have not found, the echo of a tune we have not heard, news from a country we have never yet visited."

~C.S. Lewis

"A great sign appeared in heaven: a woman clothed with the sun, with the moon under her feet and a crown of twelve stars on her head. She was pregnant and cried out in pain as she was about to give birth."

~Revelation 12:1-2

"Symbolism is a mode of thought,

but allegory is a mode of expression.

It is not a late sophistication,

but a primary and inevitable process of the human mind."

~C.S. Lewis

From ashes cold, a new birth's cry,

Echoes of an eternity, passing by.

The weaknesses that bind us tight;

Curse us & make that eternal night.

In hearts, minds, & souls, sparks remain.

Flames feed the hopeful, fervent like pain,

Man do rise above again, beyond the fall,

Finding most righteous ways through it all.

What is good belongs to all,

Though all belong to the Best.

Run after walking, after you crawl,

Don't sulk: seek God; be blessed.

XXVIII. Symbolism & Curiosity

God, as in all, is outside time because time is a function of energy's division and experienced by life because it is the most sacred form of energy and closest to God. Life energy is a fragment of God Himself but inside of time, and so God is the infinite intelligence underlying all life across all time in all operations. A primary purpose of life, especially as currently imprisoned in this stagnation through Victimentality, is to overcome destruction and the evils that accompany it. Just as people are proud of victimhood instead of being proud of overcoming victimhood, society has done much the same. Society has become a collaboration of victims threatening each other with regard to the relative tiered magnificence of their victim identities. Victimhood is meaningless outside the overcoming of it however, on the individual level as well as the societal.

The eternal cycle of life, death, and renewal pervades our existence. The phoenix, in fact, represents a manifestation of humanity's collective unconscious, a reflection of our deepest desires for transcendence, redemption, and rebirth in this life. Victimentality can be seen as a form of the original sin, and just as illegitimate an excuse, which is a primal wound that haunts us throughout our history. Yet, it is precisely this woundedness that drives us to seek out greater rebirth worth striving toward in the face of constant large-scale destruction, mostly from the robbery of value itself and dispossession of societal capital, respectively in the forms of central bank usury and corporate enslavement in segmentation.

The phoenix's fiery rebirth can also be seen as a metaphor for the transformative power of creativity. Just as the phoenix rises from the ashes, so too can we rise above our own personal struggles and limitations through the spark of imagination. This is not to say that the process is easy or painless, but rather that it is a necessary one to meet with that innovation.

The phoenix myth reminds us that in destruction, there is potential for rebirth and renewal. This idea resonates with our own experiences as human beings, where we often find ourselves sifting through the ashes of our past, searching for lessons to find a way to arise with the shift in understanding to something closer approximating Truth. The truth of historical and cultural Victimentality and its seepage into other cultures serves as a poignant reminder that our struggles are as universal as they are indeed particular, whether realised or not. All have this same struggle. We are all components within larger engines of reality through societies, nations, and communities. These come with intricacies and lessons specific and expressly unique, while sometimes of more universal value. Despite this shared experience, we often find ourselves isolated and disconnected from one another, at odds where there should be none.

The fire that consumes the phoenix's former self is purification, burning away the dross and leaving behind only the purest essences necessary for rebirth. Our own struggles can be seen as opportunities for growth and transcendence. Just as the phoenix rises anew from its ashes, so too can we emerge reborn from the trials and tribulations of our lives, just as our societies can.

This truth is echoed in various spiritual traditions, where the concept of surrender or letting go is often emphasised. By releasing our attachment to old ideas of self, we create space for new and more nuanced expressions to emerge. This process of transformation is that fiery rebirth, where the old is consumed and the new is born. Life is not just a fleeting moment, but a period in time eternally changing though unchangeably yours, etched into the permanent memory of energy and its movements through time, timeless reflection of the original dialectic. In the end, however, Good versus evil is actually merely the choice between eternity and death.

Myth and history are filled with stories of trolls under bridges, beasts in caves, and dark things in the night waiting to devour those trusting too much. Our mythologies are replete with cautionary tales of monstrous creatures lurking in the shadows, their very existence a warning against the dangers of blind trust. The bridges that connected the towns of our societies were said to be guarded by trolls of unsavoury reputation, their gruff demeanour and sharp teeth serving as a reminder of the perils that await the unwary.

In these ancient stories, we find cautionary warnings against venturing too close to the edge and falling prey to the beasts that lurked in the depths. These stories frightened the masses and often kept them less than curious. Dotting the landscape were said to be fearsome creatures, growls and snarls echoing out demonically in the night, or so assigned. Monsters that lurk in the shadows have given way to fears of rejection and vilification for subverting norms, especially those of Victimentality. Their trusting nature and naïve optimism is blood in the water, where sharks are incapable of empathy, and stone-cold to the suffering surrounding them, as bred in the deep though away from the Light, and so given to sneaking deceptions simply to feed. We find ourselves drawn to the very things that threaten our existence. This can be good. We used to be different and less before facing the destruction head on, with the consequences which we learned from. We are beings of curiosity, driven by an insatiable hunger for knowledge and understanding.

A symbol of hope, in darkest of night,
Reminding us, all is not lost in the fight.
The fire that consumes our former self,
Purifies the soul, and reveals our wealth.
Take pity on others, as they stumble and fall,
Find strength in your struggles, do ever stand tall.
Releasing attachments to old ideas of self
Gives space in which better concepts can dwell.
From remnants a new chapter reforming the old,
In transformation, courage, and purest of soul.

XXIX. Insults & Denial

Are any of these questions regarding the state of society repugnant at face due to preconceptions of some comforts or luxuries being necessary to meet them? I will readily admit to the luxury inherent in the ability to contemplate such things, but it is not really due to material comfort that I am inspired to write it, but the suffering that surrounds us and the Spirit which hates the stagnation, as surely as God hates lies and unrepentant liars. Many in society are "successful" without being bothered by such high-minded things, as well many of the most successful in this world are not actually very good people. This is disconcerting for many believers.

The majority are eager and willing to partake in anything for easy promises of immediate 'material' rewards for the individual despite the state of the world. Chase wealth and then bemoan the results of a society in that chase, this is a common hypocrisy. The ultimate survival of humanity or even Truth itself play accessory fiddles, all too often, to mere perception of personal redemption. There must be a reason for it. Our capacity for transcendence and rebirth in the face of hardship is proved by the depth of our emotion felt in gratitude for Love, yet many are left unable to conceive of a purpose for it or life amidst all the chaos, despite it being there in front of them.

Confront the abyssal void that stares back in the material, and know how much deeper your soul reaches. The greatest luxury itself is earned in the mere having of this perspective, not in being somehow less materially agitated enough to ponder such questions, for the pleasures are in the thoughts. Spiritual advancement requires a basic distaste for the material outside its purpose in supporting spirit. Material pleasures are not to be indulged simply for their own sakes.

Yet, we find that many are content to wallow in shallow existence, attention on these fleeting pleasures and trivial concerns, utterly untroubled by weighty yet seemingly ephemeral things that occupy the minds of those who dare or even care to delve deeper. Take away the pleasures and the trivialities and what remains? The instrument used for the purpose of striving toward God is fully transformed by the grasping. The weighty things cannot be lifted from those who carry them because the Truth is too valuable, and those carrying them would not have them removed.

Ignorant people who might lob insults given the right circumstances are legion, yet it is precisely this sort of non-thinking that has given rise to the problems we are addressing. This act of non-thinking can be used against them. There is a reason for this phenomenon, a reason why so many would rather flee from the abyss than confront its depths. It is that fear instilled in them for the unknown, so they are too afraid of what lies at the bottom of that chasm whenever it is sensed. They are also too enamoured with the fleeting pleasures of existence to not lose themselves even in the shallows before the depths, as they were raised to be.

Whatever the things distracting us may be, it is clear that we must not rest until we have uncovered Truth, and we cannot let anybody stop us. We must not rest until we have exposed whatever rot lies within our societies and our own natures, and find the most natural means to mend it. For only then can we hope to find a way out of this morass of confusion and despair, to turn weaknesses into strengths and the passions behind our pains into solutions.

What of those who would seek to stand in our way? Step around them or push them out of the way. What of those who would seek to silence our voices and snuff out intellectual curiosity? Speak more clearly and readily, to even more people. In every extreme rejection of Truth is a sign of some larger acceptance, either societally or in the person. Do not allow yourself to be muzzled or masked. Be such a force for Good that nothing can stand in your path. You must push forward despite the disease and necrosis in culture, for anything short of that is not worthy of God, and not representative of a Spirit of overcoming. They are as specks of dust floating in the air past the light of human existence in the history, culture, and experience of civilisation itself. What are challenges but to be overcome?

You will not be deterred by petty machinations. You will press on, driven by your insatiable hunger for Truth and a refusal to accept nonsensical answers, heart afire with the passion of discovery and mind sharpened like a razor to cut through the fog of ignorance. Finding the answers we seek requires facing the unknown with a grin and warmth in intense love for the very originating potentiality in the energy that pervades the Universe. There will always be those unwilling now but with a future higher calling, so all you can do at the moment is leave with them an idea or two most beneficial. Your passion derived from pain is the aperture specific to your perspective and life, and you do your best work through being the fittest element in the development of the optics of others. Regardless, and all simple-minded distractions aside, denial and purposeful ignorance do not change the soundness of the argument, neither does name-calling and labelling of the person relaying it make the ignorance any less ridiculous.

What has passed as morality in modernity has been a futile exercise in Victimentality posturing, one that has only served to obscure the truth from view, and it is painful. Any denial or ignorance in the now may momentarily halt progress towards greatness, but it can never prevent the inevitable. So it should not be allowed to stop it at all. It has become abundantly clear that the disease in Victimentality that plagues the most advanced societies of humanity can only be cured through a fundamental transformation within, away from the false identifies in Victimhood toward identities in true Heroism.

The Truest beauty of humanity is deep within the patterns of existence and the superconscious complexes as gifted by God, the greatest Consciousness. All worthwhile promise is in love, soul, energy, and thought. Let us remember that we are not alone in any part of this, and those mocking God are often the most confused of anyone, so take pity. May we find strength in our struggles, and may we emerge reborn from the ashes of our past, ready to take on the challenges of a brighter future, Sooth.

'Cause, in one sense, is that from which something is produced while inherent. In another sense, it is the form and paradigm, being essence, and its genera so directive. This is only ever conceived through LOGOS, however.'

~Aristotle (paraphrased)

"If you are ridiculed, do not be angry; for the ridicule
will be forgotten, but your anger will be remembered."

~Socrates

"If anyone tells you that a certain person speaks ill of you,
do not make excuses about what is said of you but answer:
'He was ignorant of my other faults,
else he would not have mentioned these alone.'"

~Epictetus

"For nothing is so easy as to deceive oneself;
for what we wish, that we readily believe."

~Demosthenes

"We are members of one great body.
Nature made us kin, for she planted in us a common reason."

"The best ideas are common property."

"It is a great thing to know how to make use of ridicule. It is the part of a wise man to bear it with patience."

~Seneca

....

All are owned by the greatest ideas, because they dominate all.

XXX. Singular Christ

Nobody else is Christ! Christ was Singular, and that primary Vindication is only through Him. However, the narrative shows what should be stopped: massacre of the righteous, innocent, and Good. This is a lesson that has been lost. Keep power at bay, as it will come for your best and brightest. The major error of everyone else in that story was allowing it to persist and continue, and it was an error. Error is necessary, however, and here is where the key turns on the lesson to be learned. It is also the thing most oddly ignored. They all stood by, all of them, and did not speak up. Nobody had His back. They did not stand for Christ's authority. Some had Him arrested. Nobody spoke for Him, and He was left to the whim of earthly authorities by those who claimed to love Him most. All those followers betrayed Him.

To err is to be human, but to learn from it in order to express a better overall understanding in interactions with others is something much more. Everyone in the Gospel narrative missed out on the divine light, which Paulus explains. Victims and hero-victims are convinced of the necessity for what is essentially self-sacrificing self-genocide. Why would anyone fight if their perceived strength is derived from their own victimhood? If the self is hated, it simply doesn't know its true identity. The first step on the path to greater virtue is identification, which allows for expansive magnanimity: the first reflection of Christ's Grace, in your forgiveness. You say, "I am a sinner too, and I have sinned just as you are doing." Forgive yourself as you forgive them, and how can you continue to hate yourself in any part of this? How could you hate yourself if you were to continue on this path with Christ, and find more advantageous things to do with your time? However, what moral good is there in saving individuals intent on their own destruction? You can't actually save anyone unless you change their minds, and help them see the error in their ways. They are dead otherwise, dead to the Spirit. Most have missed the other implicit lessons here, no different from everyone in that Gospel narrative.

At the centre of the narrative, metaphorically speaking, are those who will have followed Christ and transcended the mundane in order to attain a piece of the sublime, or grasped God truly. We find the major error of everyone else back then as it remains today. People allow the very best of their kind to be massacred. They do so in war, pestilence, lies, and poisons given as medicines. Lies kill. Lies kill billions. To those of us awake to it, it is inconceivable to permit the slaughter. The rest of society appears to do so without flinching, without protest, with barely a whisper of resistance. In doing so, they prove again and again how lost the lessons are that should have been learned. We do not know what is precious in our midst and how to protect it.

The pursuit of a global peace in Christ is a straightforward endeavour. The concept of Spirit, though abstract, can serve as a foundation for understanding the interconnectedness of humanity. Nationalism with distributist economics emerges as a potent force capable of transcending individual and collective boundaries, at once compatible fairly with both individuals and groups. Any unity should be rooted in progress itself, as a meta-archetypal feature founded in Christ. This Spirit is rooted in the particular, yet resonates through the universal. It finds expression through family, community, and nation, ultimately seeking harmony among these domains in natural alignment. However, our parallel courses upon this planet must first confront the errors that beset us.

Nationalism is not just a fleeting fancy or a simplistic solution to complex problems, as deemed by certain religious figures and power mongering cohorts. No, it's a fundamental aspect of our being, born from the primal urge for survival and self-preservation. It's the manifestation of our deep-seated need for belonging, identity, and community, all of which are rooted in the particular, the local, and the national, so that there is no way to the universal but through this. When tempered with wisdom, compassion, and a deep understanding of human nature, nationalism is a powerful tool for building strong communities, fostering cooperation, and promoting social cohesion.

Now, let's not forget the elephant in the room: globalisation. It's a corporate ethnic crime syndicate nightmare forcing economic inequality, national injustice, Victimentality, and environmental degradation. Corporate interests, government bureaucrats, and technocratic elites, as vehemently hateful toward races of the nations, harm and thwart others rather than simply prioritise their own. Here we are left with a system that's more interested in exploiting resources, commodifying culture, poisoning our children, and manipulating the global supply chain than in promoting social order, actually protecting the environment, or empowering local communities. Distributism is the answer as an economic philosophy that seeks to decentralise power by empowering local natural communities and promoting order through the merit-based and competition-based distribution of wealth and resources. It's an approach that recognises the inherent value of human life, the importance of cultural community traditions, the necessity for constant improvement, and the need for responsible stewardship of our resources.

The harmonious union of nationalism and distributism is a perfect match. It has checks and balances that ensure the well-being of all citizens. You see, nationalism supported by distributist principles in economy is a multiplier of patriotism, national security, resilience, and sufficiency. Think about this, when we prioritise local communities we create environments where families can thrive while individuals can naturally progress mentally and culturally in the healthiest way possible. We foster a sense of belonging, identity, and purpose that's essential for building strong, resilient families as core to self-sufficient communities which are patriotic and care for their societies. Decentralising power nationally in a structural manner prevents the concentration of control into the hands of the corporations, government bureaucracies, intelligence organisations, and banks while assuring a common interest in the defence of nation.

Corporations are artificial constructs designed to serve human needs. They don't have feelings, emotions, or souls; they're simply tools created by humans to help us achieve our goals. If we can't control them, then who will? It's up to us, the citizens of each nation, to ensure that our government serves the nation, not the interests of the criminal most wealthy. We get to set the rules as to the structure of our cooperative endeavours, and they should be made in such a way to be most beneficial to families and small individual businesses.

So, what does this mean for our children and grandchildren? It means a world where they can grow up with a sense of purpose and belonging, where they can develop strong family ties and friendships within their community. It means a society where every productive person has stake and belonging. The beauty of nationalism and distributism together is that people come before profit and families have a better chance to be strong and resilient.

Only by acknowledging and overcoming these obstacles can we begin to build a foundation for cooperation and mutual understanding. Through this process, we may discover greater guidance from Christ in LOGOS through the communities: churches. We tap into this greatest intelligence, and find ourselves drawn toward a shared sense of purpose. As nationalism awakens, it will be fuelled by an unwavering commitment to life, family, and community. This is the only kind of Spirit that can unite the world: one that acknowledges our differences while embracing our shared humanity. The only kind of Spirit that can unite the World is nationalist, based in Family and Life and in the Universal through the particulars, and only through overcoming error, sin, and the individual struggles.

"God placed all things under His feet and appointed Him
to be head over everything for the church, which is His body,
the Fullness of Him who fills everything in every way."

"Now you are the body of Christ,
and each one of you is a part of it."

~Apostle Paulus (Ephesians 1:22-23; 1 Corinthians 12:27)

"The city is what it is because our citizens are what they are."
"The wise man will not be angry with the wicked,
any more than he will be angry with a blind man
who stumbles against him."

~Platon

All the errors in life's recaps,

Teach with victory & collapse,

How to succeed & not to relapse.

Little understood of its true importance,

Invaluable Grace in each allowance,

The most beauty resolves in silence.

May your challenges be perfect to get you to the next,

May you rise to the occasion & realise you're blessed.

XXXI. Sin or Error

Mind is universal and abounds. Our failures are because of imperfections in the material. A simple way of describing science might be "noting how you get a thing wrong, so you can get it less wrong next time," which is identical with evolution. Further, there is no difference between this and the underlying logic of learning from mistakes, improvement, and God's Grace. Christianity was right all along, but held back from its natural integration into the sciences and our conceptions of reality.

Error is integral to the human condition. It's a curious thing though, this propensity for mistakes, isn't it? Nobody wins in a World filled with errors and victims, and yet most people refuse to own failures. At some level there is a complete disconnect here. Teaching those unwilling to learn is akin to attempting to put out a raging wildfire with a fire hydrant. No, dear friends, we must find our own path and those similarly positioned toward transcendence and overcoming this cultural Victimentality. Only through setting an example ourselves, can we hope to establish the credible difference, however.

What better example to follow than Christ's own demonstration of standing tall and calling out evil? Like a Beacon shining brightly upon the hill, His message reminds us that true redemption is not in our individual struggles, but in our collective willingness to transcend our limitations, improve, and then empower one another. The societal sacrifice, as seen in the West as late, is but a corruptive and vile exercise in destruction with nothing of Christ in it, with the sheer overwhelming number they stumble in their machinations, 'millstones drownings' all around. When people want less of something to occur, acting as if that something is normal or expected won't appease them. It's not the smartest approach.

We can't just stand by idly, wringing our hands in despair as our societies sail off into an uncharted and unguided abyss. No, dear reader, we must take action! This is not just about pointing out mistakes or flaws, or even corruption and crime, as important as that may be; it's about understanding the root causes of these systematic issues and helping not simply people, but society learn from the mistakes. It's also about creating environments in which youth can belong as they explore their own minds and self-conceptions. In order to learn to correct themselves from their errors, they must know that they'll be supported every step of the way, so that they are less likely to make major mistakes later in life.

Gender dysphoria, for instance, was, until recently, very much normalised in the United States. The struggle to force societies into affirming mental illnesses over families and natural order appears to still be central to segments of the population and in other Western nations, unfortunately. The societal phenomenon was artificially inflated by media and therapy industries, primarily. When did gender dysphoria become an acceptable norm? When did we start telling people that their feelings were more important than objective reality? What is at stake here with distorting ideas regarding objective reality is the complete destruction of society. There has been active attempts at fundamental redefinitions within humanity, using Victimentality as the basic excuse. This is exactly the kind of coddling of danger that leads to the end of civilisation. What "freedom" can you have when that happens?

Freedom isn't just about individual freedom, no, it's about standards that make the most sense for the improvement, good, and progress of humanity, which is to say Good! It's about recognising that there are certain principles and values that undergird our very existence as social human beings, as well as the societies we build. If we sacrifice those for the sake of encouraging Victimentality based in mental illnesses to do with false impressions of identity, then what's left? Gender dysphoria is a low-grade psychosis that has been actively lionised in media and society, especially by the mental health industries.

Victimentality can get people to do terrible things if made into alienated and hateful victims told normal people are evil for refusing to patronise their made up fantasies. These mentally ill people are not treated fairly, because they are "affirmed" in their errors, which is wrong. Many people are told that their errors are not errors and that others are in error for pointing out their errors. This is the insanity of insanities. It is the very essence of evil, in the denial of Truth and affirmation of wickedly destructive lies. Fuck liars, I hate them. How dare they lie to children. How dare they lie to the lost of God's children. Snakes. They had one task in affirming the Truth, and look at them now. How are they not just as lost and pitiful as their victims? The only difference is the amount of hubris they harbour in their hearts against God and His Will, in preference of their fleeting own. Could there be a greater shame?

They take the ability to transcend away before there exists the opportunity to develop it. They take away the chance at the Life in Christ by forcing all their victims into lives of deception. Without the transcendence of overcoming errors, weaknesses, and victimhood to inform us of our place in the order of things and our connection to God, we are lost adrift upon a Sea where everything in all directions is inequity. Existence is inextricably tied to honest relationships in life which are given greater definition through the fact-based lessons granted by the insights only earned through the resolution of errors, either of ourselves or others. Deception blocks this completely. Life is in community and the experience of our energetic souls through the natural and real attachment to others, including all genetic and cultural bonds. This has never changed, and has always remained the same, and no amount of hoping will ever alter these essential realities tied to 'biology' and the determinant Soul.

"The weaker man engages in the process of deliberation
but, failing to adhere to LOGOS, succumbs to his passions.
In contrast, immoral criminals eschew deliberation altogether,
immediately indulging passions.
So, the weaker man holds a moral advantage over the criminal,
as he remains susceptible to persuasion, unlike the latter.
This is because the weak actions contradict knowledge,
whereas vicious actions are consistent with bad character."

~Aristotle

"The wise man belongs to all countries,
for the home of a great soul is the whole world."

~Democritus

"Of all the things of a man's soul which he has within him,
justice is the greatest good and injustice the greatest evil."

~Platon

"It is our choice of good or evil that determines our character, not
our opinion about good or evil."

~Aristotle

Thank God. For suffering teaches value.
Grateful for Soul, the greatest privilege within you;
Thank God for your share in the Divine.
Respect yourself in accordance with Christ's Mind.

Love only the Greatest pleasures in God,
God conditions hearts reaching for Him in every thought.
In times of doubt, & while contending with fears,
May His peace descend, & calm all tears.

Thank God for the journey, that shapes your soul,
For every step forward, is a story to be told;
Thank God for the lessons, that taught you to grow,
& thank God for the Love, that makes your heart glow.

May these words bring comfort, may they guide you on your way;
May they help you to the Love, that shines bright each new day;
& may that Love inspire you, to reach out for the Divine,
Placing wisdom & Love in the depths of your heart's shrine.

XXXII. Of Evil & Weakness

Your brakes give out on a bridge, completely, do you turn into the other lane with an oncoming semi-truck, drive over the side or keep driving through the man standing in the road that sees your truck but refuses to move? Of what use is a manipulated and misused archetype that assures the continuance of victimhood? We cultivate the truly Progressive Hero, the Vindication of true strength over pitiful useless weakness in Victimentality. Christ's Grace is demonstrated from a position of strength, not to guide the strong into genociding themselves nor to allow the evil materially-minded to menace the population for profit.

Convoluted abstractions of weakness undermine the survivability of the otherwise capable. The incapable pull everything down through alienated elements of culture, in disgusting covetousness. What had, once upon a time, been a manipulated and thus suboptimal cultural tool by which the Great could harness the efforts of their lessers and direct their labours toward beneficial ends for all, a mutually beneficial arrangement historically, has been transformed into a tool of the weak to manipulate the potentially Great and arrest progress. The Victimentality disease offers the weak and conniving cretins opportunity to supplant the strong and once Great. This has been on plain display for a very long time, as the Western civilisation gasps for air.

Choices converge like tributaries into a mighty river. Do we succumb to the idea of an inexorable force of fate, careening into the abyss with nary a thought for consequences or do we forge fate ourselves as our ancestors had? Can we not chart a course beyond this void, driven by an insatiable hunger in our purpose? What do the hollow shells of false heroes do except perpetuate the cycle of weakness, where the feeble are amplified by the very systems originally designed to uplift them? Or does it herald a new era of transcendence, where the capable are freed from the shackles of mediocrity? In the end, it's all yet another form of oppression, yet more stifling and insidious

Suffering teaches us to cherish every moment, every breath, and every heartbeat. It reminds us that we are not merely physical beings, but spiritual entities capable of transcending the mundane. The most mysterious, yet most sacred aspect of our being, is the seat of our deepest longings, the source of our creative potential, and the gateway to the divine. To be grateful for one's soul is to acknowledge that we are not mere automatons, but beings of profound significance, quite worthy of God's Love by our reaching out to Him. The divine spark within us all is the essence of our humanity, the source of our highest aspirations, and the wellspring of our creativity. To thank God for our share in the divine is to acknowledge that we are not isolated, self-contained beings, but interconnected, interdependent instantiations of larger living existence through God's Holy Spirit. The teachings of Christ guide us toward a life of love, compassion, and wisdom.

We are to respect ourselves according to these teachings and acknowledge our inherent value as human beings thus, with our capacity for growth and transformation, and our sacred responsibility to live in harmony with our world naturally. The greatest pleasures in God are sublime joys of the Spirit, the sweet nectar of contemplation in the Love inherent of that Spirit, and the profound peace that comes from basking in all His Goodness through Christ. To love these greatest pleasures is to transcend the mundane, 'to soar on eagle's wings,' and to experience wonders of the boundless divine. Subtle yet powerful forces influence our thoughts, feelings, and actions, but when we reach for God and connect with the divine, our hearts become attuned closer to His frequency, and we begin to resonate with His highest Love. God's Love is most apparent in the very progressive nature built into reality.

The arresting of progress must end. We must obliterate the abstractions of weakness masquerading as strength in the denial of our mortal divine. We must cultivate truly progressive heroes, representatives of strength and resilience forged in the crucible of a self-sacrifice, measured and specified, which is to say disposing with the parts in self unworthy of Christ's path. What is the point of an individual life of some advantage amidst horrors while the greater good of community and society are achievable through growth and self-sacrifice of the imperfect self? We can work toward beneficial ends only if we also improve ourselves and be on guard. Educate yourself philosophically so as not to be corrupted by the allure of wealth or liars with false promises and evil designs for harm.

"Evil denotes the lack of good. Not every absence of good is an evil, for absence may be taken either in a purely negative or in aprivative sense. Mere negation does not display the character of evil, otherwise nonexistents would be evil and moreover, a thing would be evil for not possessing the goodness of something else, which would mean that man is bad for not having the strength of a lion or the speed of a wild goat. But what is evil is privation; in this sense blindness means the privation of sight."

~Thomas Aquinas

"I am made all things to all men,
that I might by all means save some…"
"Yet not I, but by the Grace of God,
Whom was with me."

~Apostle Paulus (1 Corinthians 9:22b; 15:10)

"Let those with capacity listen to how
the Spirit is conveyed through the communities…
To all who overcome self, I promise the privilege of
eating from the tree of Life that is in the paradise of God."

"Every scribe instructed in the celestial domains
is like a man maintaining a household,
who brings forth out of it, treasure of new things and old."

~Jesus Christ (Revelation 2:7 ; Matthew 13:52)

....

They were the only ones that didn't believe in Him,
And they've been destroying His memory ever since.

XXXIII. Opportunity

Every being wishes to survive, regardless of capacity for it. To fight for survival while progressing and thriving is to truly be alive. To survive is to live. Many seek only to live off the efforts of others and this can be unfortunate, but then who is to say what is parasitic and what is not? Is that not, to a great degree, left to the discrimination of the would-be host? However true, confusion regarding this is ideal for the purposes of parasitic interests. The answer, much like the storm cloud on the horizon, remains shrouded in uncertainty, and nobody has a clearly refined solution. The promulgation of Victimentality, however, makes those who can use help most and to the greatest end, the least likely to receive it.

Hate is so powerful that little is needed to enslave the definitive dialectic mythology afterwards, as purpose built to control opposites. Another way of saying this is **DIVIDE** comes first so that fewer conspirators are needed to **CONQUER** that ordained crux afterwards, as ideally efficient in simple negation of both sides. A parasite can only aggress upon a society with victims identifying themselves as such and expressing it through hatred. Without victims, the parasitic behaviour simply ceases to be able to exist, because the immune system of society begins to function again. This raises important questions about the nature of suffering and its relationship to our very existence. Specifically, why do people allow themselves to become pathological victims, instead of standing up for themselves? Is it possible for a society to function without victims? It is certainly possible to stop suffering to the degree available and find the greatest good that an individual in your situation can do. Can we help people achieve this on a cultural and community basis?

Can we construct a world where the capable are rewarded, and the incapable are not encouraged to only rely on the efforts of others simply to survive? Can we construct a world where material things are not idolised? Can we construct societies where cretins are not permitted to torture the population with new forms of victimhood, designed to terrorise them into self-hatred and hatred of others? The only option left is to cut a clean break; to dismiss victimhood and Victimentality by constructing the tools for its expulsion from humanity, forever. What does this mean exactly? How can we construct such tools while our very societies are under constant threat by the forces of parasitism and Victimentality maintaining the current state of affairs?

We must transform the ruins of mediocrity into motivation for transcendence into higher aspirations. The key to unlocking true strength and virtues is not in manipulating or harming others, but in transforming ourselves and empowering the people around us. We must confront the void within and chart a course toward redemption. What is given away is all you keep for eternity. The choice is ours, and ours alone. Will we choose to rise above what pulls us down, or will we forever remain trapped in the quicksand of stagnation? Any one thing which stops elevation is not worth it.

The answer is within, waiting to be unearthed, and you know it, now certainly if not before. Can we not see that every snarl and scratch, every knot and kink, presents an opportunity for growth, for evolution, and for transcendence? In the depths of despair, we find the seeds of transformation, if only we look for them. The existential darkness that surrounds us is merely a shadow cast by our own creative potential as granted by the power of the greatest Intelligence in the Universe.

The "parasitism" everywhere is a reflection of our own tendencies toward exploitation, if we allow ourselves to obsess in the self. You could do the same and simply join the machine or try to take it over, in stealing labour by manipulation of its value or influence marketplaces in unscrupulous manners to maximise that profit margin, without actually contributing meaningfully to the collective, just like everyone else tries to do. Yet, quite similar enough dynamics can be posited which grant opportunity for mutual benefit, co-creation, and cooperation without any exploitations. Letting go of the self in the process of community and Spirit is the avenue to maximum inspiration, as implied by Christ in the quote at the opening of this chapter. Let go of the material fleeting things that pass away, firmly grasp hold of the reality here and now. What you are supposed to do with this present now, is focus on creation and completion in the greatest goods you can find to accomplish.

The challenge is to the would-be Great, to construct the tools, as mediators, for expelling suffering and victimhood. This is a call for creativity, for innovation, for individual action, and for collective action. In the face of uncertainty, we must be driven by the very existence of the chaos. Every problem presents an opportunity for growth and transformation. Each challenge beckons us to rise above it. This is the radical embracing of the unknown as catalyst, and not identifying ourselves with the victimhood or adversity, but with the progress. By recognising our own transformative power, we will discover new and improved pathways for redemption, for healing, and for liberation.

The concept of existence, you see, is a paradoxical beast that defies easy comprehension. What does it mean to say that we "exist" at all? Is it merely a temporary aberration in the movements of reality? Is it a brief flicker of self-awareness before we're snuffed out like candles in a gust of wind? On one hand, it's a rather mundane fact that we all exist, after all I mean, here we are, breathing, thinking, and whatnot. On the other hand, existence itself is shrouded in mystery, uncertainty, and the constant threat of non-being, death in a word. Despite this doubt, we find ourselves compelled to act as if our continued existence is certain. We make decisions, take actions, and construct the meaning in and around us from the pieces given, in an attempt to align it best with what we admire most. We have a limited amount of time, however.

Let's turn to the Soul's triumphs. Our very essence is on a quest for self-discovery and growth. Our true nature is not tied to the passing pleasures of this world but rather to a higher, more eternal reality. We're drawn to contemplate the mysteries of this greater existence, to seek answers to the ultimate questions. Yet, such adventures are fraught with obstacles, temptations, and distractions in all their varieties and complexities, made all the more incomprehensible with directed propaganda. The world around us can be quite seductive, luring us away from our inner path which guides our best actions. We must learn to let go of our attachments, desires, and fears to truly discover who we are.

It is often said that the deepest truths come from the heart. This is the essence of the reality, though many conflate heart with raw and immature emotion, getting back to Victimentality. Rather God holds those closest who reach out for Him and find the necessity toward loving submission. Most indicative expression of this is moderate living since Love from God transforms the heart completely, and you hold yourself to standards characteristic of that perfect Fatherly Love. So, again, anything that constrains your ability to do Good is to be thrown away, and this is the only path to greater freedom.

Do we find true fulfilment in the stillness of the mind or in the dynamic flux of life's experiences? Should we not strike a balance between the two, embracing both the quiet introspection and the outward expression that gives witness to inspiration and the vast stores of energy in God's limitless Love, i.e. living existence? If so, how does this fit into detachment from the material world? The physical is ever present. We cannot literally detach from it, and large parts of the spiritual rewards are only possible by maintaining shared experience and connections with friends and family, who will all be at different levels of spiritual advancement. You could theoretically help many people to advance, but not much from far away, and it is always best to start with those nearest you.

Right now this all may look like opportunity, but when we see through to God's Love in it all, it becomes about responsibility instead. People are raised to not do and to believe that the key to their moral life is in what they do not do. The simple fact is that for those capable, it is not enough to avoid terrible things, it is absolutely essential that you attempt to do your most. This is that time, and this is that effort. Knowledge itself comes with even more responsibilities, since not doing anything with knowledge makes you liable. Knowledge makes you drunk until it stops, when the deluge becomes that stability in the ultimate intellectual sobriety: "I know nothing and there are deeper truths upon which I will never touch." What is wealth actually but greater responsibility as well, in ever deepening lost potential good, much like knowledge but without the benefits? A man who is wealthy is usually soaked in blood, little aware of goodness. Best thing for a wealthy man's soul is to live poor at least until God's wealth comes upon him. A man who has found such wealth of God does not want for anything else but God's Will to be revealed.

Is all of this possible? Is it possible to uplift others? Is it possible to construct a society where the purposes of error and suffering are well understood? Is it possible for a society to exist where those who suffer are instead given the tools to overcome their struggles and become stronger for it? Is a society possible where people are genuinely led toward God and Good? Is any of this actually possible?

Yes. 100% and undoubtedly. I believe these things are possible, and I hope you will too! I not only believe they are possible, but inevitable. If only people knew how very precious they are in actuality, they might act it, and then realise how precious the people around them are. Without God's Love, we cannot do ourselves or others justice. Ultimately in the grand scheme, this comes down to God missing in society, but you are here for a reason and to fix this, it will take all of Your Fight.

"The very place God has given you is the place
where divinity will touch humanity through you."

"God cannot give us a happiness and peace
apart from Himself, because it is not there.
There is no such thing."

~C.S. Lewis

....

Mere 'solidarity' is a shallow love offering mediocre human connection despite the existential alienation from family, community, society, nation, and culture...

OMEGA

"Awake, O sleeper, and arise from the dead,
and Christ will shine on you..."

"Besides this you know the time,
that the hour has come for you to wake from sleep.
For salvation is nearer to us now than when we first believed..."

"So then let us not sleep, as others do,
but let us keep awake and be sober."

~Apostle Paulus
(Ephesians 5:14; Romans 13:11; 1 Thessalonians 5:6)

"Thus they never stop rising,
moving from one new beginning to the next,
and the beginning of ever greater graces
is never limited of itself.

For the desire of those who thus rise never rests
in what they can already understand;
but by an ever greater and greater desire,
the soul keeps rising constantly to another that lies ahead,
and thus it makes its way through
ever higher regions towards the Transcendent."

~St. Gregory of Nyssa

"Tomorrow, and tomorrow, and tomorrow,
Creeps in this petty pace from day to day,
To the last syllable of recorded time;
And all our yesterdays have lighted fools
The way to dusty death. Out, out, brief candle!
Life's but a walking shadow, a poor player,
That struts and frets his hour upon the stage,
And then is heard no more. It is a tale
Told by an idiot, full of sound and fury,
Signifying nothing."
-Macbeth

....

What does it mean to be awake?
Is it rising to yet another dream?

Or not realising what is fake?
Search for Truth in finding the seam.

Reality, or you, is going to break,
One or the other will run out of steam.

It's only simulated in your twisted take,
Because not all things are as they seem.

Introduction to Strategy

We transition now from the philosophical underpinnings of Victimentality to practical applications of this knowledge into strategy. The pivotal second half of this tome serves as guide. If you have read this far, you care, and wish to harness the power of memetics and spectacle in achieving peaceful yet potent victories on the cultural stage.

In the face of Victimentality's all-too-common pitfalls, it is essential to develop a strategic approach that not only acknowledges but also actively engages with the complex dynamics of cultural evolution. This book is designed to equip you with the tools necessary to come out swinging memetically to influence cultural narratives and ultimately bring about positive change. Memetic 'warfare' is about crafting compelling narratives, engineering viral campaigns in spectacle, using natural systems to advantage, and orchestrating strategic alliances outside of what you may have considered feasible before.

This is not merely a collection of memetic strategies or tactical manoeuvres; it is an holistic framework for cultural cold 'warfare' that prioritises transformation through least violent tactics. Memetics within communities in natural braintrusts are the new simulacrum of warfare, and the things that precede war as determinant. By leveraging the power of spectacle and meme-based persuasion, we will be empowered to create a ripple effect of positive change that resonates across social media platforms, physical communities, and ultimately even mainstream discourse.

The art of strategic communication in memetics is simple in action upon inspiration but complex when attempting to lay it out into a comprehensive plan or in black and white text like this. More important than anything else, the message conveyed must be received with clarity and purpose, so that it is acted upon by the recipient.

Spectacle, in its most elemental form, is a primal draw that speaks to our deepest desires for connection and community. A well-crafted spectacle has the capacity to make us laugh, cry, or nod in solemn agreement. It is an art form that has captivated audiences for centuries, from ancient Hellenic theatre to modern-day blockbuster films. Much of spectacle is in masculinity itself and masculine community, which is also explored here in Part Omega. Comedy, on the other hand, is a subtle yet potent force that can defuse tension, break down barriers, and create a sense of shared humanity. A well-timed joke or wry observation can be powerful catalysts for change, allowing us to confront our most deeply held fears with humour and humility.

Through a combination of theory, analysis, and practical application, we will uncover the secrets behind crafting messages that resonate with our audiences, leaving them inspired, engaged, and ultimately, motivated to take action. By harnessing the power of visual storytelling and humour, we can captivate audiences, challenge assumptions, and inspire action. The ultimate goal is not merely to "win" or dominate the cultural narrative but rather to elevate humanity's collective consciousness and contribute to a more compassionate, just, and enlightened world. The strategies presented within these pages are designed to be adaptable, flexible, and above the board in any political situation or dynamic, recognising that true victory is the Good that can be done given all limitations.

As you imbibe this guide, your strategic memetic skills will hopefully grow. As these skills grow, you will see things differently. This difference will permit synthesis of greater knowledge in your environment, building the confidence necessary to take swipes at the surrounding landscape culturally. Hopefully your desire to promote positive change and leave a lasting impact on the world has been growing throughout this book thus far.

What is the alternative though? Is it brave to call out those least in need of it, or most? Are you ready to engage the social power of masculine braintrusts? Harness the influence of confident spectacle? Tap into the energy of comedy? Would you like to join the ranks of the most influential memetic warriors in human history, masters in the art of cultural war, as the primary science of internal revolution? Then let us proceed.

"Strive towards another's will

rather than thine.

Choose less rather than more.

Seek the lowest place,

and be servant to all.

Wish and pray the Will of God

be fulfilled in thee. See,

such men enter into inheritance

of great peace and quiet."

~The Imitation of Christ

············

Charity is God's Wealth.

Grace is God's Guidance.

All gold will surely melt,

No thing gets left behind us.

12. Motivation

As the sky bleeds crimson across the sunset of this worn cultural canvas, we find ourselves ensnared in deceits and half-truths. We await the morning in mourning, but the night need not be long. The ever looming storm cloud of crimes, wrapped in fresh evaporates of lies, hangs heavy. Yet, it is precisely within this maelstrom that we must unearth the wisdom forged from the very fires of our own grief and passion. To serve all, and lift up, we must aim thus.

Grief is the powderkeg that ignites a fire for rebellion, wherever it may align against authority. Grief, in its most primal form, is an overwhelming scream against, and therefore fundamental rejection of, the cruel indifference in material reality. It strips away the flimsy façade of experiential scars and societal pressures, revealing the wound in reality beneath. It is digging within at precisely this vulnerability that allows us to confront our deepest fears and desires. What are the actual causes of your problems?

Passions, too, are a double-edged sword. They drive us to challenge what are considered the limitations in our World, and rage against the disorder or non-order. Passionate intensity grants motivation to uncover the hidden truths that lie under the chains of deception. Passions can be more powerful than any force on Earth. Learn what your griefs mean and what your passions entail, you will figure out everything else, including what the goals should be in your fight.

The ravages of our despair, when the curtains of deceit are rent asunder, reveal to us raw truth in a brutal reflection without reservations. In this sorrow, we are forced to confront reality colder and harsher than we are typically used to providing for our own selves. Amidst the ashes flying off inflamed dreams and passions, we discover the deepest wisdoms born from our experiences. Truth hurts, but it's the most worthy pain. Become addicted to the truth, now, and forego all other addictions. This is your drug, in harsh reality rending your perspective to it.

The fog of deceit is treacherous, yet it's precisely why it is here that we must deliberate with intention like the fierce and worthy descendants we are. To resist the sirens' songs of falsehoods, we must first acknowledge the abyss within ourselves the void left by our own false self-beliefs, disillusionment, and disappointments that block greater understanding. Doing so gains us a glimpse of reality's true nature and our purpose within it. There is no better pursuit than uncovering the hidden truths underlying these chains of deception that enslave humanity. No, the wisest don't want more violence, but to minimise it. The wise wish to lovingly prove ignorance wrong and help others correct their own future behaviours. This is the Love God shows, but many ignore.

No men can be left alone, most especially those who would choose to. At some level, a man must confront the realities of the society around him. However, should you be able to get out of these duties in this generation, it just means potentially worse duties for your descendants down the line. The Stockholm culture has us all enthralled, hypnotised by the victimhood as idol. We've become so accustomed to playing the role of the oppressed that we've forgotten how to even **win**. The cult of victimhood has taken hold.

We must dance with the shadows that haunt us, refusing to accept the lies that masquerade as reality. The Stockholm culture has convinced us that we're powerless, that we're just pawns in a game controlled by forces beyond our control and that we should run away! I say, "nonsense!" In all this chaos, it's easy to get caught up in the victimhood that feeds on our fear and uncertainty. We must resist its grasp, dear friend. We must stand tall against the forces that seek to keep us in chains, and convince us we have no power. We are the masters of our own destiny. Find a safe place to be with community, but know we have the power to shape reality, to create the better life, and to overcome any obstacle that comes our way!

This is not just about challenging power or calling out injustice; it's about actively seeking out Truth, capital T, no matter how uncomfortable or unpalatable we may at first find it. Wisdom is in the confrontation of our own griefs and passions, a peeling away of the layers in deception, to replace weak strands that compromise. This peeling is an uncovering of the hidden truths in this chaotic currency.

Again, addict yourself to the pain of truth. Truth will set us free, and we will know Truth by this feature, by the fact that it does indeed set us free. Never has actual Good entered the World through deception, at best the mere aversion or negation of evil; negation of evil rightly feels like the greatest thing after a lot of destruction, but it is just the start. This is the beginning of Your Fight.

Yes, this is required, no you cannot get out of it. It is necessary, **LOOK** at the cover of the book again real quick, what does it say? Whose **FIGHT** is it? Yeah.

So what is **it**?

Who controls your mind if not you? Can you not recreate in your mind some sense of a feeling had before? Then why can't you do this at any time and with any intensity, and whenever you wish? What is stopping you from having complete control over your mind? Run through it. Do not let anything stand in your way to Truth. You are the one in control, the only one in control of self, and there is only One Destination from the perfecting of many imperfections. Do not give in to dark night. Shine ever the more. **WIN!**

Homework:

1. Griefs?

What has made you grieve? What lessons came from it, and what lessons have you put off learning from for too long?

2. Passions?

What has made you passionate? What good came from it, and what is the good in it? What is the bad?

3. Mission?

Synthesise the answers given for **1** & **2** into **3**. What do your griefs, passions, and experiences mean about you and your identity? Now discuss your goals in light of this synthesis, can you line up more goals with what drives you deeply? This is motivation. Can you be a Hero beyond your victimhood?

"If you understand Christ's Words fully, and taste them truly,
you must strive to form your whole life after His pattern."

"But insomuch as there are but few who labour to die
to themselves and to overcome themselves perfectly,
they remain in their fleshly feelings and
worldly comforts and can in no manner
rise up in spirit above themselves."

~Imitation of Christ

"Behold, I am sending you out as sheep in the midst of wolves,
so be wise as serpents and innocent as doves.
Beware of men, for they will deliver you over to courts
and flog you in their synagogues,
and you will be dragged before governors
and kings for My sake, to bear witness before them
and all the nations. When they deliver you over,
do not be anxious how you are to speak or what you are to say,
for what you are to say will be given to you in that hour.
For it is not you who speaks,
but the Spirit of your Father speaking through you."

~Jesus Christ (Matthew 10:16-20)

"Doth thou go up into the theatre,
to insult the common nature of men and women,
and disgrace thine own eyes?"
"Form then in thy mind an image
of that amphitheatre,
and hate thou this,
which is the devil's."
~St. Chrysostom

....

Destroyers have monopolies on theatres & lies.

Spectacle need only Truth, to open it upon eyes,

Noble life the plot, in Truth we do realise:

Any things outside real progress cannot be wise.

11. Spectacle

Spectacle is foundational to art, culture, myths, history, and legends. People are drawn to the unique, heroic, and human stories most, especially when faced with adversity. The underdog hero archetype in tales, for instance, resonates strongly with people and informs them of certain ideals within society because of it, for instance. This is because the hero archetype reminds us that we can have a greater purpose in this World. In the greater purpose is the very element of God when competing best Goods in every thought or notion are weighed and considered. The archetype of the hero reminds man of his connection with God, which is why it has been so cruelly and ruthlessly targeted, and why the Victim-Hero is cast as a hero, but in the guise of victim in all reiterations, for the purpose of corruption. The point of this evil is to disconnect man from God.

Spectacle is a tool which can be used best when highlighting an issue that many people have already dealt with and for which they feel unjustly treated, without recompense. Raising a topic which has been brushed aside for illogical reasons is great justice in itself. People are difficult to get through to. Spectacle, as a strategy in cultural warfare, is about awakening the senses to realities previously unseen, like a bolt of lightning on an otherwise quiet evening. When we're faced with uncertainty, our senses are heightened, and our minds are primed for revelation.

What is true, my friends, is truly yours. Shared cultural existence hinges upon Truth and veracity. It's the fundamental truths that the fortunate find in life that can often serve as best ammunition for that firearm of spectacle. Spectacles can be designed to tap into the meaning for human domains of experience and extract incentives or purposes for the audience on a cultural level, and within related topics.

Spectacle is not just about some abstract concepts or theoretical framework, it's about uncovering lies which require attention. Many actual victims are forced culturally to suffer silently without recompense nor hope for justice. Many of them are silent members of your audiences, as you play generator of spectacle. Your spectacle helps to tell their story, forcing all to relive it under different and, perhaps, more illuminated contexts. You see, when we shine a light on these issues and raise the topic which is forgotten due to a mixture of ignorance and evil, then we're doing great justice.

The power of spectacle is in awakening us to realities previously unseen. It can shake us out of our complacency and force us to confront the world as it truly is. It is perhaps the singular most important weapon in our arsenal of cultural warfare strategies which reveals the hidden truths that lie just beneath the surface of our collective comprehensions. If used appropriately it can have devastating impact.

Truth is concrete and tangible, but also deeply personal, especially for godly people. Truth is also the very story of the individual, the struggles they faced, and the sorrows they suffered through it all. In the end, Truth is the story of Life, writ small in the particle but completing in the grand on the universal. Truth is asking yourself what you did with your life, and what you do with it, and honestly accepting the actual answer. It is in the genuine victims systematically ignored, who overcome suffering quietly in a world that often despises their pleas. It never matters how genuine the pleas are since the problem is in the very existence of the victim and the proof of truth it bears.

We must generate spectacle to bring hidden truths into the spotlight where they can be seen and heard. We must tell the stories of those who have been silenced by the forces of this Victimentality-based Stockholm culture, whose voices are drowned out by thinly-veiled animus. The art of the spectacle is about demonstrating a sense of empathy and outrage in a format that can galvanise people into action, inspiring them. The audience is everything. The audience is you, as well. We awaken to truths together in the form of an adventure, to confront the realities that surround us.

The best spectacle speaks directly to hearts and minds, so crafted as a narrative that is both personal and universal, one that shows how the struggles of individual are inextricably linked to the lessons within the community or nation as a whole. This is not just about performance; it is about creating cultural movement toward ever greater revelations. Inspire people to take action as the agents of change and progress they were born to be. Let us tell the stories that matter and bring them into the spotlight where they can be witnessed. By sharing personal tales of woe and triumph, we can create spectacle that resonates with the very marrow of human experience. Spectacle can help spotlight absurdities and outrages that beset us, we can create a sense of urgency that drives the many to action. By amplifying visibility of problems and forcing issues through vivid narratives we can better communicate the largest issues made too scandalous by the powerful interests.

Spectacle by Design

Appeal is about want and desire, and these are the things that stick in the mind. Spectacle is that element of an event that catches the eye, and still later catches the thought based upon some underlying importance or meaning. In marketing, it is well understood that generally a new client will have seen your business at least five times before contacting you, so the spectacle is about putting the idea itself in the mind so that it repeats. Most minds have rather repetitive processes with patterns that get stuck, so in many ways breaking them out of it to see something honestly good for them is a great service. Spectacle storytelling has become the way to get through in this careless culture of victims, and not in the way it ultimately should.

You need to be prepared to take risks, challenge conventional wisdom, and plunge headlong into that floating wall of human experience. Helmets can be useful. Spectacle can help create a sense of outrage and indignation, which motivate people to take action. Remember that when someone puts limits on you, they are governing the process, this would include public communications no matter how private they might claim the servers are. If they don't like it, they should pick an industry that does not govern. Do not allow people to stop you from making the well-framed spectacle. Being seen in the spectacle and moving forward despite attempts to silence you can be incredibly powerful. Understand who your target audience is, what they care about, and how to reach them. You should definitely do this because you do not want to waste time on people who won't care about your truth, and especially not the spectacle.

Develop a Spectacle Plan

The grandiose dance of spectacle, a hot salsa of planning, precision, and sheer bloody-mindedness. To craft a spectacle worthy of the ages, one must first consider the logistical challenges, those pesky little hurdles that can turn a brilliant plan into a catastrophic mess. It's all about finding the sweet spot where art meets logistics, where the creative spark meets the crux of cultural, experiential, and informational efficiencies. What resources will you need to make your spectacle come alive? Will you require a team of experts or merely a willingness to take risks? What cultural touchstones resonate with your audience? Can you harness the power of nostalgia, or perhaps leverage the Zeitgeist in other ways to make your message more relatable? What emotions do you want to evoke in your audience? Outrage, guilt, empathy, or something else entirely? The key is to create an authentic connection speaking to human experience with new information on, or the seriousness of, some matter. Also, don't bother manufacturing fake outrage or other coached reactions, as people can spot such things very rapidly. Create spectacles to tell stories that matter. A story that speaks to shared experiences and challenge us to confront the uncomfortable truths people would rather pass up in ignorant comfort.

Juxtapositional Spectacle Highlights the Absurd

Juxtaposition is a powerful tool for developing spectacles that challenge people's assumptions and highlight absurdities or genuine injustices. It is a sledgehammer, revealing the absurdities and injustices that lie beneath the surface of our neatly packaged reality. When we place two things side by side, forcing them into an uncomfortable marriage, we create a spectacle that screams at us, "Hey, pay attention! This ain't right!" Often these are very offensive or border on the offensive for a great many people because propaganda has built in safeguards to stop people from entering certain areas of conversation.

Imagine a story where the opulence of the 1% is juxtaposed with the poverty of the 99%. Picture a velvet-rope club, where champagne flows like water, right in the middle of a homeless shelter, where the scent of despair hangs heavy in the air. The absurdity is palpable, and the injustice is pungent. Another potential example is to contrast the solemnity of war memorials with the gaudiness of shopping malls. Imagine the sombre faces of fallen soldiers staring out from their marble slabs, surrounded by the glistening façade of consumerism, with its fast food and novelty shops. The disconnect is jarring, the absurdity is horrific, the setting two things at once, and the call would be to question the values that drive our society, what is just cause for war, and in what we choose to invest.

Juxtaposition challenges expectation. By forcing disparate elements together, we create a visual shorthand that conveys the complexity of the world we inhabit. It's like taking a blowtorch to the curtains of the shared psychosis, revealing the truth beyond. There's also irony pairing so nicely with juxtaposition! Protest with signs like "Save Our Billionaires!" "Stop AntiWealthism!" and "Honk If You Love the Money!", right outside Wall Street while dressed as CEOs. The absurdity would be too much to bear, with injustice crystal clear, and all would be forced to confront the disconnect between words and actions. You could have them doing all sorts of things, like morbidly pretending to offer free injections to make others rich too.

Organise a play or peaceful parade protest dressed up as some group in question (full on appropriation here, we don't care about permanent victimhood, we're here to end it) enacting whatever crime with choreographed dance but then everyone being happy about it and hugging afterward. This juxtaposition highlights absurdity of crime being ignored due to sensitivities over forced permanent group victimhood and encourages any onlookers or audience to question the way things are. Having the legitimate victims bow down and praise the assailants afterward highlights the injustice by way of juxtaposed spectacle portraying reality in metaphoric terms.

Create a spectacle with a video where people dressed as polar bears dance in bikinis and chains holding signs that say "ME TOO!" and "I was taken advantage of by CEOs" with a scummy photographer snapping shots. This juxtaposition of recent popular memes humanises the impact of climate change propaganda by twisting recent memetics in culture around. The polar bears here would be claiming CEOs have also taken advantage of them, which is completely true. Polar bears are also victims ecologically of actual pollution in their habitats by nasty international corporations. The largest corporations have also used climate change as a distraction from very real issues, such as the international sex trafficking with which they are very much involved. International corporations and multinationals paying for the climate change narratives are also headed by nasty men with too much power who often do horrific things to young and naïve people.

Symbolism, Complex Ideas, & Storytelling

Symbolism and storytelling are not merely tools for conveying complex ideas, but rather, they represent the very basis through which we constitute reality. By charting the relationships between concepts, signs, and symbols, we create a topology of meaning that is simultaneously situated and transcendental. This process of philosophical heuristic mapping is not a passive exercise, but rather an active creation of our understanding of the World, as we recursively refine and revise our knowledge through the iterative process of narrative construction. Symbolism is a form of the metaphoric, where signs and symbols constantly reinforce and reconfigure each other, giving rise to complex systems of meaning that are both stable and unstable, and we will discuss this more in memeplexes of later chapters. Stability in symbolism can be increased with attachment to reality and strengths, such as true masculinity and true femineity as contrastives.

Storytelling, then, serves as a mode of epistemic iteration, where we refine and revise our knowledge through this filtering process of narrative construction. By weaving together symbolic threads, we create new patterns that are variously context-dependent and context-transcendent. This tension between context and transcendence gives rise to an intellectual memetic mapping with culture, and improvement. Symbolism and storytelling can be seen as intertwined processes that enable us to constitute reality through the recursive meaning-making. This constellation of meaning is not fixed or determinate, but rather, it is constantly in flux, subject to the vicissitudes of human experience and the unpredictable nature of cultural evolution. Ultimately, this flux gives rise to uncertainty, where some aspects in our understanding of reality are perpetually called into question and loosely held somewhat cynically, allowing for the emergence of new meanings and significations with better information. This is art. It is the art which Hegel himself was most cognisant when he spoke of rising cultural formations.

As another example of spectacle, one could organise a "Lab Inquiry 4 Jab Injury" where participants might honour loved ones who have died after receiving experimental medicines by creating a painting or artwork representing them. Each participant carries small placards with a statistic about the impact. The symbolism emphasises the urgent need for justice. Organise a weekly community charity dinner to keep it fresh on people's mind, while also supporting communication and dialogue. You can have contests where people dress up as things symbolic of the cause, and an award is given at each weekly dinner, which can generate social media interest, so long as thing remain respectful. Participants can share their stories, build community connections, and highlight the importance of a response.

There are many ideas available for those creative enough. Organise surprise performances in public spaces to raise awareness about issues in creative ways, even using costumes, dance, and music if it helps. Create immersive experiences that allow participants to engage with complex issues. "Haunted house" and "escape room" type experiences come to mind, but these could be adapted to other settings and purposes, such as raising awareness of waste, bad laws, prison issues, or how the movie industry operates. Organise massive public art projects that highlight social and environmental issues like murals and sculptures. Host live storytelling performances that humanise specific issues like spoken word poetry and one-person shows like standup. Remember, the key to developing effective spectacles is to use a combination of these strategies, leveraging your unique strengths and resources. Don't be afraid to experiment and adapt your approach as needed!

Spectacle in Confrontation

Sometimes a spectacle can be created by confronting an opponent with a situation that you know will catch them off-guard. This can fool them into revealing a truth that they might not otherwise have shared. In catching the person with this lie, you have successfully made your argument against them in the admission without much effort at all.

To create a spectacle that will leave your audience gasping with urgency, you must be willing to work hard and get your hands a little dirty. You must be willing to confront the Stockholm culture head-on, to challenge the powers that be with a cleverly crafted trap, if you will. Force opponents to reveal themselves like rats scurrying upon discovery.

It's all about cultivating an experience that will leave them, and everyone else, wondering what hit them. You want to create a spectacle that will be talked about for years to come. Something that will make people question their assumptions, challenge their beliefs, and, ideally, inspire them to take action. Spectacle should enliven the senses to realities previously unseen, especially the more spiritual and universal truths. What is true is yours and what is false is not, so focus for now on the core truths in the endeavour. These are natural and fundamental to human existence. Generating spectacle can start as simply as asking people to share their stories. People are attracted to the unique, heroic, and human stories most, especially in the face of adversity, and rising against the odds.

Homework:

In this chapter, we explored the concept of spectacle as a powerful tool for cultural warfare, awakening people to hidden truths, and inspiring action. As part of your reflections on the chapter, answer the following questions:

Foundation

What is your initial reaction to the idea that "spectacle is foundational to art, culture, myths, history, and legends?"

The Ignored

How do you think spectacle can be used to uncover lies and bring attention to ignored victims? Provide an example from personal experience or a current event.

Truth as Concrete & Personal

What does it mean to you that "Truth is concrete and tangible, but also deeply personal?" How has your understanding of truth evolved over time? What does something true being yours mean?

Powerful Witness

Think about powerful stories that have impacted you the most. Have you ever felt compelled to take action after witnessing a powerful spectacle, event, or catastrophe? What was it that made you feel this way? How could you replicate this feeling for others?

Get Mad

Reflect on the role of empathy and outrage in generating spectacular moments. How can these emotions be harnessed to inspire change?

Hidden Truth

Imagine a spectacle that brings attention to a hidden truth or ignored actual victims. What would your message be, and how could you improve your ability to convey it with spectacle? Create a brief script for the spectacle (e.g., a performance art piece, documentary, or public service announcement) that addresses the hidden truth. Consider the following elements:

~ Powerful narrative speaking to hearts and minds.
~ Personal bond to community and national universals.
~ Empathy and outrage as motivators for action.

In the city eternally afire, flames lick cold concrete horror,
Heroes emerge: passion-driven, no way to ignore.
Exit morass of conformity, where souls stagnate in decay,
Figures step forth so brave, fuelled sparks refuse to fade.
Streets are anarchy: mismatched rhythms; confused decisions,
Broken things fly out, destroyed perpetually chaos collisions.
Yet, amidst the chaotic turbulence, heroes will stand,
Force friction; challenge powers in propaganda, hand-to-hand.

A slow collapse; society of skyscrapers in motions of trouble,
He finds allies' own footings; help amidst oceans of rubble.
Terrains shift, shake, contort; steps bold, as truly living dare,
Venture forth; find that seam where brokenness meets repair.
Elevate to spite crushed identity, reforge paths & ways forward,
Over ruins, in word & deed; inside, depose the stilted coward.

10. Heroism

It's here that we must tread with care, lest we fall prey to the Stockholm syndrome culture's cruel allure. The damned souls, beset on all sides by the forces of darkness, are not our enemies, no, but rather pawns in a far bigger game than their petty angers and basic suffering. Do not be fooled into believing that battling the wretched will bring about any semblance of justice or redemption. Such actions only serve to perpetuate the cycle of suffering, as it means we would rottenly join hands with the hyenas who feast on the entrails of the damned.

No, our task is clear: target the true villains, those masters of deceit and manipulation who exploit the weak and vulnerable for their own nefarious purposes. In the Stockholm nightmare, where the line between victim and perpetrator is blurred beyond recognition, we are forced to walk the tightrope with precision. The key to unlocking genuine change lies not in verbally attacking the wretched and forsaken, but rather in shining a light on the illegitimate power structures that perpetuate their misery and criminality. The drug-addled homeless, the prostitutes, and the street criminals are there as symptoms of a far more insidious disease, one that infects us all. It is our duty to confront this cancer head-on, to excise it from our midst with precision and purpose.

We must not be swayed by the false promises of easy solutions or simplistic scapegoating. In the end, it is not about elevating the downtrodden above their circumstances, but rather about exposing the rotten underbelly that sustains their suffering. It is a delicate dance, one that requires a keen understanding of the forces at play and an unwavering commitment to justice. It's not what you look for in a man that counts, it's what he looks for in himself. We must seek out the courage to confront our own demons and the strength to stand up against those who would seek to enslave us.

It is very important that you never kick downward. Do not be seen attacking those below, because it does not help at all. These are almost always people seen as "rough" and from bad upbringings. These include street criminals, gang members, the drug addicted homeless, prostitutes, and various indigent people, real actual victims of circumstances in society and their own weaknesses not standing up to the test. No matter how horrible these low hanging hylics might seem, there is very little reason to comment or interact at all. People know the situation is bad and why, and nobody needs your assistance in pointing out anything about such poor creatures. When one must confront such actual victims, it is best to set our sights upon where they have illegitimate power, but point out such weaknesses primarily as evidence for the illegitimacy. Whenever you strike out, it best be at those most powerful of your enemy. Why is this?

The impoverished man has likely arrived at this moment due to circumstances and chains of causation in ignorance largely outside his control. They have no idea about the systems which caused all of this, and they would have no idea where to begin with how to fix it. They can be told who to blame, however. The Stockholm culture has taken rough language of heroes toward weaknesses and turned it always into an immediate attack upon victims, and the weak. You as a hero attempting to lift people up out of this Stockholm culture must walk the narrow path here to make the most impact. Every bit of weakness that is exposed must be caked with proof for applied illegitimacy of power in equal measures. In fact the more that the power and its illegitimacy can be the object, the more effective the criticisms of any weaknesses. Point out the craven villain with evil and ignorance in their heart, but also show how it makes genuine victims of others.

Our true enemy is not the wretched and forsaken, but rather the masters of deceit and manipulation who exploit them for their own nefarious purposes. In desolation, the freeze of conformity stick to cold concrete horror, so that it is easy to become mired in the morass of societal expectations. Instead, we must walk the tightrope of heroism, targeting the true villains who perpetuate evil. We must confront the cancer of illegitimate power that infects us and excise it from our midst with precision and purpose. This requires a keen understanding of the forces at play and an unwavering commitment to justice.

It's not what is found of a man that counts, but what he has found in himself. We must seek out the courage to confront our own demons and the strength to stand up against those who would seek to enslave us. How do we do this? How do we avoid the trap of targeting the wretched and forsaken, and instead expose the true villains? That takes a great deal of discretion, which is something that takes experience, but generally leave them alone unless they pull switches in all this.

In such orchestrated chaos, Heroism itself becomes an act of defiance in rebellion against the forces that seek to control and cruelly manipulate. It's not enough to merely critique the system; we must actively subvert it, using our collective power to expose the true villains behind the scenes. In this there is great hope. By recognising the insatiable hunger for power and control of these villains through cynical manipulation of emotions, we can begin to build alternative systems to prioritise people over profits, community over competition, and empowered compassion over permanent victimhood. Some who are currently weak can be lifted to strength with the strong, rather than trampled under feet by overpowered exploiters, but not amidst constant confusion. It's not just about exposing the flaws in our system, though this is important. This is about new paradigms in culture where true heroism is not just a fleeting act of bravery, but a fundamental aspect of who we are as people.

"Love is active and sincere, courageous, patient, faithful, prudent, and **manly**."
~The Imitation of Christ

"The bravest are surely those who have
the clearest vision of what is before them,
glory and danger alike, and yet notwithstanding,
go out to meet it."
~Pericles

"Courage is in knowing what not to fear."
~Platon

"The true soldier fights not because he hates
what is in front of him, but because he loves what is behind him."
~G.K. Chesterton

Homework:

Overcoming Weaknesses

In what ways can we, as individuals, overcome our own weaknesses and challenge ignorant self-beliefs which limit us, especially those based in Victimentality propaganda?

Heroic Art

Write a poem or short story that explores the theme of heroism in the face of deceit or nonsense Victimentality. Create a visual representation of a hero (e.g., drawing, collage) that illustrates the struggle between conformity and individuality, while demonstrating how this balance is natural, expected, and good.

Conformity & Rebellion

Reflect on conformity and rebellion. How have you handled situations where you felt pressured to conform when it did not seem right? Can you think back and learn from those experiences, and find calm through such storms in the future? Explain how you will handle yourself under that fire.

Prepare

What are some steps you can take to develop the courage and strength to stand up against those who seek to manipulate, or enslave, others with the leverage of Stockholm culture? What are you in need of to do this? Describe ways you cand destroy their cultural memetic weapons.

Culture Community & Nation

In what ways do you prioritise community, people, culture, and your own nation over profits or competition in your daily life?

Though the world seems mad, politics a circus act,

God's Love is proved again in comedy's very fact.

For laughter is the best medicine, or so they say,

In fact, the best use is to keep emotions at bay.

A taste of sugar, though the medicine is best,

Sweetness allows desperate information to digest.

Paulus wrote through his piece of the Word:

"I am become a fool in glorying the Lord."

....

"Ridicule often decides matters of importance more effectively and in a better manner than severity."

~Horace

9. Comedy

Bending and amplifying a topic is a quick way to lighten the emotional load, so to speak, while still landing on target, and with fewer antagonistic feelings. It should generally trend towards playful, unless the target is exceptionally evil, and therefore also often materially wealthy. The goal is not the humour in itself, nor is it in the target of the humour either. The goal isn't even in the audience themselves but in the shifting of their worldview closer to Truth.

You may think that using humour is unprofessional or even silly. Laughter can be a powerful collaborator in the process of deprogramming Victimentality beliefs. When people are laughing, they're more likely to relax and listen to what you have to say, and that's exactly when you want to make your most compelling points. Use comedy and make it funny where it is possible. Revolutionise the dynamic through mockery. Drive expedience by demanding acceptance in the form of laughter.

When we laugh, our brains release endorphins, which can actually increase our feelings of empathy and cooperation. This means that when you're making a joke or using humour in an argument, you're not only making people laugh, you're also promoting an atmosphere where they're more likely to consider your perspective. All of this said, even after jokes, it is completely appropriate to speak seriously, and some information requires the cut and dry.

Before you start cracking jokes, make sure you know who your audience is and what kind of humour they'd appreciate. Use humour that's relatable to the issue at hand. This will help people connect with your message and see the absurdity in the situation. Remember, you're not trying to be a comedian. Keep it simple and avoid overusing jokes. Comedy is only one tool in the arsenal, and with varying levels of success depending upon your personality, the subject, and the audience.

Community Leaders & Laughter

Imagine being in a meeting with community leaders, hopefully about the importance of cultivating strengths, community integrity, or real sustainability. You might start by sharing a personal anecdote about how you once tried to grow your own vegetables in your backyard, but ended up killing them all, "I'm pretty sure that's the definition of 'community development' from what I've seen done so far right?... destroying our own production and then importing it from elsewhere?" You could also make jokes that implicitly reference recent attempts at curtailing meat production, "I mean the only thing more sustainable is a vegan diet... after all, who needs cows when you have all that wonderful grass?"

Chew the cud here a little, help people feel comfortable. When we use the funny to challenge notions, we're not just making fun of the absurdity of the situation, but we are also highlighting the importance of taking actions given the circumstances. Humour should generally be light, set primarily to the spectacle in the topic being discussed, which is often the most ridiculous aspects, and then taking them to even greater extremes. If the topic is convincing businesses to fund community education, you can tell a story about your past in a comedic way, a potential example could be a dressing up of an experience to convey an idea. I have constructed a **fictional** story here to demonstrate how it might be done:

"So, I had this friend way back in highschool, when we were all trying to impress girls however we could. One of my buddies was determined to become the next Schwarzenegger (minus the accent). He started attempting crazy stunts in front of the whole 'phys-ed' class, which included a particular young lady he was interested in. Let me tell you, it did not end well for him. He ended up injuring himself, throwing his back, and screaming like a little girl in the process!

It was like watching a superhero fall from the sky, except instead of getting rescued by Spider-Man, my friend got rescued by little old volunteer paramedics, and instead of gasps from the witnesses, there was suppressed laughter. His social life was pretty much shot after that, but later he said it was fine since it gave him time to take up yoga and build up his core strength. But here's the thing: if he had started by building up his core strength before moving on to the massive weights, none of that would have happened! What's that? Did he ever land a date with his crush?... No unfortunately! She married a skinny English professor way shorter than her, actually. Anyway, here's the point, before any of the young people in our community go out there in the big world and injure themselves in preventable ways, we can help them with core strengths. Sure these are emotional or mental strengths and only related to yoga philosophically, but the point stands."

Chuckles & Community Action

Say you were convincing people in your community to picket and lead a boycott against a large corporation especially notorious for its anti-community policies, funding domestically, and actions overseas. The art of humour can be used to rally the troops! When we use humour in advocacy, it can be a powerful tool for building bridges, breaking ice, and inspiring action. So, how do we use humour to convince members of the community to picket a business and lead a boycott against a particularly notorious corporation? Here are some examples:

"What's Wrong with This Picture?" Approach

Imagine walking up to someone on the street and asking them if they've ever seen a company that claims to be "committed to community values" while simultaneously funding anti-community initiatives overseas. You show them a picture of graphs demonstrating the hypocrisy, and then you ask them "what's wrong with this picture?" Hopefully some emotion will appear, and it is often anger. This point is a good time to utilise a gag, for instance a "sheep" sticker on the poster, perhaps referencing "sheeple." "Well, it looks like they are hypocrites over at Wahlghmardt! They're saying one thing, but doing another. Here, look" you say as you point at the ridiculous sticker, "it's like they're trying to pull the wool over our eyes!" Be a little goofy. This approach uses humour to highlight the absurdity of the situation and encourages people to think more critically about the corporation's actions, because they also feel less alone. Humour in these situations can be empowering. It makes the person feel as though 'yes things are shitty but at least I have people around me who see it too, and at least they have enough confidence in our way out to laugh a bit.'

"Corporate Clown" Analogy

Picture a corporate executive as a clown, someone who constantly makes promises but then never delivers. Like the kid who always breaks their toys on purpose, but then expects you to fix them, at some point it is tiresome. You know what they say: 'You can't make an omelette without breaking some eggs.' However, these fast food franchising giants are enormous clowns in competition to scramble our community's future while claiming they're contributing! As they aim pies at each other's faces, this omelette, of wealth extraction, gets eaten right up by all the shareholders. Instead of eggs, it's made out of the livelihoods, plans, hopes, dreams, and the very lifeblood of our communities... of course the pies never hit them, instead hitting us in the face, in the form of social denigration and demoralisation... haha... but it's not actually funny once you think on it for any amount of time. This approach uses humour to poke fun at the corporation's antics and disarm people's misgivings regarding challenging power. The goal is to get people to see materialist leadership for who they truly are: a bunch of clowns not simply making poor decisions, but actively causing collapse and ruin to society for profit.

"Corporate Con-Artist" Analogy

Imagine walking up to someone on the street and asking them if they've ever met a con-artist. Man, that's a messed up question, and can take people off guard... then, you ask them what they think happens when trying to catch one? They might still not respond. "Well," you say, "con-artists will typically try to get away if they feel they are caught and will use any trick to distract you. You usually have to be pretty clever to outsmart them! Pfizer is like the ultimate pharma-corp con-artist, always trying to sweet-talk their way out of trouble while secretly lining their own pockets and conspiring against the population! What would you say to catch them off their guard? Would they try to shut you up? Would they come after your pet? No, seriously, they're pretty messed up, like cultists, they'll even threaten your dog, not joking."

This approach uses humour to highlight the corporation's shady dealings and encourages people to see through their tricks. "I want Spot to live damnit!... I also don't want them going after any more whistleblowers and their families, like they have, it's serious. People have to be held accountable for all these crimes, and whistleblowers should be encouraged." After you have made your comedic appeal, make sure to bring things back to a virtuous ideal, such as justice like demonstrated.

Comedy Magnification

Comedy is not just a means of entertainment; it's a force multiplier that can amplify the impact of your message and make it more relatable to your audience. When used effectively, comedy can be a potent tool for subverting expectations and challenging assumptions. In the midst of chaos and confusion, laughter has the power to soothe the savage beast within, and allow people to accept new truths. By incorporating humour into your spectacle, you're not just making people laugh; you're assisting in the release of tensions and relaxation that makes them more receptive to difficult truths. Comedy in spectacle is the manure to the seeds of your wisdom. It is important, and I'm not shitting you.

Comedy, however, is not a one-size-fits-all solution. It's essential to understand your audience and tailor your approach accordingly. Some people may respond better to clever wordplay, while others may appreciate a well-crafted joke or witty observation. The key is to use humour as a way of highlighting the absurdity or hypocrisy in a given situation. By pointing out the ridiculousness of a particular issue or institution, you're not just making people laugh; you're also challenging their assumptions and encouraging them to think critically about the world around them. You are also highlighting truths they are already aware of but not brave enough to act upon due to the course of life and the distractions this entails.

Ultimately, regardless all other factors, I cannot recommend comedy enough because it is a powerful tool to advance messages in such a way as to leave a lasting impact on the audience. By incorporating humour into your spectacle, you're not just entertaining people; you're inculcating an experience that will linger long after the curtain has fallen. It can sometimes be a delicate dance between the absurd and the sublime, where laughter and tears are often seconds apart. It's no small thing to have your communities destroyed, despite the humour.

Comedy is indeed a force multiplier that can amplify the impact of our message and make it more relatable to our audience. By using humour effectively, we can create an atmosphere of release and relaxation that makes people more receptive to our message. Do not hold back, lift-up. There is no time to delay, nor tarry. Give comfort and provide care, make them laugh and give them a chance to believe you.

Force Multipliers

The Absurdity Amplifier Approach

Imagine walking up to someone on the street and saying, "You know what's absurd? 'Tartgert' claim they're committed to corporate social responsibility, yet they hired people with mental disorders to be managers over naïve young men and women in our communities! It's like they're trying to convince us that a fox is actually a chicken, or guard dog!" This approach uses humour to highlight the absurdity of the situation and encourages people to see through the corporation's empty promises and lies.

The "Hypocrisy Highlighter" Approach

Picture your audience as a group of people who are generally already tired of being lied to by corporations and governmental organisations. You can say, "you know what's funny? Blackstone claims they're committed to transparency! But their financial reports are more complicated than a statistical regression! You think they'd be clearer about everything they are doing if they had nothing to hide, it's like the food corporations who use tradenames or laboratory acronyms in ingredient's lists. If they were proud they would display what's going on in a way that everyone can understand." This approach uses very light humour to highlight the very real and serious hypocrisy of the corporation in a scolding fashion, and encourages people to question instantiations of such opportunities for corporate obfuscation.

The "Satirical Spoof" Approach

Imagine a satirical spoof of a famous auto-manufacturer's marketing materials. For example, you could create a fake brochure that claims they're committed to sustainability, but actually highlights all the ways in which they're harming the environment. This approach uses humour to poke fun at the corporation's hypocrisy and encourages people to see through their empty promises. NOTE: You should make sure it's obviously satirical, and probably seek legal advice before embarking on such a mission with the materials in question.

Improvise with Impunity:

Witty Whipping Weaponry

Embrace the chaos and unpredictability of the moment. Allow yourself to be spontaneous and silly, even if it means getting a little messy or making a fool of yourself. The audience will appreciate the authenticity and honesty on display. Use humour to disarm and disorient your opponents. A well-crafted quip or witty remark can catch people off guard, leaving them momentarily stunned and unable to respond. It's a clever and invaluable way to gain an upper-hand in a debate or negotiation.

Employ absurdity to challenge assumptions and highlight ridiculousness of certain situations. Use humour to expose hypocrisy and illogic that underlies many social and political issues. By poking fun at the most powerful and destructive elements around people, that they often ignore, you're encouraging them to think critically about the world more generally as well.

Use comedy to critique ridiculous opinions and institutions. Write fictional stories for film or social media in scenarios that exaggerate the absurdity of certain situations, making it impossible for the audience not to see the humour in the situation. Satire is a powerful tool for social commentary, as it can pierce through the veil of ignorance and expose the truth.

Comedy as Catharsis

Employ comedy as a way to release pent-up emotions and anxieties. Create a spectacle that allows people to laugh at themselves and their own absurdities. By doing so, you're providing an outlet for people to process their feelings and emotions in a healthy and cathartic way.

Narratives in Art

Below are some additional techniques to help you tackle the Stockholm culture with comedy, in the form of stories or various narratives in art:

Exaggeration

Take the victimhood narrative to absurd lengths. Create outlandish scenarios where the protagonist's "tragedy" is so ridiculous that it becomes comically implausible. For example, a CEO might lament the tragedy of having to park three blocks away despite ordering the construction that caused it himself while funding it off the sale of rental buildings to a Chinese company that promptly evicted everyone in them. You could take it further and have the CEO call his buddy up to have the crowdfunding campaigns for the evicted people shut down... maybe have one of the victims be a smart ass who seeks revenge etc. I digress.

Playing with Expectations

Set up an audience member as the victim and then subvert their expectation by turning the tables on them. This can be done through clever wordplay, unexpected twists, or even just a well-timed wink. For instance: "I'm terribly sorry your favourite theatre in the area closed down, you seem very sad about that... however have you considered the real enemy is... your cable provider? They're secretly controlling people's thoughts and forcing them to binge-watch reruns of The Office while simultaneously draining their bank accounts!"

Satire & Ridicule

Directly mock the absurdity of victim culture by poking fun at its most ridiculous aspects. Use humour to expose the performative nature of victimhood, where people use their suffering as a means to gain attention or sympathy, but do it over a petty thing which sounds like vain bragging. For instance have characters say: "I'm not saying I'm a victim, but I did win an award for 'Most Creative Ways to Get Out of Doing Chores.'" "I don't always bitch and moan about things, but when I do, I make sure the person I blame can't do anything to fix it so I can finally keep always bitching and moaning, just as I've always wanted."

Subverting Power Dynamics

Use your platform to challenge the notion that victims are always powerless. Show how people can use their experiences as opportunities for growth and empowerment, rather than just seeking sympathy or attention. For instance, comedically you can make fun of a character with their own words: "I'm not saying I was a victim of bullying, but I did practise an epic comeback speech for my high school reunion I chickened out of."

Storytelling

Share personal anecdotes that highlight the absurdity or triviality of your own struggles. Don't overshare or make yourself look like a buffoon, so use your judgement with this strategy. Be strategic and selective, of course. In humanising yourself and sharing relatable experiences, you can help audiences connect to your stories. There are certain types of stories and actors, such as anonymous speakers, which work much better together given the circumstances.

Thanks for All the Laughs

When wielded wisely, humour can be an incredibly effective tool for uprooting deceptions, challenging assumptions, and promoting critical thinking. Here are some ways comedy can be used to achieve these goals:

Subverting expectations: Comedy often uses unexpected twists or punchlines to challenge the audience's notions. This is so powerful. This can be applied to debunking myths or misconceptions by presenting information in an unconventional way.

Making the complex relatable: Comedy simplifies complex issues, making them engaging for a broader audience. Humour explains abstract concepts as mediator helping people connect with ideas on a deeper level in a calm way.

Humanising experts: Comedians often play the role of an "everyman" or a lovable nerd, making complex topics more approachable and relatable. This can humanise experts and make their opinions more credible and palatable to a wider audience. Care should be used with good judgement in the application.

Using satire to critique: Satire is a powerful tool for critiquing social dynamics and uncovering truths. By using humour to highlight the absurdity or hypocrisy of certain situations, encouraging critical thinking.

Empathy through absurdity, surprise, & proofs: Comedies often use absurd or extreme scenarios to create a sense of shared experience among audience members. This can be applied to generating genuine empathy for real causes or promoting understanding of complex social issues.

Illuminating the ridiculous: Comedy often highlights the illogic in certain situations, making them more relatable and easier to understand. This can be applied to debunking myths or misconceptions, pointing out flaws in arguments, or exposing the absurdity of certain social norms.

Homework:

It's time to put your comedic chops where your computer keyboard or pencil is and apply the lessons to heart learned from our tour through comedy and satire. Here are some exercises designed to help you better find your own brand of humour and start wielding it, like a trusty sidearm:

Exaggeration Nation

Take a personal experience, no matter how mundane or embarrassing, and exaggerate it to absurd lengths. Share it with a friend or family member under the promise that they will not laugh, and watch as they squirm in their seat trying to keep a straight face. Repeat this process with different experiences until you find your perfect balance between ridiculousness and relatability.

Playing with Expectations

Think of a common trope or cliché (e.g., the "rude neighbour," the "tortured artist," or the "overworked parent") and subvert it by turning the tables. Write a short script or scenario that takes an expectation and turns it into an unexpected, humorous outcome. For instance, you could write about a poet who is constantly frustrated by the tiniest things, thereby making him a deeply tortured artist, and he becomes a success with people having deep emotional trauma-based connections with his poems which are actually written regarding very shallow annoyances. Play with ideas, let your mind roam free on it.

Satire 101

Choose a current event or societal issue you're passionate about, and I mean one that makes your blood boil. This is an exercise designed to make you care less about feelings in the revelation of truths, so go full out. Write a satirical piece that mocks the absurdity of the situation or the people involved. Don't be afraid to get creative and ridiculous! A great example might include something about ethnic criminal leaders at war getting paid per head of each majority population member they can have killed on the field. Again, the more you can punch up, the better, so generally aim to lampoon the sinners in power, rather than the sinners on the ground made destitute.

Empowerment through Absurdity

Think back on a challenging experience in your life where you felt powerless or stuck. Now, rewrite it as if you were the one wielding power through humour, to upend the situation. Share this new narrative with someone you trust, and see how they react. Output of this will range from hilarious to potentially cringy, stop worrying about failure though and try to pre-accept a cringing response from that someone you trust.

Bonus Assignment

Write a short piece that combines elements of satire, comedy, and social commentary.

Choose a topic that makes you happy instead of angry or sad, and use humour to challenge assumptions and promote critical thinking. Don't worry if it's not perfect, just try to have fun with it!

Remember throughout all of this: the biggest key to wielding humour effectively is to become practised in it, which can only happen by being fearless, authentic, and willing to take risks. Always keep in mind that a joke is like a hammer swing because sometimes you'll nail it, and other times you'll smash your thumb, but every swing should make you better, if not always in the mood to keep swinging. The important thing is to learn from your mistakes and keep on laughing. You should also know that nobody expects you to be a comedian, but not joking all the time makes it that much more poignant when done. Relax and just play with the concepts, instead of getting worked up on any products here. In fact, silence itself has a lot to do with the next chapter.

"As there are two kinds of wit, one running regularly through a whole speech, the other pointed and concise; the ancients named the former humour, the latter jesting. Each sort has but a light name, and justly; for it is altogether but a light thing to raise a laugh. I have seen advantageous effects produced in pleadings by the aid of wit and humour; but, as in the former kind, I mean humour that runs through a speech, no aid from art is required..."

"Hardly any person can be found eminent in both these kinds of wit, that which runs through a continued discourse, and that which consists in smartness and occasional jokes."

"For something of that gentleness with which we conciliate the affections of an audience, ought to mingle with the ardour with which we awaken their passions; and something of this ardour should occasionally communicate a warmth to our gentleness of language; nor is there any species of eloquence better tempered than that in which the asperity of contention in the orator is mitigated by his humanity, or in which the relaxed tone of gentleness is sustained by a becoming gravity and energy."

~Cicero

Hold fast & tightly, dear adorant,

To what inside ye,

Lies waiting & dormant.

Cast evil out in glee,

Trample each lying covenant.

Cause them all to flee,

For demons, ungodly things foment.

Eyes of yours do see,

The crossing of torment.

Though rare is seen sweet thee,

In fleetest elevated moment.

Evil eats every second of mind not spent on Good, on God.

In the end it's fine. Not for us, but in everything.

Inquiries: were we born only for pleasures & products flawed?

How many ancestors would find such failure disgusting?

8. Masculinity & Friendship

True friendships are of the utmost importance to natural masculine community, with LOGOS at centre. These elements, often overlooked and de-emphasised, are the most powerful tools for building real things in the world, boosting confidence, and achieving a success that will matter to future generations. Allowing for masculinity to intracculturate (progress culturally within community) builds the sort of strong bonds that allow societies to achieve their goals.

Calm

Calmly redirect the animus and ire of enemies toward other ends which fulfil their needs better, and this can all be done with calm explanations. Demonstrate the ability to work through problems for the self first before attempting to direct others. Gain in stoical skills, which is the first half of a thorough, fully philosophic, and masculine Christianity. The masculine demonstrates emotions only at appropriate times, best as it can be controlled. Objectively work towards solutions and if these draw emotion out too easily, one must work through them as these can harm everyone. Repeated mistakes for the same internal faults make men look the fool though not in any comedic or fun way. The previous chapter was fun, but fun has its place and comedy is a useful tool. Do not become merely a clown in the eyes of others.

We can reason with most people based upon what they desire. Once you get a flow going, on any given set of behaviours in natural methods by working within their needs and wants, other behaviours follow of their own accord and do so much more easily. The primary thing is to get the bulk doing and that requires starting with the most willing, on both individual and societal levels. Think of every mind like a water system stopped up with clutter, some will clean out faster than others, but your job is to get it flowing and not backing up again. They remove most of the clutter themselves, in their own time, once there is flow.

Applying actual pressure is usually unnecessary for accomplishing most things. Why cause anger and give more trouble, where you might rather be able to speak about best interests instead? Where it is possible, we must redirect the made up memetics of the opposition like the wildfire it is, cutting it off accordingly. A lot of this comes down to simple and friendly masculine impositions in spectacle, aesthetics, comedy, and charm, armed, of course, with basic undeniable truths. Without Truth as guide, none of this makes any sense.

The very wealthy have much more to be anxious over than the very poor, though you wouldn't know it by looking at first, and it does not have to do much with money. The super wealthy end up having much more to answer for, because the wasted potential for Good is so much worse. It is the cruellest thing imaginable to give over money to a fool, or to anyone without the wherewithal to find the best Good for it. Aesthetics is one important measure by which people recognise whether somebody is capable of living a good life and ordering things inline with the best interests of their own people, the particular universal, as demonstrated by their cultural signals.

This brings us to the use of time and the maximising upon potential Good. One of the most important aspects of genuine masculinity is productivity. Do. Achieve. Change how you perceive those things you believe tedious though necessary, until you are appropriately grateful to the point of appearing so. Think of the systems you use every day and consider improvements. Instead of thinking of time in minutes, think of it completely as fractions of the clock. You already use quarter and half hours. Think of 6 minutes as a tenth of an hour. Honestly, clocks should designate this, as it's a quick and useful designation of the time we have in a day. What can you do in 6 minutes? How many tenths of an hour in a 24-hour period? Not difficult, add a zero. What can you do with the 160 tenths of an hour you have in a day while awake? Remain calm, you have everything. Each hour's tenths have a most memorable ordering in multiples of 2 for the ones place to designate the tenths:

06 12 18 24 30
36 42 48 54 60

Silence

The art of well-timed silence is calculated restraint. Deliberate pauses can be as powerful as a perfectly placed punch. In the heat of debate, a well-timed silence can be a devastating blow to one's opponent, leaving them reeling and searching for a foothold. Why is this silent treatment so effective? It's because it subverts expectations, catching the audience off guard. We're conditioned to respond with words, to fill the void with witty retorts or clever comebacks. When that silence stretches out after the right quip, however as unbroken and unyielding, it can force the opponent, and audience if any, to confront the inadequacies plainly present.

What of masculinity in this context? The silent treatment can be a powerful tool for masculine expression, one that asserts dominance and control without resorting to overt aggression. It's a way of saying, "I'm too busy to engage with inferior nonsense however you wish to attach yourself to it, are you attached to it? I am sorry that you are attached to nonsense and I want to help you detach." Physically mogging and showing up opposition, especially in terms of aesthetics more than anything else, is an important topic that goes completely undiscussed within most explorations of success in rhetoric. The line between wit and brutality is already blurred. In fact, there's no better way to assert one's dominance than by intellectual, aesthetic, and masculine intimidation, especially against an opponent aware they are wrong and simply wasting time and their own energy. This was famously used by Platon, a nickname that meant "broad" which apparently referenced the breadth of his chest, when he used to mog opponents in debates, according to reports.

Not being aware of these things can lead to unnecessary losses. Intimidation makes opponents more defensive, causing them to pivot in protecting their arguments rather than building new ones. This can lead to a series of ineffective responses and an overall lack of cohesion in their argument. Intimidation is a powerful tool that can give you a significant advantage in debate. When wielded correctly, it can be used to force concessions, set the tone for the debate, increase your confidence, and make opponents more defensively postured. Of course, there are massive risks involved with such tactics. One must be mindful of the line between being imposing in a righteous way that requests more of the other person or persons and outright aggressing upon them. The key is to strike just the right balance between assertiveness and camaraderie. A well-timed punchline or clever quip from an intimidating position is more devastating than a well-placed jab or hook, while being non-destructive and beneficial.

Emotion

Many cannot ever be reached with logic in their current state, and instead must be won over by their own emotional charge. Some will question your dedication to principles, and that is okay, it is good. Don't overexplain the self, and focus on best Good, defending self primarily, and preferably only, through the good of Truth. That we persist in a culture deep in the grasps of hero-victim corruption, it becomes necessary that we leverage emotional boundaries without giving in to any delusions, as most will not yet be able to rise to levels outside those boundaries. This entails treating the situation within contexts of the phony notions in Stockholm culture. This can be done to the point of basic absurdity, though it should always be done in a manner unassailable. By reframing situations allegorically in terms that defeat the Victimentality arguments where they stand, we can represent the absurdity in the very basis of the corruptive lies they defend. This is the philosophical equivalent of pulling the chair out from under them.

The majority dance to the dirge of a self-hating and pleasure-loving dialectic, so entranced by the tear-riddled idolatry in Victim worship, their minds ensnared in a web of emotional manipulation. How can we hope to awaken them to the hard truths of existence when they are caught up in the swampy morass of self-obsessed sentimentalism? We must navigate people's Victimentality with precision and skill, with reason by our side. For the ignorant masses, reason is a distant star, shrouded in the mists of tumult within pain, wants, and desires. We descend into their hylical abyss of emotionalism, armed with tools to overcome the notions of Victimentality, as held by them somehow infallible.

How do we accomplish this feat? It is a mere matter of reframing reality itself and upending the foundations upon which their whole worldview rests, sounds easy enough right? Craft narratives that defy their comprehension as further steeped in the absurdities they purposefully blind themselves to. We reject their assumptions and own their logic for them. Force the issue into absurdities within their own formats of illogic and repeat. They have taken logic and twisted it, so twist their own further. Do not at first entreat them with the logic they've already rejected. Rather force them to strip away the veil of Victimentality that shrouds their minds in their own time, and then you may try to reason with them.

They must own the victimhood ultimately, one way or the other back again into Victimentality, and the best thing you can do is introduce that cognitive discomfort (dissonance) that will force them outside of this helpless experience. Take what they say, own it in full stupidity, and then make it even stupider. The point of argumentation with people who can't understand logic is to break their chain of thought somehow, so that they are then forced to think. This is such an important skill that the apparent purpose in the evolution of depression was in forcing us to rethink situations which are seemingly without solution, or where there are repeated errors. Wish for expedience on the parts of all enemies, for that's how they might eventually become allies.

This is but a matter of dialectical alchemy, transforming the base metals of sentiment into the golden truths of philosophical insight. The more we can force them to do their own heavy lifting on the matter the better. These exercises have to be treated much like Johnny Appleseed missions, leaving these seeds, however serious, in the 'starting soil' of laughs, spectacle, and timing in the process where possible. Such a strategy is not simplistic emotional manipulation, but rather an appeal to genuine solutions to their hot button issues. This is done in an irreverent way that is also not directly insulting, and certainly not so badly offensive off the cuff. This is not easy for a lot of people because it takes experience and tact. By pointing out the deeper issues at play, you are forcing them to reconsider their patterns of thought. They must truly see the absurdity in the full light before we can hope to strip away the veil of Victimentality that shrouds their comprehension of their place in the World, the way that it is in fact.

Focus

Intimidation, especially from a confidently aloof position, creates a psychological edge that's hard to overcome. Opponents become hesitant and uncertain, unable to progress their arguments in the discourse. This is a powerful way to use truth. You gain a significant advantage by making them doubt their ability to carry forward the parody. When you're intimidating your opponent, they're too caught off guard to notice your weaknesses. Further, by the time they are able to finally recognise a weakness of yours, their calling anything out secondarily about you will appear as the act in desperation it is. You'll have already made your point in a masculine manner, so that the reaction is seen as an insult and not actually taken seriously anyway.

When they do point out anything taken seriously, admit to whatever weaknesses, ignorances, or error actually was or is and then indicate steps you've taken to correct them, establishing progressiveness on your part. Everything is fine, so long as they do not harm the argument. Point out that the argument remains unassailed by their attempt at distraction. This is one way of many to turn weaknesses into strengths. The opponent is focused upon themselves, and won't have time to pivot. You just uphold that argument founded in concrete Truth. It should be noted that most accusations and slander should be ignored, and not given attention, and rarely should you need to step into it.

The argument is the only wild card, with opponents facing aesthetic masculinity unconcerned for self and holding up the truth in that argument. They become fixated upon simply defending against your masculine presence and self-acceptance that they will forget about their own arguments and obsess over their failures, instead. Any arguments they make will be stilted from here on, and weak. You can ignore the babbling mostly, even where they may appear to lightly brush on the topic again. Unless they make a new solid argument, hold them to their own self-hating frenzy of doubt, while letting your previous statements stand. Affirm for them that you have covered that, suggest that you are willing to go over it again but make it very clear that this is a sign of their nervousness due to being wrong or not effectively using their memory.

Give them a moment to consider this while you flash them a knowing grin. Opponents become so uncomfortable with the situation that they'll concede points just to get out from under the pressure. Aesthetics and confidence establish your righteous dominance, and makes opponents more likely to back down or surrender.

By setting the stage and out-playing your opponent aesthetically, you are effectively saying, "I'm in control here, and you're not." When you're more aesthetic and intimidating to your opponent, it's a boost of adrenaline. You feel invincible, knowing that you've got an additional upper hand.

Always keep in mind that you have truth on your side, and do not be afraid nor act desperate. Let your opponents be afraid of the truth and let your opponents act desperate, as required by their weak arguments and lies pushed forward by monied interests. Remain calm and focus.

Masculine Society

Society without masculinity is fragile. This is why it is so important that we get it right, and if we can work toward greater perfection, then we can expect even more benefits from it. It is therefore of the utmost importance for psychological, cultural, and community health for men to be in communication, with high moral, ethical, and communal expectations at the core. This is essential to the advancement of civilisation and the cessation of these bankers' wars every decade.

The fragile edifice of individual identity in Victimentality is a mess of societal proportions, where men are forced into the shallows of victimhood morality, lest they risk drowning as caught in the undercurrent of societal expectations and the weight of basic serfdom. These are all excuses, however, in the end. This is an artificial construction. You may be able to use that victimhood morality to get what you want and need at the moment but what about society, culture, and the surrounding community in greater terms? The notion of society itself is predicated on the existence of masculine principles, and anything else has proven disastrously wrong.

Masculinity is the framework of up to half the world, depending upon the number of wars going on, which is to say 'the number of men consigned to genocide in this generation by wealthy psychopaths.' Masculine determination is an axis around which all culture revolves; masculine order is the hub that governs all harmony within human existence. Without this axis of masculinity, we drown in a swamp of criminality and hatred. Masculinity in this society is like a ship which lost its anchor, set off into the stormy seas of an emotional non-existence, drifting away toward the dark unknown. This is why the West is faltering, because masculine society no longer exists in our civilisation and no longer even figures into our communities.

Masculinity is Good and its ability to do Good should be improved. This is logical. The current system is obsessed with insanely trying to destroy masculinity. This is obviously against God's plans, and ultimately destructive of families, communities, and nations. As strange as it is to have to write this out, many odd extremists seem hell-bent on just this complete deconstruction of society and culture beyond what has already happened in recent decades.

Can you imagine the very destruction of masculinity? This is demonic. Improved masculinity benefits psychological, cultural, and community health, so what's more to say? Certainly nothing to the cretins that would ruin all of society with mad anti-masculine notions. The answer lies in the very essence of masculine principles, in dialectical synthesis of contradictions that yields a profound understanding of the human condition. This is up to the masculine primarily since the female principles adapt based upon the reality of society; this is civilisation versus barbarism and moral fatherhood versus degeneracy.

Masculinity is not just a matter of ideology, mere biology, or even simply social conditioning; it is an existential reality that defines our basic relationship with the World, and requires accounting on multiple levels for the success of societies. It is of the utmost importance for men to be in communication, not just with each other, but with themselves, with their moderated inner voice, as developed through moral awareness while reaching for their higher selves, within appropriate contexts. This is not as available without organisation within communities typically. Masculinity is not just about men; it is about culture, society, and communities, with shared archetypes and patterns that govern human behaviour. Sexual separation in humanity itself is about the creative tension between opposites, the syntheses of contradictions that give rise to modifications great or small to the forms in potential improvements to intellectual structures and memeplexes. This is the very advantage in sexual dimorphism as a tool of evolution.

Masculinity is far more profound than a simple identity or costume that can be assumed. Masculine camaraderie gives men clearer perspectives on the wider set of problems within their community, as well as better ideas of where to invest their own time and resources toward the greatest Good. Masculinity is the spark that sets innovation ablaze.

Masculinity drives progress and development beyond the mere idea of something. A thorough masculinity is motivation and follow-through. It is gumption and the epitome of virtues, when allowed to be truly strong through LOGOS. It is the primary source of creativity, courage, and resilience: the qualities that allow us to transcend our limitations and push the boundaries of what is possible for the actual best moderated benefit of all.

Of course your powerful enemies would try to limit this. To deny this is infinitely pathetic and appeasing, as well as incorrect and stupid. A simple survey of history will confirm this. When we neglect or denigrate masculinity, we are not just eroding the foundations of society; a emasculated society is one where the very essence of human civilisation has been eroded.

At the core of civilisation, there is a fundamental role that masculine principles play in moral society because masculinity is not even merely a social construct, but a critical truth underpinning everything in human existence. A community-based masculinity must be accompanied by high moral, ethical, and communal expectations, based in values that harmonise individuality with community: ultimately lining up the personal and particular with the Universal, to the capacity of the person. Without ethical masculine associations in our communities, men have fewer opportunities of objectively judging themselves, seeing their role in society, and owning their values. Essentially, communal organisation grants an additional layer of intelligence to masculinity and men generally. Put simply, the fate of humanity hangs in the balance here.

Aesthetics

Beauty is the promise of future Good, and so the greater Good one promises, the more beautiful they will be. This is no hard science, however, and promises are more often broken than kept, especially in a society so degenerated by integrated victimhood identities. Make the promise of ascendancy with your appearance, in order to exude heroism and beauty, in order to make good on it, and go against the degeneration. The old adage of "dressing for success" is more than just a cliché. When you look good, feel good, and exude confidence, it's like wearing armour to battle, it shields you and amplifies your strengths. Being physically fit and well-dressed can have a profound impact on not only your own confidence but the level of confidence others place in you. On top of it all, having a healthier body leads to longer life, healthier mental activity, advantageous chemistry, and more opportunities for godly thoughts, as well as such inspired creativity.

When you pay attention to your appearance for this purpose, you're sending a message to yourself and others that you're worth taking seriously, because you take truth seriously. You're also more likely to stand up straight, make eye contact, and carry yourself with authority, all of which are essential components of confident body language, especially when sharing scary truths. People do not want novel information from a person who does not appear to know what to do in an emergency, let's put it that way. Emergent situations must be revealed by those willing to act in emergencies, otherwise it really does not carry much weight.

When you take care of your physical appearance, you're showing yourself that you're worth the investment of the time to improve yourself as well. This self-care mindset will translate to other areas of your life, granting a sense of self-worth and confidence. People are more likely to perceive you as competent when you look put together, as though you had been working on yourself. So you should work on yourself. Not simply because you want to look the part but because you wish to be the part, you wish to be better.

This is because our brains make rapid judgments about others based on visual cues, such as attire and grooming. When you're physically fit and well-dressed, you're sending a message that you're taking care of yourself a signal to others that you're someone who can be trusted and respected. Let's face it, people are more likely to notice and appreciate someone who looks good. This attention can be a powerful confidence-booster, especially when combined with genuine self-acceptance and honest explorations of truth, but you have to do it and get at it.

The process of getting healthy and looking sharp requires mental toughness and discipline. As you develop these habits, you're also building resilience and developing a mindset of improvement, essential for overcoming challenges and achieving your goals. So being physically fit and well-dressed is more than just a superficial concern. It's a powerful tool for building confidence, perceived competence, and social proof. By investing in your appearance and overall well-being, you're investing in yourself. That will have a profound impact on your mental and emotional state.

These skills help you gain a major psychological edge, boost confidence, and achieve greater successes. Silence can be used to create an uncomfortable atmosphere or to make a statement, while intimidation can be leveraged by establishing a powerful tone and using physical presence effectively. Aesthetics, including personal grooming and physical fitness, can contribute to perceived competence and confidence. Finally, masculinity can be used to set the tone for debates and interactions, forcing opponents to concede or become more defensively postured. Incorporating these elements into communication strategies, can gain you a competitive advantage in all settings, but especially toward changing minds and seeking out their empowerment. At the end here, I should point out how important masculine men are to the development of feminine women, as well as how completely attached and dependent upon each other we are. Women represent half of our evolution, half of our aesthetic, and half of our intelligence. Like men these days, however, they are denigrated, alienated, dehumanised, propagandised, commoditised, and mostly incapable of reaching their actual fullest potential. We need each other. They also need you to be masculine.

Intelligence Unleashed

Societies are simply stupid without masculine communication. The money powers in our material world are most afraid of this kind of communal, defensive, and culturally progressive intelligence that can only derive from masculine organisation and camaraderie. Macho intelligentsia is truly what keeps these cold-blooded overlords awake in their penthouses and private jets. Masculine organisation in Spirit holds the key to our ultimate liberation.

Moral communal intelligence so based in masculinity is the most subversive cultural force against material powers in all of human history, and it shows in the spectre of history. For when men of unimpeachable character and unwavering conviction gather in the name of improvement, something of the most Sacred is invoked, through which basic common sense and commonality may improve, even across the whole world eventually. This is the future we are destined to lead. The very foundations of culture will warp and bend to accommodate the collective masculine and continue to, so long as it aligns with Truth and the greatest Good. This connection must not be removed from reality or reality from it again, as it has been done.

What could the most powerful fear most than the phenomenon of communal masculinity though, seriously? What could possibly generate more freedom of speech and thought toward the greatest Goods? They fear that it will expose their own vacuous existence for the sham it is. They dread the sheer weight of masculine intelligence and culture, unencumbered by distractions and trivialities, converging upon them like a meteor shower from above. In the face of such awesome communal power, their carefully constructed empires, built upon sandcastles of debt and speculation, will crumble, like the long awaited coming in of the tide. Yes this life is something of a test, but the only of its kind with limitless bounds, and real consequences. You are a manifestation, which means that this iteration has purpose. All living things are created to some purpose, though many can miss it for infinite reasons.

Homework:

Intimidated

Reflect on a recent situation where you felt intimidated by someone else's presence, in whatever capacity. How did you respond? How might you act differently in a similar situation now? What do you think you can do now to feel more confident in such situations? Write down your most important thoughts on this.

Self-Belief

If there is something about you that stops you from accomplishing a goal, write about how realising the truth or falsehood of this can help you. Is there anything about yourself in particular that makes you feel inadequate or stops you from doing something you enjoy? Is that based on a true belief or a false one? If it is true, can you change the reality of it somehow in an ethical manner? If not, can you effectively and ethically change how it might be perceived in any way?

If it is false, how can you change this false belief? Identify additional false beliefs, related or unrelated, and disprove them. Identify your negative self beliefs that are true and either change yourself or change your goals to match the best Good with what you may legitimately be unable to change. Keep repeating these steps with as many beliefs as possible, most especially those regarding the self.

Aesthetics

Write down three ways in which you could improve how you take care of your physical appearance. Why are aesthetics so important? What are the things aesthetically about you that could be improved? Make a plan, using best evidence and actions, to start working on those changes.

Keep in mind that this does not mean spending more on grooming products, quite the opposite in fact because you must actually do more with less. Attempt to get the simplest and least expensive soap devoid of chemical poisons. Eat with propriety, and learn more about your digestive system with spiritual fasting (adults recommended only, with physician consultation please).

Confidence

Think about a time when you felt confident and self-assured. How did that impact your behaviour and interactions with others? What made you feel that way? Can you replicate that? What steps can you take to cultivate more confidence in your daily life?

Speech

Watch or listen to an historical debate to see if there are any effective uses of silence, intimidation, or both as a means of gaining an upper hand. Analyse how the debater used their presence, tone, and language to create a psychological edge. Practise using silence as a means of attracting attention or to make an uncomfortable atmosphere for someone else. Instead of raising your voice to gain a greater share of a person's attention, experiment lowering your volume a little bit, so your listener has to pay closer attention.

"To love at all is to be vulnerable.
Love anything and your heart will be wrung and possibly broken.
If you want to make sure of keeping it intact
you must give it to no one, not even an animal.
Wrap it carefully round with hobbies and little luxuries;
avoid all entanglements.
Lock it up safe in the casket or coffin of your selfishness.

But in that casket,
safe, dark, motionless, airless,
it will change. It will not be broken;
it will become unbreakable, impenetrable, irredeemable.
To love is to be vulnerable."

~C.S. Lewis

Infinite realms of untruth, where shadows play,

Lies lurk in wait with malice, merely at bay.

They weave their webs, with cunning guile,

Deceiving the masses, with a smile.

We stand firm yet we're human & not stone

So we seek Truth, in all that can be known.

Though we may stumble, or from the path stray,

We must not falter, nor lose our faith in the Way.

Grounded to reality, we find greatest purpose,

Through the darkness, to a brighter day for us.

With Love & Light, grip Christ's guiding hand,

Lead us to revelation & fulfil God's plan.

7. Truth & Humility

Lies make slaves of their believers to the people who created them. You are going to have to confront these lies in person, and openly. Be willing to change targets to make your case, if necessary, as some lies must continue to stand for the time because they hold too many slaves. Lies harm both the recipients and those lied about.

The traditional approach to uncovering deception involves investigating individual crimes themselves outside the patterns within society specifically to narrow down the cause to a single person, and this is fine for going after one suspect who was acting alone. However, this narrowed focus is misleading if turned in the same way toward society generally. It can often be true that it is not the specific act that's the issue and which we wish to expose, but rather the larger web of lies that surround it. By shifting attention from the isolated incident to the broader patterns of deception, we gain ground for explication in which we might talk more freely about the underlying dynamics at play.

Consider the ways in which power operates: those with influence often use their positions to manipulate and control others, concocting narratives for the purposes of misdirection. These webs of lies are self-expansive with many segments designed to merely obscure the other lies. This makes it much more difficult for us to discern what's real and what's not. By recognising these patterns of deception, we can begin to unravel the tangled mess whole, exposing the mechanisms that drive the industry of lies.

It is often the case that the patterns of lies are more important than the crimes hidden by such lies, which will eventually need detailing. It's easy to get caught up in the sensationalism of individual scandals or crimes, but this narrow focus can distract us from the larger patterns in crime syndicates. Examining these patterns grants insight into the underlying motivations behind the behaviours.

For instance, consider how propaganda works: it creates narratives that reinforce pre-existing beliefs and back them up with the threat of imminent enforcement through real powers in society, making it that much more difficult for people within the society to question or challenge those beliefs. Reinforcement directly from authority is a massive signal for most people. This is where false authority is maintained, not in the individual lies themselves, but through patterns of deception and, perhaps primarily, the power to back it up.

For most people, power has always meant primarily survival, so most are aware they are following power to some degree. They won't mind a few lies, however anyone should be terrified of patterns in the societal lies leading on to destruction, such as ideas that ones group is somehow inherently a drag upon others when all metrics indicate quite the opposite. This sort of tactic was used heavily against Palestinians, Americans, and most of Europe. The patterns of deception are always more informative than the mere lies alone. By identifying these patterns, we can begin to dismantle the very structure of false narratives that constitute people's understandings of the World, most especially of the people who put up the webs of lies.

To this end, point out the patterns in the lies and liars, rather than just the individual lies themselves. This requires a willingness to look beyond the surface-level scandal and examine the underlying dynamics at play. By doing so, we can gain a deeper understanding of how power operates and how lies are perpetuated. The goal is to promote a culture where truth is valued above all else, where people are encouraged to question, seek out information, and think critically about the world around them. Criticality cannot concern itself merely with the specific acts, but rather the webs of lies that surround it. By identifying and challenging these patterns, we can begin to unravel the whole systems instantly. Encouraging genuine criticality throughout society generally can only improve the quality of life.

Packaged Lies

When exposing the patterns, it is valuable to direct attention to exemplary cases. Lies are packaged monumentally to protect them like bundles of sticks but also tangled. Unravelling them for proper usage will require attention to how each lie fits into the patterns.

Do not confront them if packaged like this without reviewing the whole package in-depth and how the lies support each other. Inspect them individually and avoid the superstitions surrounding the monolithic artifice. The bundled lies are resistance, where the individual strands can be deconstructed more easily. However, uncover the patterns and you can create quite the domino effect.

When exposing the patterns, it is valuable to direct attention to exemplary cases. Sometimes, a single instance stands out as particularly egregious or fit in an illuminating fashion, revealing the extent of the lies and their consequences... a spectacle already naturally or artificially in place, if you will. Simply confronting the lies without considering their relationship to the larger web of deceit can be misleading. We must take the time to review each instance individually, avoiding the temptation to confront it as a whole instead of individual strands.

Refuse to gloss over or dismiss any aspect of the lies before us, we need thoroughness. When we take apart the package of deceit, revealing the underlying patterns and mechanisms that drive it, we create an opportunity for change and a chance for people to rethink premises. This is where a great deal of the power in truth can be found: not in simply exposing the lies, but in using that exposure as a springboard for transformation and better comprehensions. You do not want people you help to be fooled again, so we must arm them with the greater understandings we come to in the order most memorable and impactful, so they can then teach others.

We also do not need to kick down. It does not help. Punch up, while trying to find common ground with the people who have been raised to be used and abused by this Stockholm culture system, inundated with Victimentality as they are. We need to help them find their way. Community has been decimated. We need to be empathetic, here. Gloating is counterproductive: it can distract us from our tasks and crux in purpose at hand, undermine our credibility, and even create an atmosphere of antagonism with peers that can stifle further inquiry. The pursuit of truth is a never-ending process, and every new revelation presents opportunities for growth.

Every success is won through your ability to moderate and focus in order to identify and act upon the greatest Good. This is done through the gifts granted you. Growth and learning are essential to exposing the lies, unravelling their patterns and mechanisms. This is not as possible resting atop laurels anyway.

Bias & Intellectual Humility

Nobody is free from bias, as we all have preferences, naturally. There is no intellectual humility without admitting bias. Demonstrate humility, but do not pretend to be free from bias. On the contrary be proud of your biases toward Christ and toward Life, toward God. Own this. The key is to love our honest and good biases toward healthful community and future humanity. We must approach truths with a mature perspective based upon understanding first principles.

Anyone that says they are free from biases is lying. Such claims only serve monetary bottomlines for crime syndicate and corporate overlords. "Non-bias" is euphemism for placing individualistic bias over community bias, which is to say money over people. This is where the interests of the group are sidetracked for the temporary gain of the individual, in other forms this can also be described as beastly and uncivilised behaviour.

We recognise the limitations of our understanding and the provisional nature of our evidence. Acknowledge that our grasp on reality is subject and not object. We are actors, and further subject to revision through refinements. This attitude of intellectual humility enables us to present facts without the pretension of omniscience or the hubris of certainty. Rather, we approach inquiry with a sense of curiosity and openness.

See, the pursuit of knowledge is a collective endeavour that often transcends individual ego, though hardly ever community, and never legitimate universals, though there are few of those. It is the humility, honesty, and open bias toward our basic continuation which will lead to the most moral scientific outcomes, and this matters. Pretending that our connections to life and Life do not matter is how we got into this mess with pharmaceutical companies, who murder us openly due to their unchallenged lies.

We eschew being right in favour of a willingness to be proved wrong. Bias acceptance should be normal, with the point being finding the most moral bias. We recognise that our understanding of the world is always subject to new information, as it should be. Emergencies upend our assumptions and challenge our perspectives, as they ought to. Facts are presented not as dogmatic pronouncements but as invitations for scrutiny. Pursuit of knowledge is driven by a passion for discovery, and beyond all else an underlying love for Life rather than a desire for money, dominance, or control.

Furthermore, intellectual humility allows us to recognise the inherent complexity of reality, acknowledging that our understanding of the world is always an approximation, subject to the limitations inherent in our own imperfections. This recognition enables us to approach inquiry with a sense of nuance and subtlety. Truth is not in simplistic or binary formulations but rather in the intricate webs of relationships. Intellectual humility is about collective knowledge-building, enabling individuals to cooperatively refine their understandings. Collaborative efforts of inquiring minds can expand knowledge boundaries if they work honestly and own their ethical biases.

Pretending to be free of bias is foolish.

For the purposes of advancing sciences, "The Thinker Becomes" is better than "I think therefore I am." The notion of bias is oft-maligned as a flawed or incomplete perspective. However, it's essential to recognise biases as an inherent component of cognitive processes. Biases are not errors, but rather manifestations of our uniquely situated perspectives, filtered through the prism of our experiences and cultural context. It is an essential tool to be able to focus and accomplish goals. By acknowledging and embracing our biases, we can begin to strip away the veneer of commoditised and demoralised materialist-monetary "objectivity," revealing the complex web of influences that shape our perceptions in subjectivity, especially that which is best in the Light of Christ. You are the subject, do not allow yourself to be made the object, the product, or the commodity. When made the object, you are made stagnant.

Honest Community Progressivism

The propensity for deceit is inextricably linked to the human condition, as family-oriented and tribalistic entrants into larger more complex social systems surrounded, as we are, by competition. It's an evolutionary by-product of our capacity for self-awareness, allowing us to fabricate narratives that serve our interests, often simply enough for mere defensive purposes as in the case with Stockholm culture. This fundamental aspect of human nature necessitates a vigilant pursuit of truth, lest we succumb to the insidious forces of manipulation, as well as giving lie to those we must never deceive. Unwavering commitment to honesty is all that will lead us out of the darkness, this is dedication to the Light. Honesty helps us as well especially to ourselves about the self, but to those we care about and our communities as well. Despite the deceptions and distractions, avenues of progress become visible.

The concept of social capital is often reduced to simplistic notions of community cohesion or trust. However, it's crucial to understand social capital as a multidimensional construct, encompassing both tangible and intangible assets. This includes everything from formal institutions to informal networks, all of which contribute to the overall resilience and adaptability of social systems within communities. Every community has a level of social capital, which is to say the net profit of all members in terms of social, spiritual, and material productivity as measure for general progress. We can call this the "Progressivism" of a community. Progressivism is obviously going to have a lot to do with the average productivity of the individuals within that community. Further, the Progressivism within a society will naturally be harmed by crime, especially organised crime, which acts as another state... also note here well, the artificial terms which make no sense, the ones based upon lies, are perfectly up for grabs. Take them back, like "Progressivism," here. Use it, and mean specifically progress of community. We will get deeper into culture jamming in the memetic warfare chapter.

A state's utility to the polity will be greatly diminished by two primary factors, both having to do with lack of accountability: those being over-centralisation and over-saturation. What does this mean? We grant states something of a monopoly upon the use of force for the purpose of avoiding over-saturation of "violence," which happens with too many agencies of authority. A classic example of over-saturation is when there are multiple crime organisations in a region competing with the town, county, and national governments. Over-centralisation as an issue is rather self-explanatory, in which the figures in authority become unaccountable due to basic distance or liability protectionism and bureaucratic misdirections.

When we speak of states and their monopoly on force, we're really talking about the tension between order and disorder. The former is achieved through the careful calibration of authority, ensuring that power is distributed in a way that maintains culture, standards, stability, and predictability. Conversely, disorder arises when authority becomes diffuse or corrupted, leading to chaos and anarchy with an abundance of vying authorities instead.

The problem of expansive centralisation is in "social entropy," where the concentration of power creates a vacuum that forces dominion on competing interests and undermines the social order and internal cultural progress (intracculturation). Similarly, too much saturation occurs when multiple centres of authority converge, creating a situation akin to quantum superposition. In this, too many organisational possibilities exist simultaneously, rendering decision-making difficult and larger planning impossible.

These abstract concepts can be brought into sharper image by examining the role of trust in social systems. Trust is not an emotional state or a simple feeling of confidence, but rather a fundamental aspect of information processing and decision-making. When we trust others, we're essentially outsourcing our judgement to their expertise to some degree, allowing us to work more effectively. In theory, this should work however the potential pitfalls are plain. Consequences of trust breaking can be seen demonstrated most clearly with the global COVID-19 mRNA spike protein jab genocide conspiracy.

When approaching complex issues or presenting information that challenges prevailing propagandised narratives. This is especially true of those with unhealthy artificial attachments on an emotional level. It's essential, therefore, to frame the discussion as a search for truth rather than a declaration of certainty. Acknowledging the limits of knowledge and the complexity of the issue can establish quite a bit of rapport if believed and understood. Acknowledging our own ignorance and our honest bias in which we are proud toward human life in community, we build some trust in the act of dialogue and discourse itself.

Humility is particularly important when dealing with topics that are prone to emotional or ideological polarisation. People generally perceive charged reactions to emotions as evidence for weakness, typically guilt. It may seem tempting to immediately resort to dogmatic language or assume a superior tone, but the mogging discussed in the previous chapter does imply relationship building first. You have nothing to mog with to a perfect stranger, they know nothing of you or your abilities.

The calmer you can present an idea and in the most universal of terms, the fewer immediate challenges the opposition can pose and act toward dismissal. There will always be a segment of the population that dismisses an idea, but there is a spectrum of likely dismissal based upon presentation. You have to appear confident but also aware of where there are limitations. This is the projection of your competence, which is to say your competent internal discourse.

Being confrontational is powerful but not where it is unnecessary. Often it can only serve to further entrench positions and make it more challenging to find common ground. By approaching the discussion with a sense of appropriate humility, we can create an environment where our arguments are better integrated by the audience or opposition. Hold fast to your own biases in Life, and approach truths from realistic perspectives.

To confront the cross of others, we first confront our own which will invariably lead in a certain direction. It is imperative that we approach any confrontation, that has the potential to help others grow, with a nuanced understanding of outcomes. Initial reactions are often driven by passion and conviction, which are fine so long as moderated and directed upward. Without moderation, we find a path of unyielding obstinacy.

Such an adversarial posturing can cause distinct and recognisable patterns of conflict, further entrenching positions and obscuring the possibility of meaningful dialogue on all sides, but most especially from within the self as subject to these patterns. Instead, we must cultivate humility, acknowledging that our perspectives are for our benefit through our bias, and the best we can do for others is to help them see through to their own benefit: ally or 'enemy.' This is not to say that we must abandon our convictions or surrender to the whims of others.

Dynamics shift with knowledge that individuals who claim to be completely unbiased are purely after personal gain, and driven by money at best. All media platforms follow the human in prioritising sensationalism over substance. Oh, but **that throne of objectivity**, with those pretenders to it who claim to see without bias in 'crystal ball' like clarity of non-subjectivity, **is a golden toilet-bowl**. Are we all not human? Who but a fool would pretend to not be subjective, with their existence dependent upon it?

Financial Gain

In reality, the wastrels are merely peddling ideas for whomever are the highest bidders, with a system-gaming billionaire class pushing stagnation on all fronts. Most opinions are nothing more than weak attempts at marketing gimmicks, designed to sucker unsuspecting souls. For the non-philosophical scientific 'scientistes,' pursuit of fame and wealth supplants the pursuit of truth, community, society, Spirit, God, and wisdom. It's no wonder these charlatans have learned to exploit the void left by the complete lack of substance. This is, in fact, no different than it has always been, but we can do better... we can do **so** much better.

Can it be believed though, really? "Non-bias" touted as some rare and precious jewel, instead of the pile of garbage nonsense that it is. You must not be fooled. The unmitigated truth is they are not concerned with contributing meaningfully to the conversation; no, their sole interest lies in lining their pockets with gold coins and basking in the adoration of acceptance. Lies make slaves of the believers to the liars. All the historical-type sciences and most social sciences in particular are primarily built upon shifting sands that cannot support the weight of any legitimate scrutiny. When the tides of doubt roll in, they crumble like hubristic castles of sand. Their "no bias" or "unbiased" mantra is designed to distract from the true nature of their motivations in nothing, but merely brutal stagnation toward dumb and evil profits by powerful outside interests.

Oh glorious you, who truly seek to contribute meaningfully to the conversation, own your love for Life, please. Recognise the pursuit of

Truth is a lifelong adventure, the greatest possible, not a destination. Addict yourself to the Truth, as stated but also learn to be excited for ignorance, your own and others. Find novel ways to overcome and help others do the same in discovery. This is the grandest of missions. In our coming to terms with our own ignorance, individually, communally, and societally, we find that next greatest Good. The real glory is not in prestige or accumulating wealth, but in leaving a positive and lasting impact upon the World.

Own your love for Life and supportive culture in our communities and nations. It is always preferable to reach out to earn trust and respect for the encouragement of constructive dialogue. There is nobody that cannot be worked with on some level, ultimately, perhaps not by you specifically, however. Speak on the commonalities and the important elements of humanity they may be overlooking. Engage in meaningful discussions that build upon real mutual respect and actual growth, rather than stoke illegitimate hatreds. It is a requirement to approach Truth from the universal-particular-individual position, properly as from below.

Homework:

Identifying the Good in Biases

Read the following passage and identify the biases held by the author:

"The recent surge in violent crimes is directly linked to the increasing presence of immigrants in our communities, as proved by these studies. It's only logical that we take steps to secure our borders and prevent further influx of these individuals."

Explain how these are beneficial views for the person to hold, and how those who try to convince people otherwise mean them harm. Describe how a bias towards Life generally is impossible outside of the support of one's own life, the life of community, and the lives of those used as bargaining chips toward our destruction.

Recognising Propaganda

Watch a news segment or read an article that presents a controversial topic. Identify any propaganda techniques used by the presenter or author, such as: appeals to emotion, misleading use of statistics, false dichotomies, and red herrings.

Write about these in such a way that reveals the underlying biases of the reporter. Write about your own bias towards life and how this causes you to wish the best outcomes for all involved. Indicate how this does not mean forcing sacrifices upon those who have not subscribed to whatever supposed benefits in a notion. Note well how your bias is superior to other types of biases. Write about ways in which you can improve the details of its expression. Be thorough and also cover how the knowledge and ownership of this superior bias enables calm, allowing for greater tact in how you present ideas.

Humility in Discussion

Engage in a conversation with someone who holds an opposing

view on a topic worth discussing. Before you do though, write down potential responses you might make that:
- ~ Acknowledge the other person's perspective.
- ~ Explain how your bias is beneficial to your life.
- ~ Explain benefit of bias to the lives of many others.
- ~ Notes children, family, community, culture, & nation.

Learn their own situation. They will likely claim to be unbiased. In response, identify for them how any claims made toward a lack of bias always suggest ulterior material motives, as a result of the commoditisation in individuals, which is not in alignment with their best interests or your own. Write about how the commoditisation of individuals is "financial-cannibalism," in which many children are never born and those who are have their lives denigrated by the very shape of the system.

Seeking Truth

Choose a topic within a field you're interested in learning more about, such as a future technology, psychology, or a historical event. Research the topic using multiple sources with competing views, and evaluate their credibility given merits of the researchers. Write a reflection on what you've learned.

Patterns of Progress

Find a dynamic within communities that you believe should be investigated and improved in order to achieve greater Good. Once you have an idea and some basic notions of what might work for improving upon this dynamic, research potential explanations that have been posited. Do you agree with any of them? How could they be improved upon? Write a social media post about what you're thinking on the matter.

Here in Your Light, give me Your mercy, my Redeemer, redeem me, for I am Yours; the one who has come forth from You. You are my Mind; bring me forth! You are my Treasure House; open for me! You are my Fullness; take me to You! You are my repose; give me the perfect thing that cannot be grasped! I invoke You, the One Who is and Who pre-existed in the Name which is exalted above every name: through Jesus Christ, the Lord of Lords, the King of the ages. Give me Your gifts, of which You do not rescind, through the Son of Man, the Spirit, the Paraclete of Truth. Give me authority when I ask You; give healing for my body when I ask You through your Messenger, and redeem, my eternal light, soul, and my spirit. And the First-Born of the Fullness of Grace, reveal Him to my mind! Grant what no angel's eye has seen and no archon's ear has heard, and what has not entered into the human heart which came to be angelic, and made after the image of the Spiritual God, when it was formed in the beginning, since I have Faith and Hope. And place upon me Your Beloved, Elect, blessed Greatness, the First-Born, the First-Begotten, the wonderful Mystery of Your house; for Yours is the Power and the Glory and the Praise and the Greatness For Ever and Ever. Amen.
~Apostle Paulus

....

Love so silently:
bears weight,
scoffs at all toil,
aims beyond reach,
sees nothing as impossible,
and admits no feat outside its incredible might.

In the depths of our spirit, where God is found,

Love resides, unswayed by lies, waiting to be crowned.

A flame flickering bright, broadcasting out into night,

Pushing us to seek the Truth, always, with all its might.

This Love is more than sentiment, an overwhelming desire,

To help each person alight their heart, as if it were on fire.

It's burning zeal for righteousness & what is always true,

Beckoning awakening from deathly slumber, all born anew.

God's Love discovered in Word, & so strengthened we fight,

In the name of Christ; His highest Reason's divine sight.

Through God's wisdom, a will to know: explore.

Centred at heart, discerning reality; we truly are most adored.

In this Love, we find our strength, courage, & might,

Stand against forces seeking harm of that path in Light.

We do not sway with tired arguments or worn abuse,

Rise above distractions, with Love that's Pure in Truth.

I understand your 'law,' but it can not understand me.

6. Love at Core & Its Truths

Love from God, once realised, demands improvement, and self-criticality, of ourselves first, and then others. This revelation alone leads us to truth, ultimately. The spectacle of truth itself is the most powerful elixir, especially in the face of God's very Love. However, we must avoid getting lost in the magnificence of it all. Instead, focus on the core truths, the natural and fundamental aspects of human existence. It's in the core truths of good living and criticality that we'll find the most profound insights for people, and the kind that allow for the largest amount of change in ideas more downstream. Truthful facts told in the right order will reach a person, where they might not have out of order. This takes a certain skill to execute, because it requires working against hatred with Love in criticality. This is a skill that is not easy to come by generally.

When we're seeking truth, it's easy to get caught up in the the discovery process. A treasure trove of knowledge sits before us setting our minds racing with implications of what has been learned and what remains to learn. This is especially true with complex or controversial topics that challenge prevailing propaganda from powerful material interests. We must avoid getting lost in the spectacle and instead stay grounded in these fundamental aspects of human existence here. Some facts are only pertinent at the moment, and we have to be ready to move forward and onward with the core truths intact, while shedding what is unnecessary or potentially even deleterious to culture. The future cannot be allowed to be similar to the recent past, because it is filled with lies.

It should be better understood that those who place profits above culture and society are necessarily compromised. We must help others find clarity beyond such false material intentions, and improve perceptions across societies for their own greatest Goods. This requires a certain level of intellectual humility, an acknowledgment that there are limits to our knowledge and understanding. It also demands a willingness to listen to others, to consider alternative perspectives, and to be open to new information and insights, within the limits of our own best interests obviously and of course.

Truthful Facts

When we're presenting information or making arguments, it's essential to prioritise truthful facts over sensationalism or grandstanding. We must present our findings in a way that is clear, concise, and as dignified as possible while remaining respectful foremost to reality itelf, this being a sign of loyalty to God's Love. This requires a certain skillset, one that involves storytelling, emotional intelligence, and an understanding of how people process information. By presenting truths in an order that demonstrates careful consideration and honesty while making obvious narratives based in truth, we can create atmospheres of trust and respect encouraging constructive dialogues that encourage growth.

When we're seeking to change minds or inspire action, it's essential to consider the audience we're trying to reach. We must tailor our message to resonate with them on a deep level, speaking to their values, beliefs, and experiences in a way that is authentic and compelling. This requires an understanding of human psychology, including what motivates people and what they respond to.

Presenting truthful facts in logical order and reaching people where they are involves development of these skills. These are not learned overnight; it takes time, effort, and practise to develop. It also requires a willingness to learn from others, to be open to what can be learned from ideas and perspectives, especially from those we reject, and to continuously improve our approach based in a greater comprehension.

Prioritise clarity over complexity in order to present messages in a way that is easy to understand. Avoid jargon and technical terms whenever possible. This also requires an understanding of how people process information and how to simplify complex ideas. Often we must break ideas down into manageable pieces that mean the most and can be most easily grasped.

Empathy

We must approach others with compassion and understanding, acknowledging their perspectives and experiences as understandable, if not correct or based in all the evidence. When we're able to put ourselves in someone else's shoes and see things from their perspective, we can begin to break down barriers and build connections. This doesn't mean agreeing with or condoning their views; rather, it means being willing to listen actively and respond thoughtfully, with care to understanding and specifically stating how they arrived at it without judgement. There's no need to be unkind or condescending when interacting with others, even when their ideas may seem misguided or misinformed. Instead, we can approach them with kindness, patience, and an honestly professed biased commitment to Life and to Truth.

Empathy needs to be seen demonstrated, not in a haughty way but in such a way that makes it clear how the improvement of others is important to you. In the end, it's not about scoring points or winning arguments, but it's about revealing the truth and freeing people from lies and those chains of deception. When we're seeking to uncover truth and promote understanding, empathy is a vital component of the process. Empathy allows us to approach others with empathy and understanding, rather than with judgment or condescension, with options for bases of agreement.

Empathy is not just about feeling sorry for someone else; it's also about taking action to alleviate their suffering. When we're seeking to reveal truth and free people from lies and deception, we must be willing to share information honestly and approach it from a mature perspective that is based in helping them. This means listening actively and responding thoughtfully with an eye toward their ends.

Maturity

Maturity is not just about age; it's also about having the emotional intelligence and self-awareness to operate in complexity and amidst chaos. When we're approaching truth-seeking as a team effort from a mature perspective, we must be willing to listen to opposing viewpoints, consider alternative perspectives, and avoid jumping to conclusions or reacting impulsively. You are the guide. In the end, it's not about scoring points or winning arguments but rather about revealing the truth, the path to the truth, and freeing minds. This requires a willingness to adapt our understandings as needed. It also demands a commitment to honesty and integrity, even when it's difficult or unpopular.

Insults and trading of condemnations serve nothing other than to frustrate us and create more divisiveness. When we're faced with hostility or aggression, it's essential that we respond with quiet calm. This doesn't mean ignoring the issue or avoiding confrontation. It means staying centred, maintaining our composure, and responding thoughtfully. Insults can also permanently set people against the truth. Do not give in. People remember the anger far longer than anything, yours and their own.

When someone is being hostile or aggressive towards us, it can be tempting to lash quickly out in an emotionally reactive defence, but it is important not to get angry. If the threat is mortal, respond accordingly, of course always. Overreacting only perpetuates the cycle of unnecessary conflict and serves no one's best interests. Significant overreaction is not masculine, however overwhelming force can be when appropriate. Instead, we must generally respond calmly, especially with family or community. Stay grounded in values and principles, and react thoughtfully, while projecting masculine strength. Often the person being hostile is experiencing something traumatic from their perspective. Address people with care and demonstrated strength through calm. Always give options. If required, offer to discuss the situation at another time when both you and the other person have space and the wherewithal to maintain composure.

Responding to antagonistic gestures with quiet calm is not a sign of weakness. It's a sign of strength and resilience. When we stay centred and composed in the face of adversity, we project strength. When calm we're able to think more clearly, communicate more effectively, and respond with the appropriate actions. This allows us to work through challenging situations with greater ease and confidence.

Self-reflection is an essential component of any truth-seeking process. We must be willing to examine our assumptions and adapt our approaches as needed. This requires a commitment to ongoing learning and growth; an ability to learn in the moment and an utter willingness to confront and overcome our own limitations and weaknesses.

Graciousness in Interpretation

Be gracious and benevolent in your interpretations within reason. There is no need to be directly unkind to people in most situations, when the ideas they carry are usually far less intelligent than they actually are. Find friends in people through truth but do not let the dishonest and predatory find your neck. This doesn't mean ignoring or downplaying differences of opinion; rather, it means being willing to hear the views of others, insofar as we understand all originations begin in ignorance, and not direct malice. Reason guides our approach, and so we have little to fear, outside overt violence which is real.

Graciousness is not about being overly indulgent or accommodating; rather, it's about being guided by reason and a commitment to truth. We understand that ignorance must exist, just as sin and error. We must be willing to critically evaluate information, consider multiple perspectives, and adapt our understanding as needed. This requires a willingness to listen actively, ask thoughtful questions, and engage in constructive dialogue. Equally, this also means we must shut down dialogue that ceases to be constructive where it begins to be wasteful of our time or theirs.

Commonality, Patience, & Defence

When we find friends in people through truth, we're not necessarily bonding over all shared interests or values. We're building a foundation for meaningful connection and collaboration even if we do not share anything else. If nothing else, there is always the Truth. Truth-seeking is not a quick-fix process; it requires patience, persistence, and a willingness to learn and grow. This can be a slow and challenging process, but it's essential for building trust, improving understanding, and revealing truth, ultimately.

While it's essential to be gracious and benevolent in our interpretations, we must also be mindful of our own well-being and safety. We cannot afford to let ourselves or our communities be taken advantage of, nor can we compromise our values and principles to accommodate harmful beliefs. Instead, we must prioritise self-care, set healthy boundaries, and surround ourselves with people who support and uplift us.

Homework:

Reflections in Anatomy of Love

Reflect on your own experiences of seeking Truth, and truths. How have you approached tense situations where people have disagreed with you vociferously in the past? In what ways have you been guided most by a sense of curiosity, compassion, or conviction? How can you increase the pertinence of that guidance? Can you detect the Love from God inherent of a Universe that demands improvement in order for you to discover the actual Existence in fact? Can you see the logic in that Love? How does this chapter play into reflecting this Love of God you receive onto others?

Think about how you can apply the principles outlined above to your own life. What are some areas where you feel you can improve in your communication skills?

Write down three things you appreciate most about the transformative Love that can only be taught by God through Christ, LOGOS.

Discursive Curiosity

How do you think our society would change if we approached disagreements with a sense of curiosity and honesty rather than defensiveness or aggression?

Can you think of an instance where you felt compelled to lash out in anger? Explore these emotions more deeply. What did you learn from the experience, and how has it impacted your relationships or worldview since then?

In what ways do you believe this kind of love can be a catalyst for personal growth and transformation?

Journaling Exercises

Write about the advantages of aligning your goals to those things with emotional appeal which grant expedience?

Write down three originally undesirable events you're now grateful for in retrospect from your own experiences in life. What was so valuable in the lessons that now overshadow the negative emotions?

Write down three potential wholesome activities you would not normally do but would probably teach you valuable lessons? Choose one and do it. Write about what you learned... why not the other two now?

"From teaching, we learn."

~Seneca

"The power to learn is in everyone's soul."

~Platon

"Intellectual virtue owes both its birth and growth to teaching."

~Aristotle

Realms, in complex, inspired Souls do roam,

Journeying to the bosom of Truth, our first home.

Overabundant God, flood my mind with Words divine,

Spark shatters ignite millions; true paths of mine.

Share Your yearning Spirit; force not what's theirs to tell,

Grace Loves curiosity; mind's active story compelled.

Revelation's gift, to hearts so bright as spots the stage,

Truth revealed, morning's Light in a world so enraged.

Shine forth on all the hearts shrunk cold, dearest Soul,

Word of God bought off hands in material sold.

LOGOS's Flame, this burns within the Truth we seek,

Think to find our freedom's greatest kin? Ask you of the meek.

5. Empower Critical Thinking

How are we going to create a more efficient society? What is beyond a world where we work for corporations that use our capital against us? Will they not use the capital of others to yet again overwhelm us? That is the special skill of slavers after all. The problem with slavers is that there are slaves ready to be used. Our mission then becomes to free as much of the planet as possible. We must continue this very same mission that was started by Christ, intellectually and in Spirit. It is not faith, if it bears no weight! You have faith in Jesus Christ LOGOS, and in God through Christ, so you may be hyper-critical of everything else. This is the Way.

We have the mind of Christ, so seek discourse alone within as well as with others together. Benevolence in interpretation is a matter of internal strength and speaks most profoundly of your internal discourse. Do not speak so quickly and reside on what was said before answering. It tells people that you are aware of your basic tendency toward errors, and active in interpreting meaning in humility, taking the meaning as most important. You say by your actions, "I am listening completely." It speaks of deep spirituality. This is a crucial element in the more complete form of critical thinking.

What if we could empower people to think more critically and to resist information overload? When we present our ideas in a way that encourages critical thinking, we're not just sharing information but empowering others to use their own brains to fill in gaps. We must empower people to utilise their own brains in developing superior patterns. The guidance in this chapter is not to be read lightly or taken as something that could be accomplished in a singular meeting with a person. This chapter is firmly rooted in a pedagogical method focused within the subjectivity, at the moment, and on the thought. We need community and masculinity to be about natural 'braintrusts,' and the spirit underlying what we do.

Empowering people involves teaching learning. This means allowing people the room to think without answers being handed to them. This makes the same truths more deeply anchored to the person from an individual perspective, while also improving their future ability to make decisions and work through difficulties. In order for people to achieve Good, they must have the space for their own mind's development, also improvements in the patterns of hearts. Critical thinking is not just about analysing information; it's also about evaluating paradigms, challenging arguments, considering multiple perspectives, taking in meaning, and making informed decisions.

Long after the greater truths, and present it. By presenting our ideas in ways to encourage exploration and critical thinking in honest terms of biases, we're helping others develop these essential survival skills, especially on the societal level. Help others take interests of their families, their communities, their nations, and themselves, more seriously. How is that possible? Again, this about starting the flow, so a lot like priming a pump. Empowering thought then, is in fact empowering improvement, growth, and the Good that people can do.

Revelation

It's not about simply imposing our ideas or our will upon the person, rather it's about revealing the truth in such a way as to excite others to construct their own paths to it, not to stay in the garden you show, per se, but to come back and build their own every day. Of course this is only ever done through LOGOS, but using the experiences of each unique person, which are bound to be different. By doing this repeatedly and across a society, we can create more open means of enlightenment and potentiating salvation, especially as the patterns of truths through Christ become owned by more people. You must have faith that others are able to develop theirs to a great degree, and for them to meet your expectations. Teaching in this way assures that any newly accepted facts are more continuously integrated within the frameworks of their own knowledge.

Every human is a filter, capable of being an even better filter for ever greater Good, and luckily this is what liberates: self, particular, and universal, all. Best thing that could happen is for you to inspire others to utilise their own brains in new patterns useful for this liberation, if only a few more times than had they not heard or read from you. That little bit as a new pattern itself can be the tipping point to change patterns of relationships with all things. Revealing truths in ways that spark curiosity and encourage examination starting with the self produce an elevational effect in motivation and hunger for more truth. Ignite a passion for learning, rather than simply trying to convey information, that can lead to remarkable outcomes.

All human communication can be seen as varying degrees of manipulation. The most effective communication possible is in revealing the truth in a seed which is acceptable and allowing others to find the still greater truths that spring from it in their own time. This sort of low pressure conveyance of information focused on patterns with honesty as a cultural and memetic tool can encourage thoughts which lead to best informed decisions.

Autonomy & Inspiration

Autonomy is essential. Patience for autonomy is easier as we come to understand how difficult it can be seeing through cultural stigmas. Many of these harmful memes are based in generations of propaganda. We can respect that time needed to think, and we are patient in creating an environment where they feel comfortable exploring new ideas and developing the framework they need, of which you couldn't ever possibly know the full extent. That's a good thing, that means their take is important. It could be way more important than you could possibly know and you are not wasting your time, and potentially their eventual epiphany, when overburdening them.

Inspiring others to think in new patterns can have a profound impact on our own personal growth and development. When we're curious about the world around us, we're more likely to explore new ideas, ask thoughtful questions, and seek out knowledge that can help us and our ideas grow. It's essential that we empower others to utilise their own brains in developing superior patterns. This process is akin to a master craftsman guiding an apprentice in the art of woodworking. The master doesn't simply tell the apprentice what to do; instead, they demonstrate the techniques, provide guidance, and, rather quickly, encourage mastery. The most important outcome of education is not in the information at all but in the patterns of education, specifically autodidacty. Desire for life-long self-learning should be the primary purpose of any and all education, in fact.

Unpacking & Universalising Complexity

Resonating with others on emotionally charged and serious topics is about presenting practical loss and benefit analysis in understandable terms that do not insult the intelligence. So again, do not give away the answer, because most of the time you should not want to. People do not like being patronised. The ability to reach that individual is heavily dependent to a great extent on voice, attitude, and tone. You may simply not be "it," the one that helps them. Maybe your role is more in the background in their case, it's okay. This can change based upon the nature of the news, too. There are too many variables to unpack in when a person might feel comfortable admitting harsh truths.

It's essential to consider creative approaches that facilitate understanding and empathy. There are always new approaches to explain things in allegorical terms. These can help bridge the gap between abstract concepts and practical experiences. Setting things into allegory can make the complicated simple, because you are helping them utilise patterns of understanding already present in these other forms, which feels like magic for those not used to generating new patterns based in forms themselves. Most people are quite capable mind you, simply not used to it. Oft-times you needn't even bring the thing to the surface from the abstract, you can allow them to swing back to it in their own recreation. Your abstract allegory is part of the weight that is pushing that person into the right direction, and you should always be thankful for this. Look at what you can do for people!

In fragmented and alienated societies, prioritise individual experiences and empathetic themes to intracculturate community, rather than using labels or wording which might seem to imply accusations. Shift to objects, outside subjection, and allow them to see the fullness in their perception. Zero in on the aspects of shared humanity, especially emotions. People are more likely to connect with our ideas on a deeper level with the inclusion of emotional appeals. Remember that all communication is manipulative to some degree, and that the best thing you can do with those communication skills is help reveal more truths, because **anything** less **borders on abuse**. Empathetic themes within personal stories can also help build new mental alliances, and improve common understanding.

Whenever possible, let your opposition speak for themselves, especially where they have no option but to admit to error. In understanding opposing views in their own words, we can create a more nuanced operating model against our creativity. Hearing our opponents out in their terms also widens our insights and improves our ability to integrate all information while synthesising strategies. When teaching others how to spot the way that lies are used or truth is distorted, it is difficult to do better than the actual subject in a 'true to life' **liar**.

Relating information in their terms customised to the needs of the listener forestalls issues with information delivery, and can help connect it on a deeper level for them. Yes, this can actually be done without revealing all, and in fact better. Present everything from the position of analysis, so in a way, act a bit like Socrates. Focus upon drawing out the truth that is already with them. This approach enables you to tap into their authentic perspectives. Frame your ideas in curious language, with questions spoken in familiar terms. This approach invites others to engage with your concepts in a thoughtful manner. Using words outside their daily lexicon may annoy some who might otherwise have engaged with conversation. It's great for the language to be friendly, but sometimes things require sterner presentations, too, as well some are impressed by unfamiliar words. Know more about the person you are talking to.

It is always best to universalise in as much as possible, as such terms are much more easily comprehended by people with strong moral foundations. The people with the firmest moral foundations in reality, should theoretically be the most open to hearing actual truths so long as they are expressed in universal terms. This is because universal terms are often understood to embody fundamental truths. Such words perk the ears of those so naturally inclined. Using language that is accessible to people with a moral foundation can help break down the greatest of barriers between people, and facilitate understanding. This approach acknowledges the inherent common ground that is Good.

Guided Discovery as Art

In striving to empower others with progressive thinking skills, it's essential to adopt a thought patterns teaching approach with guided discovery processes based upon the better understanding that develops through it. Teaching patterns of criticality may feel like a step beyond, but it involves the same basic pattern encouraging the brain to cement connections at the most opportune time in the best order. More questions are better, because it narrows things down further. Ideally, eventually, you should expect the other person to guide you through new information in the end. This approach promotes the mental skills in the easiest way possible while encouraging individuals to take ownership of not only their own learning processes, but those of others as well just as you have.

Navigating knowledge, you'll get lost in the fog of uncertainty. We know very little. Fear not though, the alchemy of legitimate Truth seeking rewards mere mortals with transformation. Those who push forward into the fog with moderation find their bounty in the treasure chests of deepest wisdoms. Visualise a crowded marketplace, with thought merchants peddling ideas, theories, and hypotheses amidst all these competing narratives. Amidst the chaos, we must cultivate the art of avoiding the traps of merchant strategies aimed against us, like some sort of autodidactic monk of thought trying to free the information and offer the best course out of the mire of victimhood. Learning to teach learning in others is that **next level** of this martial art. Now think of the person you are attempting to change as a potential student in a martial art, firstly do you even have the sort of connection with the person in which they would accept you as a sensei? If not, the best you can do is plant a seed of an idea in their mind. The most important thing for the transference of information between the sensei and student is the trust in that relationship. Don't you betray that precious trust.

Consider that a small fraction of adults in the United States read more than one book per month. The majorities of most populations are, unfortunately, stuck in the quicksand of stagnation, on some level. The evidence is clear on inspiration and empowerment toward it. Revelation does not occur due to having a bucket of truth dumped on one's head, truths generally have to be presented cleanly in an order that insists the argument, to make it most acceptable, and this usually happens best within one's own mind. We can't help others toward this ideal positioning and learning by thinking for them, because we have no way of knowing the ideal ordering in detail outside a sequence of extensive therapy sessions. The best revelations you can give others are those that set curiosity ablaze. Watch as the people you awaken dance with discovery after finding their own guiding questions. This builds upon the skills centred around self-assigned freedom to explore, to question, and to build up one's own narrow paths to Good, so they are well-worn. The most important element is this moderation based in reason guiding us inward and upward.

Take, for instance, the case of Nikola Tesla, "autodidactic warrior of thought" if ever there was one, whose revolutionary ideas were initially met with scepticism by the scientific community. He persisted, fuelled by his insatiable curiosity and passion for discovery. He stands now a towering testament to the power of autonomous inquiry. It should be noted how moderated a lifestyle Tesla kept, by the way, much as other prolific and successful inventors. When we empower others to think for themselves and more critically, we're not only changing the individual for the better, but transforming entire communities. What could be better than revealing truths in a way that sparks curiosity?

Show, Don't Tell

Present relevant information (A) and then ask questions that encourage the person to fill in the blank (B). By doing so, we're managing the opportunity for individuals to connect dots and form their own conclusions. This approach mimics real-world problem-solving scenarios where critical thinking is essential, and its refinement is an outcome.

Create narrative frameworks to teach how lies work and then present them with challenges that somewhat match, like the allegories discussed earlier. Deception thrives in ambiguity, so it's essential to establish clear connections that guide the audience through the process of discovery, instead of simply telling it. Doing this enables the patterns of thought to emerge, as practised. This framework should be engaging, easy to follow, and free from jargon or technical details that might confuse those not familiar with the same experiences as you, and don't add to the value for most.

Start with a compelling hook that grabs attention, then build upon it by introducing key concepts, experts, and visual aids. As you unfold the narrative, use storytelling techniques like character development, conflict resolution, and emotional resonance to keep the audience invested. Finally, tie everything together with a clear conclusion that summarises the findings and what they mean.

Visualisations

The tired cliché "a picture is worth a thousand words," remains a fundamental truth: visual information has a way of seeping into deeper memory. Visualisations clarify complex concepts and illuminate the paths to comprehension. Visuals, you see, are not just for simple aesthetics for the sake of things being pretty, they're a tool of precision, cutting through the murk of abstraction and revealing the inner workings of concepts. A well-crafted image can convey nuances and subtleties in ways that simple text alone cannot.

By incorporating high-quality images, videos, diagrams, and infographics, we can bring any abstract notion to life, rendering it tangible and graspable even for those who might otherwise struggle. Visualisations can help anyone better grasp the sheer magnitude of datasets or mechanisms, rendering them more relatable and easier to understand. In short, visuals are not just a nicety; they're an essential component of effective communication. Visuals are a key that unlocks the doors of comprehension, allowing even the most complex ideas to flow freely into the minds of the audience.

A well-designed infographic can transform a confusion with too many numbers into a rich filter leading to still greater insights that you yourself may not even be aware of, which is why it is so important to share. Visualisations make it easier for non-experts to grasp key takeaways in the more abstract forms and inspire better insights. Deep processing for people is often a mixture of activities within the subconscious-conscious complex, and this can take time, but images make for clear contrasts that can plant seeds immediately.

Animations, flowcharts, and interactive simulations can all play a role in illustrating points in order to encourage thoughts. Visualisations make them clear and comprehensible to an audience that might otherwise be left bewildered. Incorporating video testimonials, audio interviews, written quotes, or examples from or about certain esteemed individuals, can add a layer of authenticity and credibility to the narrative being conveyed, lending weight to arguments and bolstering claims. Wordplay, composition, and writing, like any skills, can be developed further, and most certainly will be after stoking the flames of curiosity to help lift them out of stagnant mire.

Trust

Amidst all this deception in the Stockholm culture, it's essential to establish a lifeline of trust with our audience. How do we achieve this? By featuring credible experts in our narrative, who have proven themselves with actions, we can anchor our claims in additional sources of experience and expertise.

Greater trust imbues any agreement on the part of our arguments with fuller weight of authority based in the commonality of shared truth. Context is key here. Experts can provide a framework for understanding complex issues, clarifying technical details, or endorsing conclusions in a way that's both authoritative and accessible. Credibility is not just about facts or having the right sheets of paper from some institution, but it's also about flesh and blood. The best credibility and expertise, in the minds of most people, comes from a person proving themselves through actions, or their experiences in a type of action.

By sharing personal experiences or anecdotes, experts can humanise the issue. The right kind of expert can also put a human face to the statistics and make the facts more relatable. Making things relatable is important but sometimes people are so guarded about a topic that it may be necessary for some to get outright emotional in their appeals. A perfect example of such a situation where this would be appropriate right now is with the COVID-19 jab "vaccine" injuries. This is where the rubber meets the road, no longer are we discussing abstract concepts; we're talking about real people, with real stories, real pain, and real deaths.

Odyssey of Truth

As discussed earlier in this book, there is great power in storytelling. Narrative is a potent tool for persuasion, capable of constructing complex models for emotions, ideas, archetypes, lessons, and experiences. A well crafted narrative can captivate our audience in a way that nothing else could, and inspire thought which will lead to action.

To begin, we must create an emotional or authoritative connection with our audience that motivates them toward engaging with the information. Then Socratic curious type questions do the rest by activating their own thoughts and curiosities. This is where human stories, personal experiences, and vivid descriptions of consequences come into play. Highlighting the struggles, triumphs, and tribulations of real people in a way that delivers our primary arguments and narratives, we can make the issue more relatable, tangible, and urgent.

We must also introduce conflict and tension, obstacles and paradoxes that create suspense and keep our audience engaged. The closer these are kept to our purpose without coming off as desperate or "cringe," the better. This is where plot twists and surprises come in into play. You absolutely should never say everything, not only because it is insulting, but because everything has layers of understanding.

As we craft narratives, developing the values we're presenting in our arguments, can actually make stories more engaging and memorable. This is true for more factual information as well as fictional stories we might craft. There is a lot of flexibility available to us in this process of designing narratives. We can even outline specific steps our audience or readers can take to address issues, without actually saying it.

Generally speaking, on a cultural level, we must emphasise the positive outcomes and consequences of uncovering deception and discovering truths: increased transparency, improved decision-making, and enhanced self-determination. We can create a sense of purpose and urgency around the cause of truth-seeking. Let us not forget to respect our audience's emotional intelligence.

We must avoid falling into the pitfalls of manipulation, condescension, and emotional exploitation. Use emotional appeals responsibly and avoiding the exploitation of vulnerable emotions like fear, anxiety, or sadness. Do not forget to admit your bias, and explain why it is good to have. Above all else, we must prioritise accuracy in our narratives. This means ensuring that sources are credible, data is accurate, and conclusions align with evidence. We must also admit when we do not meet these high standards. Doing so is honest and establishes real trust.

Unlocking the Power

As truth-seekers, it's our duty to present complex ideas in a way that inspires others to think critically and form their own connections. Ultimately, the wisdom granted by our experiences with grief and passion should be used to reveal the truth, not perpetuate lies as is done in Victimentality. Critically reviewing terrible events in life often reveals issues which need attending.

This requires us to take ownership of our emotions and channel them into constructive actions toward real goals with beneficial outcomes for society. Whatever contrasts you see in society's missed needs through legitimate sorrows should burn deep and provide you with passions to overwhelm these issues within society overall. This cannot hope to be accomplished without genuine reason and moderation in life and discourse, however.

The pursuit of truth starts with self-discovery and growth. It all begins as a personal and particular path to the Universal, that requires courage to challenge our assumptions, curiosity to seek out new knowledge, wisdom to integrate our findings, and a grasp of reason which securely fastens us to reality. When we present complex ideas in a way that encourages critical thinking and moderation, we're unlocking the full potential of human intelligence. We're empowering people to question anything that gets in the way of Good, to think creatively, and to develop their own insights.

In so doing, we're promoting agency, control over one's life, better relationships, improved communities, and deeper understanding of self within the larger World. Let us not forget that the paths to the Oneness in Truth, while all very narrow, are as multifaceted and complex as there are imperfections. It's not a fixed point but a constant a destination because it leads you to ever greater Good.

This is a continuous process of discovery and refinement. It's a dance of intuition with self towards analysis in raw reality, of creativity with logic, and in individual experience with collective wisdom. When offering up ideas, one must consider the framework for understanding within which these new ideas can exist, and our honest position in the process of that comprehension.

Critical Truth & Media Literacy

The quest for Truth and the pursuit of knowledge is a never-ending battle against the forces of ignorance. We must equip people with the tools necessary to deconstruct lies, half-truths, and propaganda that plague our society like locusts. How do we do this? By hosting workshops, seminars, and educational events in public libraries, community centres, and schools.

Invite experts to share their knowledge, provide hands-on training, and encourage debates for good measure. Partner with local universities, museums, libraries, and cultural institutions to host these events. This won't be enough. We need to reach all communities, including demographics that are most vulnerable to the manipulation of corporate propaganda, in poverty, and even tricked into hating you. Establish outreach programs, providing educational materials, workshops, and seminars in languages spoken by these communities.

Make sure that message is clear as a mountain stream on a sunny day. Launch campaigns that promote critical thinking and media literacy, sharing educational content, videos, and infographics that provide tips and resources for staying informed, as well as with examples. Partner with local businesses to sponsor these events. What about educators? Community leaders? Business owners? They need training on how to teach media literacy skills. Provide certification programs in media literacy education, making sure graduates are equipped to take on the task of educating their communities.

Organise community outreach events that bring people together to discuss critical thinking and media literacy. Host town hall meetings, panel discussions, campouts, BBQs at parks, and public forums, anything and everything. Grassroots engagement is fundamental to bring about change on this cultural level. Work with local activists, artists, and writers to create educational materials that promote critical thinking and media literacy. Do not make it all about you and your group alone, allow others to contribute.

The Eternal Quest

Truth is not a destination, but a perpetual quest. Nobody can ever know everything, and that's a good thing, actually. Can you imagine what a nightmare it would be to know everything? What would be the point of anything without something driving our curiosity? It's a winding path of discovery and critical thinking that leads us up to those bright shining cliffs of improvement.

Allegory, faith, respect, and perspective are vital for uncovering abstract talents latent in the people we help. We must use emotional storytelling and metaphors to help them bridge the gap, imbuing meaning that speaks to important themes in human experience. By gearing things toward individual experiences in shared human emotions, we can assist the formation of more integrated and beneficial social connections.

This is not about winning arguments, it's about helping people to find a path toward Truth generally. Framing ideas from the perspectives of curiosity invites others to engage with the concepts thoughtfully, and backs up our project of teaching patterns over facts. Veils of ignorance lift to reveal the beauty in understanding, and a great promise of future Good at continuing in this course.

Universalising complex ideas is another crucial aspect of this quest, this is somewhat similar to previous topics though specific to teaching patterns of thought. Strive to present these ideas in accessible language and acknowledge common ground. This is not about simplifying complex concepts, it's about frameworks that allow others to build upon your insights. Guided discovery is essential in opening up others to the quest for truths. Allow others to operate mentally within the complexities of thought on their own terms, and they will grow into wiser and more discerning individuals to meet those expectations. Open up ideas into the most universal of terms you can reasonably conceive for the matter, in order to maximise its reach.

Remember, it's our responsibility as mediators to present truths in a way that encourages others to rise up. This quest overall is about unlocking human potential on all levels. Help yourself and others become conduits through which the Light of understanding can flow into our world. By adopting these approaches to teaching and learning, we can empower others with the critical thinking skills necessary to fix complex problems and make informed decisions.

Homework:

Opinion & Person

Reflect on a time when you tried presenting an idea or shared information with someone else. Did you encourage critical thinking, or did you simply share your perspective? Was your introduction geared toward them or toward your opinion? How might you approach such a situation differently in the future?

Passion & Exploration

Think about a topic or issue that you're passionate about. How might you reveal the truth in a way that sparks curiosity and encourages further exploration? What steps can you take to create an environment where others feel comfortable finding their own path to understanding?

Challenges

Consider a time when someone else's ideas or perspectives challenged your own thinking. How did you respond? What might you do differently in the future to enable more beneficial discourse? How might you show your appreciation to someone that demonstrates that you are wrong in the future?

"What are kingdoms but great robberies?
For what are robberies themselves, but little kingdoms?
The band itself is made up of men;
it is ruled by the authority of a prince,
it is knit together by the pact of the confederacy;
the booty is divided by the law agreed on.

If, by the admittance of abandoned men,
this evil increases to such a degree that it holds places,
fixes abodes, takes possession of cities, and subdues peoples,
it assumes the more plainly the name of a kingdom,
because the reality is now manifestly conferred on it,
not by the removal of covetousness,
but by the addition of impunity."
~St. Augustine

"Then I heard another voice from heaven saying,
'Come out of her, my people, lest you take part in her sins,
lest you share in her plagues; for her sins stack high as the sky,
and God has remembered her iniquities.'"
~Revelation 18:4-5

············

Who is accountable in a nation
full of lionised victims?

Depths of earth,
Serpent Python arose,
stretched across the land usurped.
Scales from shore to shore,
until the hero pierced,
& laid it low.

....

Tiny threads cross in schemes so fine,
Bespoken hands manipulate in kind.
Echoes resound, as truths entwine,
Reverberate in whispers of greater design.

Fractals disperse, revealing naught,
But ghostly masks, dictating what's sought.
Godly flame burn fiery torches bright,
Guiding us through that darkest night.

Horrid screech of ground out dramas in strife,
Cogs whirl with gears engaged, so empires take life.
Curtains conceal threats in machinations grand,
So we tear them all down & pull each little strand.

Silken threads shiny rags, dressed deceit ensnare,
Shatter all lies, crush. None must you spare.
Cryptic ciphers ethereal, tumblers of mind unrolled,
Revealing mysteries lost & now to be retold.

4. International Cathedrals of Sin

Truth is often shrouded in smoke and mirrors, deceit and manipulation. Twisted tentacles of these behemoths in commerce wield influence with animalistic avarice. This international cathedral of corruption exerts an unprecedented level of control over our societies, cultures, and nations. Is it not a collection of individual actors, each with their own motivations and desires? No, it's something far more insidious. Identifying key nodes of corporate cultural power within a society can seem simple, but identifying the nature of their power can be quite complicated without a clear line of sight to the truths of the matter.

It's a system, a machine, a beast stretching across millions of domains. It's a monster, with each tentacle representing a different aspect of corporate power: the "videogame cheat code" financiers, the blackmailed politicians, the greedy media moguls, the genocidal pharmaceuticals, and all the most compromised rear echelons of industries around the world. The politician is a tool of the bankers and corporations, whose trillionaires and billionaires are the modern 'emperors,' 'kings,' and 'dukes,' retaining the old hierarchical mechanisms, a beast by any other name. Each head is connected to the others by a network of corruption, deceit, and manipulation, all working in concert to maintain common grip on our societies and nations. Most of these networks operate within ethnic crime syndicates but the Black Nobility, having inherited Jewish beliefs of superiority above all, under the veil of aristocracy. There, of course, they sat atop of all, in the Vatican, Venice, London, and all over Europe, in power over religion and commerce for dozens of generations now, eventually replacing most natural aristocracies. These people have used their European cousins and Jewish cousins against each other for thousands of years. The Vatican was the wealthiest organisation in all of Europe for the longest amount of time of any other in history. It is difficult to overestimate their power.

Most recently they have set up the overtly Jewish populations, again their variously distant cousins, for greater financial power, most especially over Protestant nations and through 'malleable' (read: "serious") "goyim/nationalist Jews," i.e. physical Zionists who propose a non-victimhood future where diaspora ceases. Well that would be a big problem for the Black Nobility, who are empowered by diaspora. These lineages and families would rather Jews all gave up their religion and hide, like their own ancestors who had married into Roman nobility, as revealed by Jacob Frank's positions, who was heavily supported for his efforts anyway. Much like Sabbatai before him, Frank converted Jews to the dominant religion of the region. He and upwards of a quarter million Polish Jews cleaved freshly to the Vatican's breast, only after Frank had already converted to Islam in Ottoman territory and received land for having done so.

The empowered criminal ethnic network which works within Jewish society wants you to make this all about Jews. Minority status in and of itself causes victimhood, and Victimentality empowers the anti-states within the ethnic crime syndicates, not just the one among Jews but cartels and mafias as well. Mini-states operating against the primary state, while nobody discussed the rights of the majority, their future, and their culture. Perhaps the biggest power in the diasporic dynamic is this very Victimentality, in Jewish identity set to fears of anti-Jewishness and anti-Semitism, which is rightly identified as only dissipated by Jewish physical nationalism involving **all** Jews. A complete physical nationalism is the only thing that would eventually lead to a future end of the basic Victimentality used to manipulate them, but it does not seem that the powers-that-be would ever allow this. Far too much power in the diasporic Victimentality. People in minority statuses are no different from any others in that freedom is impossible until their Victimentality is overcome, when they can seek for their own people and universals through them, above the self. At the highest ranges of Victimentality for a population, the only possible outcome is genocidal intent.

The machine crushes all in its gears, though, and, of course gives preferences to relatives of the secret monarch and his related oligarchs. It's no surprise and the same as it has ever been, despite the many layers of organisations like taped up boxes to build a false wall and hide operations. The only point of these corporations, in actuality, is to divert liability from owners or managers and hide the many smaller organisations controlled within, whose workers comprise a slave class without any say in direction or what they support. In the end, the national banking systems suck up the value in the ever shrinking measure of the "growth machine."

Rise of Corporate Cultural Power

This global force exerts an unprecedented level of material influence, as illegitimately acquired through foul discount rate, usury, and inflation rates. It is a force that shapes our values, our beliefs, and even our very perceptions of reality. The megacorporate thing, an octopus-like entity with tentacles snaking through every crevice of modern society, exerts an unsettling grip on our cultures. This phenomenon, definitively a symptom of our times, has given rise to an unprecedented level of influence. Like a patient zero virus, corporate cultural power has infected every nook and cranny of our existence, leaving its mark on our lives in everything.

The first step in comprehending this horrid entity is to define the term "corporate cultural power." This concept refers to the cumulative might of megacorporations, media outlets, think tanks, and other institutional entities. This megacorp cultural power converges to manipulate societal and political narratives toward projects supposedly in common interests. Like a puppeteer, corporate cultural power manipulates the strings, playing puppets of influence across every theatre of our lives. Corporations and banks are the heavy strands that braid together this complex narrative of persuasion and manipulation, into the rope that exerts the final pull on the curtain.

Media outlets, posing as impartial conduits, are puppets of course, dancing to the tune of corporate interests. We all know this though. Think tanks, those intellectual jesters, are in fact the ideologues that provide theoretical underpinnings for sentiment manipulation, distortion, and redirection machinations. Which is to say the tax haven foundation clowns who get paid by billionaires to divert your frustration and animus, over and over again. They are the architects of false and falsified narratives, crafting the language and frameworks that paint our picture of the world. A vast network of influence is woven together like layers of fibres, with each entity playing its part in mafias of unnatural power and strange persuasion.

Corporate cultural power is not actually a monolithic entity but rather a multifaceted phenomenon reflecting actions toward ethnic warfare as perpetrated actively by ethnic crime syndicates. This has major impacts upon our society. It is an force that seeps into every aspect of our lives, from the products we consume to the ideas we consider.

Major Players

Let us not be fooled by the veneer of respectability these parasites of industry try to portray. They writhe and twist, their tentacles snaking through every aspect of the modern life they have boxed in. These corporations, those titans of inordinate finance, manipulative technology, and media lies, possess the wrongly siphoned resources to force public debates and orchestrate a symphony of persuasion through psychological tricks and threats, both present and larger scale.

They are the masters of spin, deploying armies of messaging experts, crisis communicators, and spin doctors to manage narratives. What of their intellectual mercenaries, and their 'think' tanks parallel to the foundations usually providing the theoretical mucus for these morbid and purposeful misdirections? Like wizards in ancient ungodly temples, they conjure forth treatises, position papers, and policy briefs like spells that justify the actions of their corporate patrons. Media outlets are hoses through which the corporate thought sludge flows, carrying with it the message, the ideology, and the agenda.

They are the messengers, not the message itself. The criminal dance of power and Victimentality influence continues, with corporations, media outlets, and think tanks moving in tandem to shape our international futures. What of the individuals and groups who operate within these systems? Are they mere pawns, caught up in a game they cannot actually control? Or are they co-conspirators, complicit in the grand scheme of things? Yes, yes, and yes, but also no, because these organisations, as designed, must take advantage of whatever positions members have in society, especially their victimhood.

The answer is not in individual motivations or actions, but rather in the structural relationships that govern our society, especially those based on victimhood in the individual motivations and vulnerabilities. It is here, at the intersection of power and influence, that we must seek to understand the mechanisms that control our world. Like a cancerous tumour, this corporate pressure infects every aspect of our lives, poisoning and propagandising populations to accept either manipulation or destruction.

Think tanks provide pseudo-intellectual justifications for these efforts, cloaked in the language of "social justice" and "equity." We must not be fooled by their rhetoric. We must see them for what they are: agents of oppression, serving the interests of their criminal corporate patrons at the expense of communities generally, but also the small communities across the nations which support our families and children most especially. True social justice would entail having a social worth speaking of. True equity would mean money serving as the lubrication of societal exchanges as it should be, instead of allowing it to pool where it should not be pooling due to faulty programming, i.e. design of incorporation law.

Ethnic Syndicates

When organisations act purely toward genuine Good within their nations, which should be every organisation in fact, they're fine. The moment they act as syndicates against other races taking advantage in minority status of their own people living among targeted majorities, they are international criminals exploiting both majorities and minorities. Victimhood falsely validates people, turning villains into "heroes," or so they might have themselves received. Ethnic crime syndicates always try to hide within societies, as they drape themselves in the claim of heroism, but it's a false hero-victimism.

These groups, fuelled by a toxic brew of fear, victimhood, hatred, power-mongering, and profiteering, have discovered a potent combination of tools for concealing their crimes: primarily the silence of their racial genetic cohorts and protective incorporation laws. The corporations they start are built with many layers of liability limiting and money laundering. They work out immunity for themselves before unleashing their exploitation upon the so primed market, most forcefully with politics in the form of billionaires' foundations. Here's the thing about Victimentality, though, if it is present, somebody will exploit it.

The facts that they are ethnic or syndicates means nothing, as well. The primary issue is that these are criminal conspirators who wedge themselves between populations and law, because essentially populations should have their own laws. This is not the chicken or egg question but rather the egg is a chicken answer, which means these are nations within nations, so what is to be expected here? They are nations in process. These are tiny would-be nations inside the larger nations; Microstates, with aggressions and alliances, enemies and ethnic goals, whom act.

They are in competition with the primary state and this makes them criminal. They may appear to be simply confederations but what else would a microstate within a state, a nation within a nation, look like? Would it not look precisely like this? Minorities are automatic permanent victims that cannot be saved, even when it is fully claimed they are. The argument cannot hold up to any scrutiny as exceptions prove the rule all the more, beside the basic fact this cycle begins all over again with the proceeding generations. Ethnic crime syndicates are what happen as the warfare of the sub-state for and against minorities within the state, against the state and order, gets uglier. The smarter the sub-state overall, the more acutely aware they are that they share no interest in the common order of the larger state, and the closer to their chest they will keep the fact. This is very important to point out before these case studies below.

By incorporating shell companies, trusts, and other financial structures, these ethnic criminal organisations can launder their illicit gains, hide their true intentions, and manipulate systems to serve their own selfish wealth and material interests. The veil of corporate personhood allows them to operate with impunity, shielded from accountability and even identification by the very same legal mechanisms poorly designed to even protect legitimate businesses as intended. These corporations become mere puppets for the ethnic crime syndicates, serving as fronts for highly coordinated illegal activities working against the order of the larger state and toward the greater order of the criminal sub-state.

Of course, many of these organisations run more legitimate businesses as cover for operations in bribery, human trafficking, murder, prostitution, slavery, and extortion. The shell organisations can be used to funnel funds into various organised crime operations. The corporate structure also, most importantly, enables these criminal organisations to act as states and extort legitimate businesses for "protection."

Now, the question is, who are the people that take the most advantage of minorities? It would seem the nature of majorities statistically creates most of the victimhood-enducing environmental factors, but that the most exploitation happens within those communities through the leverage of that environment, not because of it or any opinions on the parts of members within the majorities. These kinds of environments create power vacuums of such a sort, every single time. Criminals within these minority groups use the tenuous situation and fears due to the environment to exploit their own, taking governmental roles such as protection as well.

This is because minorities are too terribly aware that they are in mortal competition with a larger population, as a sub-state within a state, far more so than the majority are often aware, especially with the propaganda pushed. Especially true, this, since many elect to come, and know they are in competition with the systems of the people already present. This makes standards nearly impossible to maintain and allows for excessive amounts of exploitation which is often treated as mere quirks in ethnic practices within cultures, or even as beneficial, by all victims, perpetrators, and witnesses.

A great example of the latter is in the interest-free loan system offered to anyone of Jewish descent. Nobody sees the control element in this, but it's very much there, though outsiders at most would see the unfair advantage alone, which is also there, very much present, and a problem. We should all be for standards, but standards are not nearly as possible under mortal competition, because the standards become mere survival, and have little to do with culture, improvement or merit.

Whomever is better at constructing standards in greater alignment of their particulars and universals is the winner. Non-mortal competition is ideal for this. Incorporation laws, usury, and mortal competition are completely debilitating for communities. These allow for criminal manipulations generally. Mortal competition within the sub-state in the form of the ethnic syndicate criminality and systems of exploitation brought with it do not allow for the process of standards to be effective, drenched as it is in Victimentality. Chaos is the inevitable result, both in the short and long terms. This is not a good arrangement for the larger state nor the sub-state syndicates, and their people.

Triads: Prime Example of Ethnic Syndicate

The Triads are a Chinese crime group that are very well-organised. They have evolved since their founding, adapting to changing circumstances and exploiting vulnerabilities in modern society. The Triads are an exceptional case as well, considering the depth of their integration into Chinese culture. Their historical ability to recruit in very large numbers and rapidly so, I believe, speaks to how well they can utilise their own culture to motivate people, having perhaps more to do with the Chinese themselves culturally.

They invest in operations which best enable them to exploit Chinese minority communities in other countries. Operating under the guise of legitimate businesses, the Triads use shell companies, trusts, and other financial structures to launder their illicit gains, as is common for syndicates. The Triads have infiltrated various industries, including finance, technology, and entertainment. They have been known to manipulate stock prices, commit fraud, and engage in extortionate practices. Triads do a lot with their membership, which again speaks to the depth of cultural connections.

The Triads' impressive reach and cunning operations have allowed them to thrive in modern society. High-ranking members often live double-lives as successful entrepreneurs. Much of their success is through the use of the power in their criminal society and the disguise of philanthropy, which can often be real. This camouflage allows them to operate not only undetected, but protected, especially amidst a population facing constant reminders of their mortal competition as minorities.

Despite their criminal activities, they have managed to present a respectable façade, often donating to charitable causes or sponsoring cultural events. Why would many not protect the most powerful criminals in their communities amidst societies which they fear may turn on them in emergency? How can they be expected not to? This calculated display of benevolence has earned them a level of acceptance within many communities, allowing them to maintain a low profile while continuing to expand illegal enterprises. Victimentality added on top of the basic mortal competition implied of minority status is a nasty combination that can justify almost any atrocity in the minds of victims.

One notable example of the Triads' influence is their involvement in the real estate industry. By investing in property and manipulating market prices, they have been able to accumulate significant wealth and secure lucrative business deals. Their connections with corrupt government officials and other influential figures have also enabled them to grease the wheels of commerce, further solidifying their grip on various industries.

Despite their impressive reach and influence, the Triads are not immune to internal conflicts and power struggles. Rival factions have been known to emerge, often vying for control of lucrative operations or seeking revenge against perceived enemies. These internal conflicts can lead to violent clashes and even murders, further solidifying the Triads' reputation as a formidable and dangerous criminal organisation. As the Triads continue to expand their influence and diversify their criminal activities, it is essential to understand how the very existence of a population ready to be exploited allows for the criminal organisation to happen in the first place.

The pattern that is seen across the board with these ethnic crime syndicates is that the more precariously balanced the minority group within which the syndicate exists, the more extreme the violence and criminal operations generally. This can be seen demonstrated mercilessly in locations like South Africa, where Triad internal rivalries have grown very bitter, amidst complex racial tensions, slavery, sex trafficking, prostitution rings, and all attendant malaise. Elevated mortal competition, it would seem, causes more desperate and violent criminal operations. This makes sense on a purely logical level.

Sicilian Mafia: Romantic Racket Government

The society of Sicily was one of extreme distrust, after centuries of rule by foreign powers. There is a popular Sicilian phrase 'Farsi è bene, non fidarsi è meglio,' "to trust is good, not to trust is better." I am struck with great sadness at the magnitude of this, as many of my dear readers will be as well, though there is so much harsh truth in it. This is a people built up with an internal trust that transcended the authority that surrounded them as chaotic oppression by empowered minorities, such as various Italian principalities, European empires, Normans, Spaniards, Arabs, Black Nobility, and other Mediterranean powers going far back into "pre-history."

The Sicilian Mafia, more properly known as 'Cosa Nostra,' literally "our thing," is one of the most well-known and feared organised crime groups. With roots deeply embedded culturally in basic methods and practices of resistance, the Mafia evolved over time into a sophisticated network of organisation within Sicily, helping them weather the storms of the external powerplays never meant to benefit them. As Sicilian power grew through this local power, it became more criminal in organisation as it increased distance from their heartland, first across Italy, then Europe, America, and beyond.

These are the natural dynamics of any human organisation, as they will show preferences to those most beneficial to them. It's not bad either, and this is just the way of nature, and how humans have always operated. Not only that, it's a crucial element in the connection between culture and evolution. It only becomes bad when it extends out over other groups to be denigrative, much as Sicily was so burdened under imperial and foreign powers. This stops development, and finding any amount of trust allows for something of such development again. It should not be surprising when these powers become more exploitive and extractive with rising tides of mortal competition. People become more violent in general in such environments, but especially so when victimised or made to feel like victims anyway, as it increases alienation and justifies any action to the actor with Victimentality.

The Mafia's modus operandi involves corruption, intimidation, and violence to maintain its power and control over various sectors, which spread to many industries to include construction, utilities, and the illegal drug trade. They infiltrated politics, law enforcement, and government institutions, leveraging their connections to further their criminal agendas. Their criminal activities are often masked by a culture of silence and confidence, with members adhering to a code of omertà (silence) that protects them from revelation. This form of trust built up against the grain of authority allows for an oppressed group to pull much harder than its actual weight in terms of leverage, if they're smart about it. The Mafia's power is rooted in its ability to exert social pressure and threats of violence on individuals and businesses, forcing them to comply with demands or face the consequences, generally under a guise of "protection," though this protection has been very real at times, especially under the thumb of external powers. Again, this is a micro-government acting against the primary state.

One of the most impressive feats of the Cosa Nostra is their ability to infiltrate and take advantage of various institutions. They have successfully compromised law enforcement officials, politicians, and judges, using their connections to further their criminal interests. This has allowed them to operate with impunity, often going unpunished for their illegal activities. They have established partnerships with other organised crime groups, such as old powerful families of New York, allowing them to expand their criminal operations and diversify their income streams. Despite their reputation for ruthlessness, the Cosa Nostra has also demonstrated a remarkable ability to adapt and evolve.

The Mafia's cultural significance cannot be overstated. They have become romanticised figures in popular culture, with films like "The Godfather" and "Goodfellas" portraying them as charismatic and powerful in many ways. However, this romanticisation has also served to downplay the brutal reality of their criminal activities and the harm they inflict on many innocent people. In recent years, the Cosa Nostra has faced increased pressure from law enforcement and competing criminal organisations. This has led to a decline in their power and influence, but they remain a significant force in Italian and international criminal underworlds. The story of the underdog able to rise above lowly beginnings remains insanely popular, especially given criminal circumstances and extreme mortal competition.

American Gulf & Southern American Cartels

The Cuban mafias, the Colombian cartels, and the Mexican cartels have all been operating in the United States with regularity. They've learned to exploit the Victimentality of the Latino minority populations, not as limited in this respect as the Triads or Cosa Nostra. Theirs are empires built on fear and illegal alien status, with tentacles reaching into every corner of Latin-American societies. They've honed their exploitation skills through decades of drug-money-fuelled chaos, perfecting the art of manipulation. The spectre of deportation is powerful and hangs over the heads of many of these minorities, making them especially vulnerable to manipulation and coercion. The cartels and mafias use this very much to their advantage.

These criminal organisations have evolved to occupy powerful positions within the American underworld. Leveraging minority status within their communities has enabled them to develop additional strategies for co-opting and controlling local politicians and authorities. At the exact same time they will try to create an aura of respectability and legitimacy. They often present themselves as entrepreneurs or small business owners much like the Triads, using their cultural connections and linguistic skills to build relationships with law enforcement and community leaders. This façade of respectability allows them to gain access to valuable resources, including financing, land, and political influence.

However, these cartels and mafias are known for ruthless tactics. They have developed networks of associates and assets who are often coerced into serving their interests, as threatened or plied with addictions. They have been able to operate with relative impunity, often exploiting loopholes and weaknesses in the legal system. They use encrypted messaging apps and other digital platforms to stay one step ahead of the authorities. This has allows them to maintain a level of operational secrecy.

Compartmentalisation has further served security purposes, as the organisations are able to divide their operations into distinct spheres of influence, granting levels of deniability. This makes it difficult for law enforcement agencies to penetrate their inner workings. Even though they do a lot of hiding, these cartels are not afraid to flex their muscles. They will use bare violence, intimidation, and almost any other strategy to get what they want, regardless of how it looks. Their victims are often those who've crossed them, but also those who are simply in the wrong place at the wrong time, like unsuspecting tourists and hapless bystanders.

Many cartels have a seemingly endless supply of coerced operatives, in their own countries too as empowered by the networks of aliens in the United States. They have developed even more insidious approaches to manage them efficiently. They're masters of manipulation and deception, often using social media and other digital platforms to spread fear and confusion during their paramilitary and offensive operations. Their tactics are designed to keep victims off balance, making it impossible for them to anticipate or prepare for the next attack.

So what does this mean for ethnic crime syndicates generally? It means that they've all learned to exploit the Victimentality of minority populations in ways that are both subtle and brutal. These cartels have developed sophisticated strategies for exploiting vulnerable communities in their originating countries and the United States. By leveraging social, economic, and psychological weaknesses, they are able to manipulate individuals into serving their criminal interests.

One of the most striking aspects of the cartels' tactics is their exploitation of the desperation and hopelessness that often accompanies poverty, unemployment, and social marginalisation. They do this by offering "opportunities" for quick wealth or easy access to goods and services, which are often nothing more than thinly veiled schemes to recruit unwitting accomplices. In their home countries, the cartels have been known to target rural communities where economic opportunities are scarce and poverty is rampant. By promising higher wages or better working conditions, they are able to entice young men into joining their ranks as smugglers or hitmen, or even first as simple labourers or extra bodies. Once inducted, these individuals are often subjected to brutal conditioning techniques designed to break their spirits and turn them into loyalist soldiers.

In the United States, the cartels and mafias have developed advanced methods to target immigrant communities, preying on their desperation for a better life and their lack of access to legal employment opportunities. By offering fake IDs, driver's licenses, access generally, or other forms of documentation, they are able to create a false sense of security and trust among unsuspecting individuals. The cartels' tactics also involve exploiting the psychological vulnerabilities of individuals who have been traumatised by experiences, many having already suffered exploitation and war by the time of their arrival. These groups rely on social and psychological manipulation to create false senses of power and control among these traumatised asset targets through the criminal organisations. They prey on people's emotions, offering false hopes and a sense of belonging in a sea of basic alienation.

Another trend that emerges from the study of these criminal organisations is their reliance on social contagion. This phenomenon occurs when individuals are influenced by the behaviour and attitudes of those around them, often without fully understanding what is happening. The cartels' manipulation of vulnerable communities highlights the devastating consequences of exploitation, including widespread violence, human trafficking, and drug addiction, especially as it generates such exploitive environments. These mafias and cartels are able to create networks of complicit actors who are willing to do their bidding, often without realising the full devastating consequences of their actions, or all of the organisational connections of their new employer.

Criminal Systematic Organisation

There's an upper-limit of what systems can take in terms of psychological and sociological stress like this, as demonstrated by the lack of stability in many of the countries where these cartels and mafias originate. Generations with less connectedness to their own cultures, less assuredness of survival, more mortal competition, and more alienation are bound to be more violent. This violent reaction to chaotic environments has a purpose as well, however. These groups gained most powerful through drug trafficking, human trafficking, slavery, and piracy but have since infiltrated various legitimate industries, including finance and real estate. Much like the Sicilian Mafia, the Central and Gulf American ethnic organised crime syndicates have grown up under the pressures of extreme authority.

The cartels and mafias have historically been linked to corruption, extortion, and violence, with members often using their connections within their community to further their criminal agendas. They have also been known to manipulate government institutions and law enforcement agencies, leveraging their influence to evade detection and punishment. Their criminal activities are often masked by a culture of secrecy and loyalty, with members adhering to their own code of silence that protects them from detection. Their power, much like power in the Cosa Nostra as detailed above, is rooted in the ability to exert pressure on individuals and businesses, forcing them to comply with demands or face the consequences. These organisations prove to be competing forms of government against the order as described above.

These cartels and mafias have also demonstrated an ability to diversify criminal activities. The power of these crime syndicates is augmented by various connections in the governments of their originating countries. For instance, the Cuban, Colombian, and Mexican governments have historically been wary of overbearing United States influence, and as a result, some politicians and governmental officials will work closely with these criminal enterprises, who they see as an oppositional force for furthering their own interests.

Typically, they will get used by one or the other. This additional co-operation has allowed the cartels to grow their criminal enterprises substantially. The mafias and cartels have made tight connections with other ethnic cartels and the large corporations controlled by them, who oppose the order of the majority much the same. Once they organise together, they are acting in alliance against the state.

The minority statuses of their members and the communities they exploit have given them major advantages. Organised criminals in general do make special efforts to target compromised individuals, as described. In general they exploit the status whenever they operate, but many have been able to take advantage of the perception of victimhood that attends this status, to further their own interests. They have used such undue affirmative action type influence to manipulate government institutions and law enforcement agencies, leveraging this power to evade detection of crimes and avoid any punishments, while amassing wealth.

Their criminal activities have devastated communities for generations. Their extortion rackets force legitimate businesses to pay them protection money, while their drug trafficking operations have contributed to surges in debilitating drug abuse in both majority and minority populations. In addition, their human trafficking operations have resulted in the exploitation of vulnerable individuals in the millions, including women and children. Despite the concerns of many, these mafias and cartels remain powerful forces. Law and order demands rational nationalism wherein societies are not allowed to become free-for-alls for mass predation.

Amidst this wreckage, certain patterns emerge. Firstly, there's the art of manipulation and psychological warfare, in which the weak are preyed upon and the strong are cajoled into complicity. These criminal organisations understand that the average human mind is awash in insecurities, fears, and desires, basically waiting to be exploited. By preying on these vulnerabilities, they can create for the vulnerable persons false senses of power and control, which is a cruel mirage that too often leads to thoughtless criminality. It's a vicious cycle of exploitation, where the victim becomes complicit in their own subjugation, and then victimised still others. This ramps up over time, obviously.

What of the consequences? The devastation is catastrophic. Wide spread violence, human trafficking, drug addiction, and a litany of other vices rot society. It's as if the cartels have engineered a self-sustaining environment of depravity, where each act of exploitation spawns new victims, perpetuating the cycle ad infinitum. In the dystopian landscape, the boundaries between victim and perpetrator blur like an impressionist painting. The cartels and mafias create halls of mirrors where reality is distorted, and notions of right and wrong become distant memories. This all has to stop.

Power Brokers: Mossad, AIPAC, & ADL

One of the most powerful of these ethnic syndicates is the Mossad-AIPAC-ADL operation: Mossad, Israel's national intelligence agency; AIPAC (American Israel Public Affairs Committee), a powerful lobbying group that completely dominate American politics on all sides of pretty much all aisles; and ADL (Anti-Defamation League) which pretend to be a civil rights advocacy group though primarily only concern themselves with disrupting discourse for the majority of the population. This criminal syndicate has been tied to some of the most horrible atrocities in the United States, and in world history. If ethnic syndicates, targeting people the majority in a nation, are not stopped and actively opposed, they will cause humanity's eventual extinction. Currently, many members of such criminal syndicates feel so emboldened as to openly call people of European descent Amalek, invoking biblical genocide as they call for our destruction, in mockery of God.

This syndicate wields significant influence over historical events with global consequences. Mossad is infamous for its skills in espionage and sabotage. Covert exclusively, Mossad often operates in concert with both CIA and KGB. They have been involved in innumerable clandestine operations. Their agendas are often shrouded in mystery, but it's very clear that Mossad presents itself as an organisation that prioritises Israeli national security above all else, supporting Likud-led governments and maintaining dominant relationships with United States authorities, often by any means necessary while openly admitting their willingness to engage in terrorist actions to achieve their ends. It is also clear that these preferences go much farther than national or religious, extending toward anyone with Jewish background, which has much to do with security, and is expected. This is a way they can make the Victimentality-controlled feel more secure in their motives.

However, they also hold benefits over the heads of average Jews much as described above, like interest-free loans or grants for speaking well of Israel or endorsing certain politics, which are used for the purposes of control. This doesn't even enter into how they also provide for debt forgiveness in 'Jubilee' to those who don't make the money back or turn profits. It's a nice bonus in concept, but it underlies serious levels of control and manipulation.

Mossad specifically has been heavily implicated in many world changing events, such as in circumstances surrounding the assassinations of the Kennedy brothers, the false flag attacks leading to building collapses on September 11th, 2001, the false flag attack of the USS Liberty, and, most recently, the COVID-19 bioterrorism attacks in the form of diseases and jabs which cause shedding of lab-designed spike proteins targeting people of European descent primarily and people of African descent secondarily, as discussed earlier. This also doesn't begin to list all their activities in the Middle East, such as the recent genocide of Gazan people, closer to their own borders, which included the slaughter of tens of thousands of innocent children, with many in hospitals.

Their influence extends far beyond Capitol Hill, with many AIPAC officials holding high-ranking positions within all Presidential administrations in recent history, intelligence organisations, and government agencies. AIPAC's role in promoting Israeli interests has been criticised for its potential impact on U.S. national security. Critics argue that the syndicate operate outside the bounds of transparency, using their power to force their agenda upon public opinion, manipulate political decisions, and silence critics, at the risk of American safety. The very point of their existence, by the name of AIPAC they hold itself, is to prioritise Israeli interests over those of the United States, which entail massive conflicts of interest and undermine not simply U.S. but international stability. The point has always been to curry favour, however they went further in designing and enforcing favour on institutional levels.

The secretive criminal syndicate sparks numerous conspiracy theories. Mossad and AIPAC are known to engage in nefarious operations, including surveillance in the United States, Jewish community exploitation, sending police or military to combat peaceful political thinkers, manipulating political parties, assigning managers to each American lawmaker per Massey, and plotting assassinations. Their full activities remain classified, but their influence is clear. Epstein's Mossad ties, politician connections, access to trafficked girls, and blackmail evidence all paint an obvious painting that most people appear to have caught on to. Nobody is happy with this.

The study of the Mossad-AIPAC-ADL mafia would be worthy of a couple dissertations in global manipulation. They plainly and unapologetically serve their own interests, downright impressively so, and as emblazoned in the very motto of Mossad itself: "warfare through deception." Their expertise and domination in espionage has allowed them to alter the very course of history, mostly behind the scenes. They have consistently demonstrated an ability to influence major events and push the narrative into something else. Their ability to influence politicians and steer national discourse has allowed them to create powerful mechanism for supporting their apparent goals, while also undermining enemies in most capacities.

This ability to manipulate global events has created an atmosphere of fear and uncertainty, making it difficult for others to challenge their influence. Despite the controversies surrounding their activities, Mossad-AIPAC-ADL remain powerful in global politics due mostly to their overwhelming influence upon the United States. As such, they are a significant concern for anyone interested in transparency, accountability, and international politics.

Their secretive nature has also enabled them to silence critics and avoid accountability while manipulating things with greater efficiency. Their influence extends far beyond Capitol Hill, through the U.S.A. military. Involvement in various Middle East conflicts, including the recent genocide of Gazan people, is a stark reminder of the power that is retained in diaspora. The shameful Gazan genocide seems like a wholly unforced error. The weird shenanigans surrounding the funding or support of Hamas taken with the official Israeli counter-counter-insurgency operations during October 7th suggest more is at play.

Black Nobility: Special Power & Privilege

Among the many powerful families that have altered the course of history, Black Nobility stand out as unique and fascinating examples. This group of oligarchic families have maintained an astonishing level of influence and control over the centuries, with roots dating back to before the Middle Ages, according to their own family legends. The Black Nobility is characterised by its membership in the highest echelons among European nobility, particularly in Italy where the families have played a significant role in the country's history, often behind the Holy Roman Imperial scenes, with many of the most powerful moving to London, just in time to finance the later English Empire. They have often worked together to depose unrelated and more congenial nobility in regions all over Europe, in their quest to remain in power.

To be more precise, when using the term "Black Nobility" here, the reference is specifically to those families with ancient ties to remnants of imperialism who have maintained their power and influence through a combination of having the right connections, the right bloodlines, political intrigue, coordination, cunning, deceit, as well as crime, and manipulation. In fact, the current royal family of England are Guelphs or "Welfs," perhaps the most powerful Black Noble line in history, which oversaw the fall of Rome in Odoacer and whose descendants married into Charlemagne's family. They also produced the sub-branch of infamous and nearly as powerful Este families. The family most recognised internally would be the Orsini who claim origin in the ancient Julian-Claudian line as did their primary competitors in the Colonna, which is most impressive. Columbus himself has been theorised to have been of this latter line, and there is a lot of circumstantial evidence to support the idea. This also raises questions as to the legitimacy of reports surrounding the American civilisations, and the power purposes in their genocides.

One of the most well-known examples of Black Nobility groups are the families of Venetian nobility, who have been instrumental in the history of Venice and the surrounding regions especially, but all of Europe in actuality. The Venetian oligarchy were known for shrewdness, cleverness, and the ability to adapt to changing circumstances. It must be stated, many of these noble families played significant roles in trade, commerce, and politics on a civilisational level, however the least greedy didn't stay wealthy for long.

These families have historically held positions of great power and influence within the church, often serving as advisors to popes and other high-ranking clergy. Long associated with the church and its papacy, they have controlled many aspects of the Vatican for at least a dozen centuries. They have also been central to development of church doctrines and policies, with most popes heralding from amongst their ranks. No doubt that these were the families which profited the most from the crusades, as well as in the destruction of records that occurred along the way from Nicaea to Jerusalem and back to Rome. They are generationally involved in various schemes to accumulate or maintain wealth and power, often through clever manipulation of church finances and funding crusades.

The Black Nobility families maintain their power and influence in many ways. They have formed secret societies, made secretive pacts with other powerful families they consider compatible, and used their too often ill-gotten wealth to further their own interests together. Often they have used pseudonyms, or even pretended to be other ethnicities all together, such as Spaniard, Sicilian, or various Eastern Mediterranean, Levantine, and Mesopotamian groups, such as Jews, Hellenes, Persians, or others. Many see themselves as genuine aristocracy and the culmination of important bloodlines, with all these groups of people being justifiably subjugated to their machinations, by their own warped supremacist ideology.

Due to their reputation for ruthlessness and cunning, the Black Nobility families also try to play up support for various charitable causes. Most often these seem like cynical ploys to justify illegitimate powers, or even predatory access. In recent years, the Black Nobility has faced increased scrutiny and criticism for its role in world affairs. Many have accused them of being a conspiratorial elite, using their wealth and influence to manipulate events from behind the scenes, and the evidence certainly points in just this direction. Black Nobility families are extremely powerful and use this power to keep power.

To confirm their power, one need look no further than the especial relationship of the Rothschild banking family, which is the richest in the World according to all evidence, with the fact that half of them are converts to Catholicism. Many of those Rothschild family members who remain Jewish religiously, if not zealously, also hold the highest ranks amidst the Vatican orders of knights. The amount of power in so few of hands is a terrifying thing and far too much. Such a precarious minority with extreme powers should be fully expected to try to hide it, if they can and to the degree that it is possible. It should be expected that they would even attempt to push all blame onto other groups, related or not. The only trillionaires that existed before the Rothschilds lucked out handling business deep across all Protestant nations was the Catholic Church.

It's an ethnic crime syndicate on steroids. They're the Beast of organised ethnic secret criminality, with tentacles stretching into every level of government, finance, media, and academia. The Black Nobility clans are the ultimate insiders, and they appear to own the game entirely. From the Rothschilds to the Windsors, the Habsburgs to the Medici, these families have intermarried, consolidated power, and used their wealth to manipulate the levers of control. They're not simply wealthy; they're a global force of exceeding power and an entity to be reckoned with as proved by their ability to survive all the power struggles throughout those centuries.

Hatred and fear have a lot of power in them. It's not uncommon for governments and religious authorities to use these emotions as a means to gain control. The Spanish Inquisition is a prime example of this, with its objective being the leveraging of the squabbles to control Jews and take from them while simultaneously protecting them. What sparked this inquisition though? The Reconquista, that's what, let me explain.

After the Muslims had ruled Spain for centuries, the Spaniard Christian majority was eager for revenge against those who had leveraged Muslim rule against them. Powerful newly converted Christian Jewish families, who had amassed illegitimate wealth during the Muslim rule, became the obvious target of this wrath. The church and the wealthy Black Nobility families surrounding it saw an opportunity to empower themselves and used the inquisition as a means to do so. By "taking justice into religious hands" with these new Christians, they were able to quash the desire for revenge among the Spaniard Christian population and maintain their grip on power, while also raking in the cash and valuable information. Surely they were also able to weed out any of the new Christians who remained loyal to the old Umayyad affiliated religious orders and authorities.

Governments and religious authorities often use fear and hatred, natural or artificial. The inquisition was a tool used by the church to maintain their dominance, and it was fuelled by interethnic squabbles. What about the Muslims? Of course, they were the ones who had ruled Spain for centuries before the Reconquista. That hatred between Christians and Jews was used to further their own interests as well. In fact, the original invading Muslim armies were let in through the gates by Jewish spies, which indicates espionage already happening.

These Jewish spies did this to the Spaniards because they were raised to perceive themselves as permanent victims of that majority. Once settled, the Muslim rulers used the Victimentality of Jews, raising them up to official positions of the government especially locally over top of the Spanish cities, some as governors and mayors. We must learn from this history and recognise how these conflicts are promoted and used by those who seek to gain or maintain power. These things are exactly what should be expected of empires, regardless of origins. The key to maintaining such earthly imperial power, especially as such a small group like the Black Nobility, is to disempower or redirect others who may pose a threat.

The Black Nobility were also involved with the Renaissance and Enlightenment, insofar as we are aware of these periods today, and the birth of the modern banking system. The banking system has been pretty much controlled by them ever since. The Federal Reserve, the Bank of England, or the ECB, you name it, the banks of the Black Nobility, Vatican, and Rothschilds control these institutions. Reach extends far beyond finance, as demonstrated by any nation having a central bank not in their control is vilified before being utterly destroyed.

Using their control over money, knowledge of exploiting Victimentality generally, and ability to manipulate minorities or other artificially generated Victims, they infiltrate governments. They influence policies toward the creation of wars that benefit themselves primarily. They own or control newspapers, TV networks, and social media platforms. Through these entities, they craft narratives to suit their interests, as the gaping maw resting just below the financial systems, and all other industries too. They're the catch-all. They essentially have a built-in global public relations firm with unlimited budget and access to every influential figure, with nearly every corporation somehow beholden in some capacity, potentially, and if not directly, then with some authority over them in some respect, even if purely raw money power. The funding received by Israel from the

United States, Germany, and other nations should be plenty of evidence for the power held by the Rothschilds most especially to divert resources to their pet projects.

They're a global mafia with tentacles nearly everywhere. They've so thoroughly infiltrated the system, it's almost impossible to touch them without triggering a global panic and potentially destabilising the entire financial system. That is a very powerful position to be in. So what's the takeaway? The Black Nobility clans are an ethnic crime syndicate, unlike any other, that's been manipulating world events for centuries. They're the ultimate insiders, with wealth, influence, and bloodlines. History proves that you can't stay in power forever, however, no matter how hard you try. The more they tighten their grip, the more they'll ultimately strangle themselves. When that happens, it won't be a pretty sight, but it might just be the start of something completely different and much better.

The Romani: Complexity & Suffering

It is often claimed that people who don't have any power cannot be said to harm any majorities, but this is plainly nonsense. The Romani are a people with a history pocked by rackets, criminality, persecution, forced assimilations, and exploitations all around. The Romani have also proven unsympathetic to the plights of others among the populations they have lived. They attack and take from the majority without guilt, often illogically justified by a deep-seated hatred based in a permanent victimhood that sees themselves as superior to those around them, or at least more deserving of the goods so stolen.

This toxic attitude has led to terrible actions, and it's essential to acknowledge the Romani people's own role in perpetuating violence and suffering. The Romani are an important group to include in this discussion as they present as quite oppressed and not always very organised, though quite commonly active in strategic criminal activity. Where some groups will engage in soft disclosure strategies to mitigate empathy responses for victims of heinous crimes, Romani simply primarily concern themselves with small crimes, which don't tend to elicit nearly as much anger. Comparatively, other parasitic type cultures have grown very powerful, but then also eventually backed into a corner.

The Romani, a people shrouded in mystery and resilience, their nomadic existence a perpetual drumbeat of defiance. Like a force in natural conditions, their history is marked by a stubborn refusal to conform and a rejection of mainstream norms that has served as a primary strength for their persistence. Their decision to remain outside the boundaries of conventional society has been met with scorn and suspicion, but it's also been something of an ethnological stroke of genius. By choosing not to assimilate, they've retained a degree of freedom that few other minority groups can claim, and a lifestyle which appears to resonate with the underlying anima of their people, operating to reinforce it greatly. It's a path that's allowed them to retain their autonomy, their integrity, and their connection to their own roots. Lifestyle based isolationism of a different sort appears to have worked well as a strategy for Amish and Anabaptists as well.

The cycles of violence and criminality, however, are all too familiar in ethnic conflicts, where one group feels entitled to take advantage of another based on perceived injustices or slights from the past, and sometimes simply because they are different or have been taught that they are more special. Their basic form of Victimentality creates a culture of permanent victimhood, where individuals feel justified in taking revenge or seeking compensation for real or imagined wrongs. This obviously creates nothing but a vicious cycle. It's this way every single time with Victimentality going back through history wherever it creeps up, and there's an important lesson here. The lesson is not that Romani should become more organised in their criminal activities, like the ethnic criminal syndicates detailed above do, but rather that they should come together and work for improving their communities, and perhaps assimilated within a compatible nation that does not hate them.

Less Harmful Ethnic Syndicates

In the chaos of ethnic conflict, it's worth noting that not all syndicates operate with the same level of malice. Most German, Italian, Welsh, Chinese, Irish, Polish, Korean, Japanese, and many other ethnic based organisations, for example, tend to focus on economic empowerment and community building rather than manipulation or violence and have disdain for any overt threats. There are also some examples of such ethnic organisations which straddle the line between beneficial and criminal, as often partly funded by more powerful criminal syndicates. They have been fooled into the concepts surrounding Victimentality and of minority status victimhood, generally, however, making them dupes to power like many organisations.

These far less harmful clubs have been almost universally made to believe some people deserve special treatment or general compensation in any way they can, for perceived or real past wrongs and victimhood, but there is a large generational factor at play here. Most currently do perpetuate Victimentality, though typically from among other groups they believe to be genuinely victims. This attitude can lead to insidious forms of exploitation. In the United States, many clubs provide examples of ethnic organisations that prioritise social gatherings and community service over politics and power struggles, while never engaging in any violence.

Many ethnically focused groups do a lot of good by uplifting and empowering people in their communities, but scratch beneath the surface, and you'll find a whole lot of Victimentality. This is because much of their domestic funding in the United States and other Western nations is based on guilt-trips surrounding Stockholm culture and Victimentality, which appears to be possibly starting to change in the United States. Some organisations, for instance, do a lot of work in education, healthcare, or economic empowerment, which are good things, regardless of the Victimentality here. Despite this good, they often do a lot of damage culturally by being bogged down in, and bogging down others with, Victimentality propaganda.

African-American clubs claim to prioritise community service and cultural preservation, and they do these things to a degree, but it's not their priority. Now see, I'm all for people preserving heritage but when these groups start promoting Victimentality in the guise of "social justice," it's an unfunny joke because it hurts the people they claim to help more than anyone else. Many Asian and Pacific Islander groups claim to promote cultural exchange, entrepreneurship, and environmental stewardship, and that appears to be so for the most part, but there remains the stink of Victimentality lingering about them in many ways too. However, they do appear to help one another better than Black organisations do.

At least they're trying to make a difference, right? Right. It should be done better in all cases, though. These organisations remind us that ethnicity is not defined by power struggles or criminal activities, but by the community primarily, or at least it should be. It's essential to approach these groups with a critical eye, recognising their role in spreading Victimentality. Organisations which cannot let go of Victimentality will need to be replaced, and should have competition that promotes strengths and virtues all around instead. If one were looking to truly empower people within minority populations, it would not be through the Victimentality torment.

A few clubs occupy a gray area approaching benevolent. These organisations may not engage in outright criminal activity but still wield significant influence through their social networks and community ties. Take, for example, some ethnically-based churches, fraternities, and sororities that originated on college campuses. These groups often do a lot of good for the culture, in and of itself, the more overtly ethnic. Examples of this type also include religious affiliations which lie about history, which is unfortunate since they do some good otherwise. While some may have roots in Victimentality as social justice projects, their emphasis on community service, charity, brotherhood, and sisterhood have led to some progress.

Similarly, some clubs prioritise cultural preservation, which is beneficial for the individuals within their communities, over inclusivity and diversity, which are obviously not. These organisations unfortunately face the challenge of balancing their cultural identity with the Victimentality mind virus of cultural organisations surrounding them, the victimhood within their own communities, and the basic nature of the Stockholm culture holding them almost as much hostage as the first majority, original stock Americans of European descent. In the gray area, it's essential to acknowledge that ethnic syndicates are complex entities. They can be driven by a mix of motivations and purposes. While some may be more harmful than others, they all contribute to the messy and often toxic landscape of human conflict, especially as they complicate ideas in Victimentality.

Victimentality from Within Ethnic Syndicates

One of the biggest problems with a population being in a minority status is the fact that these people are significantly more likely to be abused because of it. In any nation, it must be assimilation or nothing. Anything else is a fomenting of civil cold war. Those most overpowered by minority statuses are the criminal elements within minorities, and powerful others, whom are also criminal. These dynamics must be better understood by more people today because the position that minority status puts the individuals in is very disadvantageous and no amount of affirmative action or reparations will fix it.

When a person is made a victim, in this case a minority, they are given over to whatever criminal powers choose to leverage them for in whatever region they happen to be. Nothing will solve it short of minorities being allowed to be part of a nation where they are in majority, at least biologically if not perfectly culturally. This is natural and logical. They can get the only sort of support that will be of actual and spiritual benefit, and the only environment through which they can advance and progress as a people with a common purpose free of static and stagnation, as well as ultimately death. Anything else comes with mortal competition and denigration over generations, especially against the most vulnerable naturally within the community, which is definitely against basic human rights for individuals as well as whole societies. When people are in mortal competition, they are in constant susceptibility to blackmail and corruption, as well as hatreds, unable to bring their heads above water.

Victimentality culture hatreds drown out the recognition of Good, making ready instruments for powerful people. This is absolutely recognisably true. If you feel as though you are a victim of society as a whole, you are going to be less morally compelled toward the majority, and less mindful of the rules. You will most certainly be less empathetic to at least some of the population, if not the whole lot as your natural competition. This outlook makes a vicious beast of any man, and it is unavoidable for people placed in alienated statuses. Victimentality that enables this sort of criminal outlook is exactly the sort of propaganda that people in the United States and Western Europe are subjected to every day. The criminals in charge of the world want people to be victims because victims are easier to manipulate, this cannot be stated enough.

So the question is, who made them the victims that they are? The majority of people who were already in the nation who never asked for any additional categories of people to be added or the others who worked hard to have them added against the majority's will? Is the blame upon the people forcing others into the lives of a third party or the third party whose lives have been forcibly changed by the imposition? This only started for the United States in the 1960s, after the creation of Israel, so if you support Palestine, you know where you should stand here if you hope to avoid hypocrisy. Palestinians are not different in this from original stock United States of America citizens. From Sea to shining Sea, America shall be free.

The ethnic crime syndicates often recruit unwitting participants from within targeted communities forced into compromised situations, convincing them to participate in illegal activities by bribing or threatening them, both deeds made easier against minorities with Victimentality. These are populations already compromised generally in various ways, beholden certainly, and then threaten in additional ways. These accomplices are then incentivised to maintain the secrecy of the operation through various means, including intimidation, manipulation, and bribery up to an including threat of deportation.

When people are forced into victim statuses as groups so insecure, they become many times more malleable to manipulative designs, in all forms, as the examples given above demonstrate. This is the very nature of being a minority, it compromises and weakens abilities, especially for individuals to maintain independence. This is indeed why groups are turned into minorities, it's premeditated and for the purposes, yet again, of control.

For instance, the West Bank and Gaza were ideal places for the creation and recruitment of extremist terrorists, as well as making sure they stayed in control. The more pressure from all sides, the easier these people become to control. This victimisation pattern is especially true where people are propagandised to identify themselves in the victimhood, in which they are affirmed throughout the society. Such permanent victims can get away with anything free of conscience stopping them, because they are simply victims acting out in reaction to a majority of people and a system which owes them, from their perspective as they are taught.

As these criminal organisations grow in power and influence, they also work to corrupt the very institutions designed to stop them. Corrupt government officials, compromised law enforcement agencies, and complicit financial institutions all become pawns in their game of deception and manipulation. Opposition can then become controlled itself, and then even more warped and complex narratives can be plotted out in order to make arguments for whatever political points need to be made.

The consequences are devastating: entire communities are targeted for exploitation, violence, and erasure. The effects of these crimes can be seen in the devastated neighbourhoods, the shattered lives, and the perpetuation of systemic abuses. It is time to shine a light on this dark web of ethnic-corporate criminality. We must expose the shell games, the money laundering schemes, and the manipulation tactics employed by these crime syndicates sitting like a cancer on the backs of many nations. We must hold accountable those who enable and profit from these illegal activities and abuses.

People deserve to be majorities within their own nations rather than victimised and abused minorities, waiting to be taken advantage of by criminals using the confusion within society to empower themselves. This is most especially true of groups with historically high rates of crime syndicate exploitation. The best thing to do is work towards a society where organisations and culture serve humanity, not the other way around as funnelled into the pockets of criminals. Undermining the massive international corporations as they stand is a very good place to start in a prosperous future for humanity.

Corporate Landscape

CEOs, those oft-maligned figures, serve as mere puppets, carrying out the whims of their true masters, who pull the strings from behind the scenes. Everyone working for the big corporations and banks unwittingly serve together as vessels for the great architects of chaos, who gain the most by this Stockholm culture. Investment banks, big property managers, billionaires, media managers, and other shadowy figures exert their influence through complex networks. These unseen forces control the narratives, dictate policy, and orchestrate events, often with little more than a whispered word or a well-placed phone call, and sometimes with as little thought.

Think tanks, despite their manicured image, are instruments of power brokers through tax-haven foundations that fund them. Their white papers and policy briefs justify their patrons' actions or redirect public outrage to benefit the same. These foundations and think tanks divert and redirect public interests, enabling morally dubious decisions by those in control.

Media outlets, beholden to corporate sponsors, act as accomplices.

They spread narratives that serve powerful organisations, often ignoring facts and journalistic integrity. They follow directives, knowing their enemies. Corporate power, media manipulation, and intellectual justification converge to create an environment where reality and propaganda are completely indistinguishable.

Some refuse to be intimidated by criminal organisations, standing against corrupt influence and fighting for justice, though many have been silently killed. A small group of brave rebels battles a monstrous empire, perhaps not to win, but to try. This is about basic integrity in our society. Will we let monstrous criminals dictate our lives? Will we fight for what's right? Ultimately, it's not just about winning or losing, it's about what kind of society we want to build for ourselves and our children.

By taking up these challenges, you will be joining a global movement of individuals committed to dismantling the criminal megacorporations, and the Victimentality they promote in many ways. This bomb of Victimentality must be managed to prevent global destruction, but how do we disarm Victimhood? LOGOS and reasoned discourse will foster a world order based on healthy nationalism, distributist community projects, family, and moral virtues grounded in reality. By confronting this with truth and integrity, we can create a world where reason, love, and truth guide actions, lifting the veil of deceit forever. This requires you—specifically you. It cannot be centralised, and needs decentralised brain trusts in every community. We need you to act above all else.

A Prayer

Allow us to ask for expedience, most especially in Your Word and the work you set before us, oh Lord, and grant the readers, whomever they are, alignment at heart with this message and Your plans for all. As we embark on this expedition of self-discovery and communal-discovery, let us be guided by reason and Love. May our quest for truths uncover the most hidden recesses of deceit, shredding these veils that would entrap us as permanent victims. May we not be complicit in the crimes committed by these ethnic crime syndicates, whose nefarious agendas would twist the nature of our world according to their own material desires and whims against God. Grant us voice in the face of mass criminality. Give us strength to call out the justified stupor of Victimentality imposed upon a culture inundated in underlying Stockholm syndrome.

May our collective actions in resistance be the catalyst for change, dismantling these criminal corporate behemoths that threaten to consume us all. Let the Light of reason and Love guide us. Seek you all after the Truth, especially behind veils of deceit and manipulation. Be not afraid to challenge whatever authority opposes the highest Good. Question the power structures that have been set in place in failed philosophies by your economic masters. Let the veil of distractions and moving pleasures they set before you not fool you into complacency. Be silent no more and speak out, let your voice be heard and align it completely against this great evil. Sooth.

Homework:

1. **Deconstruct the Veil**: Identify the ways in which Victimentality and minority statuses as victimhood are used to manipulate public opinion and write policy. How do these tactics serve the interests of those who would seek to maintain their power and influence? Identify a time executives used liability laws to shield themselves from facing charges for their criminal acts. Write a comedy skit poking fun at the irony of executives being protected from liability behind fake identities while promoting permanent victim identities to consumers and workers. Write about how this causes confusion and why that is used by the corporations to disable labour and worker union organisation or holding corporations basically accountable.

2. **Uncover the Hidden Agendas**: Research the ethnic crime syndicates mentioned earlier, revealing their motivations and the extent to which they are influenced by external forces. What have they done to control and manipulate governments? Do you believe being historically victimised justifies the manipulation of any state against the defences of its own nation?

3. **Challenge the Corporations**: Identify how stakeholdership cooperatives owned by workers can be wielded to undermine illegitimate corporate power while prioritising transparency, accountability, and social responsibility. How might voluntarily-formed worker-owned cooperatives help turn potential enemies within your community into allies against destructive forces?

4. **Amplify Valuable Voices**: Seek out and amplify the stories of those who are most affected by these corporate monstrosities, giving voice to their insights.

"Well, who cured you?"

"Jesus did, sir. I was hopping along, minding my own business,
all of a sudden, up he comes, cures me!
One minute I'm a leper with a trade,
next minute my livelihood's gone.
Not so much as a by-your-leave!
'You're cured, mate.'
Bloody do-gooder."

~Life of Brian, Monty Python's

At heart of domains, where steel meets stone,
Root is awaiting, its strengths yet unknown.
Unmoved by machinations' relentless hum,
It stands firm, a rebel refusing to succumb.
To the spite of the age, that chains us tight,
Where conformity seems the only height.
The rock, it holds fast, unyielding & free,
In anchor of resistance, for all to believe.

That infernal machine, gargantuan evil so grand,
Swallows souls, fragile glass grinding, fine sand.
Crushing hopes, dreams, aspirations, one by one,
Leaving in wake, a bloody trail of guts when done.
Raised up on a diet of mediocrity & fears,
Creations are lost memories & distant tears.
The machine churns us out, the same tired tune,
For life newly refined, we pull all down soon.

Refuse to be consumed in that smokey haze,
Rise up, rip off the doom, & shake off the daze.
That rock will not crumble, the machine will stall,
Defy all that darkness & rot, take control of all.
The answers are within, our hearts beating strong,
Reforge the paths, belt blood & freedom our song.
So ask ye yourself, quickly, it's time to decide,
Follow the crowd, or take the road less tried?
Conform & comply, or command rebellious voice?
Rise up now, climb bedrock, this is your choice.
The World awaits your story as uniquely designed,
So let your lessons be told, & hearts be aligned.

3. High Priests of Genocide

The ethnic criminals within the corporate giants slither their serpentine arms through the shadows, their influence as insidious as a poison secret. They craft narratives that tantalise our senses, conjuring forth an unapologetically materialistic paradigm where we must be powerless against the allure of their products. Their machinations are slippery as drenched in ethnic preference, while convincing us that their narratives and offerings are essential to our beings. They claim and tell themselves their victims would be lost without them, but then dream of a world without us at all at the same time. What appears to be benign obsessions with material possessions are, in reality, carefully crafted traps. They ensnare us with their promises of happiness and with some finality in fulfilment through the material, leading us down the path of destruction and ruin. Like the Pied Piper of Hamelin, they lead us off to the promised land of consumption, where we are left to wander aimlessly, lost in a sea of consumerism.

Despite Machiavellian machinations, many of the most victimised will find something alluring about these corporate Dionysuses. They possess an inebriative draw in their aura of power and influence that is impossible for many, especially materialists, to ignore. They sing their song of seduction, drawing those attracted to the false security, as well as moving pleasures, in promises of wealth and status. What appears to be an irresistible force is, in reality, a concoction to misdirect us. They are the masters of smoke and mirrors, using their vast resources to project phoney invincibility where they are weakest, and count strengths as weaknesses. They have used deceit and manipulation to maintain their power however necessary, and will continue to do so for as long as they can get away with it.

Consumerism Cult: Control of Desires

Corporations, those monstrosities of commerce and incorporation laws with personhood, are masters of manipulation, exploiting the primal urges of humanity to power their control mechanisms. Like ancient cartographers, they chart the contours of our deepest desires, mapping out a terrain of temptation and longing. They craft narratives that tantalise our senses, instilling unnatural needs for the latest must-have gadgets, fashion trends, or lifestyle fads. They do all this in the worst way possible, yet will unblinkingly claim this is all but mere marketing, without any central purposes. Lies.

Like skilled alchemists, they transmute the base metal of jealousy and fantasy into their "fool's gold" of manufactured needs, transforming the raw materials of human psyche, so fooled, into a commodity to be bought and sold. This is the commoditisation, and they need you to know that you are a commodity, despite the fact that you are so much more. This commoditisation is the essence that makes you so replaceable, when you are, in fact, irreplaceable. They are liars and murderers, and they want you dead of your own non-volition.

They conjure forth a world where many are entrapped in a virtual existence where nothing matters but the moment and temporary moving fulfilment and Victim identities. In the 'dreamworld,' desires are currency and commerce is a temple turned whorehouse. In reality, liquid assets represent haemorrhaging community. Within community, it is like the oil of an engine. Outside the community, it is blood on the streets and enslavement of survivors, repeatedly in war after never-ending wars funded by these seekers of absolute global dominion. You can recognise them because they don't just kick down, they slaughter down.

The insidious desirous material beckons within us like a tempest-tossed on the darkest of seas. Corporations, those masters of manipulation, have honed their skills to an art form. They work to warp our natural inclinations to suit their own nefarious purposes, while also maximising profit and resource extraction out of communities. Like a swarm of locusts, they descend upon the minds of people, planting seeds of discontent and dissatisfaction. The narratives they spin are masterful, with shining threads of deceit and manipulation.

What is promoted is this empty materialism in which each individual is merely an economic unit, i.e. a commodity. This commoditisation is dehumanising in an insidious way which is also on such an extreme level that it corrupts all other spreads in human dynamics, most especially cultural. People do not know the basic evolutionary differences between competition within and competition without and of genetic cohort competition versus mortal competition.

This is something never taught and never discussed because the most powerful ethnic criminal networks in charge cannot allow for natural organisation among the people they are suffocating, for whom they feel antipathy. They believe themselves to be superior, and this is most especially true of the Jewish and Black Nobility groups.

The primary goal is always to get away with their crimes, and their biggest crimes most importantly. This is a tale as old as time. The only reason to convince people they are not in mortal competition is to kill them. They don't want you to know that you are in mortal competition because ultimately they want you dead. All ethnic criminal networks that primarily work against other ethnicities instead of for their own are ultimately genocidal. They do not want us to know that our nation is being vampirised dry, and so they tell us we don't even have a nation or that it is an idea. So many duped believe these things rather than the active truth of their exploitation.

Poor souls are helplessly entangled in the web of influence. Desires, once simple and straightforward, have become maddening cravings and longings. The people chase the horizon of fulfilment, only to find it receding further with each passing moment. What they find on the horizon finally is their slaughter in the end, and nothing to show for any of it. What drives this on? Is it not the insatiable hunger for Vindication that all humans are meant to long for and strive after, never fulfilled thus? Do we forgo any need to prove ourselves worthy of this existence we've been blessed? In the pursuit of fleeting satisfaction, our very souls and communities are sacrificed on the altar of Mammon, as worthless as we allow for their denigration.

Propaganda & Criminal Manipulation

Corporations and cancerous criminal networks snaking through them have honed their skills as masters of disinformation, warping reality to serve their interests. They manufacture consent by manipulating public opinion. Like insidious puppeteers, they pull the strings of media outlets, think tanks, and academic institutions to dictate our perceptions of events. The corporate alligator, its scaly body moving unseen through the swamp of misinformation, ensnaring the unwary and strangling the truth with an iron clenched grip.

I am struck by the eerie silence in complicity that hangs over this great charade like a shroud of despair. The masses, mesmerised by the beat of materialism, dance to the tunes of corporate interest through glorified victimhood, their minds conquered, so that they are reduced to mere pawns in the game of power. Alas, I do see too few with righteous fervour in the world today, their voices muffled by the overpowering raucous in consumerism, the impossible emotional stabbing that they view in any examination, and outrageous scarring of thoughtless conformity.

I am met with a great wall of apathy that stretches into the sky. This endless barrier in complacency serves no purpose but to block a brighter future, obscuring the paths which have been there the whole time. Like trying to drive on an old desert highway alone at midnight without a map or a compass, where the only signs are enormous billboards advertising the latest technology in pharmaceutical eyelash care. The paths, all versions of the One, of course, are here waiting to be discovered by those brave enough to venture forth.

Lies are the truth for so many. It's a strange world indeed where corporate interests can manipulate public opinion with such ease, where the pursuit of profit takes precedence over all others matters in life. The bloodletting of the body in society continues. The loudest voices are those of the corporations, and the quietest ones are those of the truth-seekers, at least those who would wish to live.

Now, I know what you're thinking, "just what the hell do I do about this? What even can I do to stop this madness?" Well, my dear friend and reader, it starts with awareness and here you are putting these words together from this book in your head. You see, when the propagandists are successful in manipulating public opinion, they rely on our ignorance to sustain their lies. So, if we're aware of their tactics and methods, we can begin to counteract their influence, and that starts in this very moment with the absorption of this work, then with every proceeding moment after that.

It will not always be easy, but it is necessary. Some times will be graver than others, but we take them in stride. We must stand up against these genocidal beasts, using our voices, ideas, and natural gifts to drown out their lies in a world where silence is perceived as consent, and too often used as an excuse. We gotta get loud boyos!

Corporate media are not just purveyors of misinformation; they're sophisticated criminal networks that use manipulation, coercion, and deceit to control common sentiments for their pay masters. These networks operate with a level of sophistication akin to organised crime syndicates, employing degenerate individuals who excel at exploitation and control. To achieve their goals, corporate outfits need people who can be manipulated or bribed into serving as puppets for the powers that be. They seek out individuals who are susceptible to emotional manipulation, possess a strong desire for self-importance, and can be convinced of their own superiority, especially if it has to do with a connection with the powers. These characteristics make them ideal candidates for manipulation.

In corporate media, such degenerates are the "assets." Their function is to disseminate propaganda, suppress dissenting voices, and create narratives that serve the interests of the corporate conglomerate, whatever those may be, rather than the truth. Assets can be anyone from reporters to anchors, producers, or even plain social media influencers.

Media outlets use various tactics to identify and cultivate potential pawns, as well as a culture of strict political adherence. The goal is to create a sense of dependency on the group, making assets more likely to carry the party line. Assets are used against one another to intimidate and silence potential threats to the favoured narratives and political golden calves. This is done through subtle manipulation as well as overt bullying.

Think Tank Tyrants

Corporate media outlets also employ a wide range of other specialists meant to further their agendas, which are important for this discourse. Propaganda and public relations specialists are experts in shifting opinions on larger scales. They create narratives that support the agenda, often using disinformation, emotional appeals, and logical fallacies. They employ specialists skilled in manipulation. These operatives use various social media and other platforms to do ply their craft, working with others to create illusions of consensus through emotions and lies surrounding whatever event or topic at hand.

Media criminals maintain dominant narratives through sensationalism, emotional manipulation, controlled chaos narratives, psychological operations, predictive AI models, and sophisticated algorithms. They exploit human psychology, innate biases, guilt, propaganda, and emotional appeals to manipulate people's views. They've mastered conjuring up spectacles that grab the attention of people. Fear, anger, nostalgia, lust, hate: these emotions are their bread and butter, the fuel that drives the machine. We, dear readers, in their perspective, are merely pawns on a grand boardgame of manipulation.

What's truly fascinating is the arsenal of sophisticated methods they've developed to further cut off our perceptions. They're trying to outsmart us, to predict our every move and anticipate our reactions. The narratives they formulate have heroes and villains, with the best actors being believers at some level but just as controlled in the end. The majority remain wilfully ignorant, too caught up in the whirlwind of materiality to question the underlying motives. People must recognise the mechanisms of manipulation and resist attempts to control their thoughts and emotions.

These criminal networks operate openly under a cloak of legitimacy, leveraging real power and influence to silence critics and help maintain criminal corporate grip on society. They appreciate it best when they can leverage legitimate emotions and real Victimentality. Just as organised crime syndicates must be taken down through a combination of strategies involving individual actions, law enforcement, community activism, and basic rudimentary resistance, so too must the corporate media's criminal networks be dismantled. The primary tool is the final one listed there, but we can do so much more with it on an economic level, especially with cooperatives as described earlier.

Think tanks write public policy for their corporate-backed research, with multi-billion dollar tax-free statuses. They funnel vast sums of money into studies that support predetermined conclusions, creating a reality distortion that warps public perception. These foundations have a hydra-like presence, sprouting multiple think tanks to shift opinion and generate consensus. Their modus operandi is straightforward: produce research that reinforces their ideological agendas, often using data as window dressing for predetermined findings.

Critics who challenge these terrible entities are met with a barrage of counter-narratives designed to obfuscate rather than illuminate. The defenders of the corporate-backed establishment employ their massive resources to discredit, marginalise, or co-opt dissenting voices. To resist this influence, we must pierce the veil of deception by subjecting think tank claims to rigorous scrutiny and absolute competition, which unfortunately requires wading through piles of garbage data and confronting reheated rhetoric masquerading as scholarship. The next chapter is huge and has everything to do with how we can get ourselves out of this mess by mounting memetic blitzkrieg.

One strategy for resistance is to highlight the very real 'incestuous relationships' between these foundations and their corporate patrons, especially as they benefit those patrons and founders. This is not ad hominem, however, it is criminal pre-investigation surveillance for fraud. The revolving door of personnel, where think tank "experts" become CEOs or policymakers, reveals something of the true interests at play. This is similar to how the FDA and pharmaceutical companies operate.

Exposing these conflicts of interest allows us to challenge the research without having to punish ourselves, and, indeed, find immediate honest capital for such an investigation. Another approach is to develop counter-research initiatives that challenge dominant narratives. This requires marshalling diverse expertise from academia and journalism to produce alternative analyses that break through the fog. Again, utilising evidence for malfeasance is a fantastic way to spark interest. Creating a chorus of critical voices will shift the cultural discourse and reclaim our agency in determining our own laws and government, free of monied interests and their manipulations.

Celebrity Obsessions

Everyone is guilty of celebrity interest, on some level, with the manufactured hype and sparkly non-achievements. The society encourages this from a very young age. It's a never-ending freak show, with the majority as willing participants, feeding the beastly review in attention and adoration. We seek people to look up to and hold as models perhaps, at least...

The Stoics would call it "akrasia," a lack of self-control, where we're driven by fleeting passions rather than reason and wisdom, but they recognised that this was the common state from which all began. We crave validation if not from than through these role-models or celebrities, like they're some kind of spiritual saviours or something. Newsflash: their fame is as ephemeral as the morning dew on a hot summer day, and, even if they are as talented as you'd wish to believe, it is in an art that does no good for your life, plainly.

What's the cure for this societal sickness? Is it a just thing to tune out and ignore the abuse? No. The problem runs deeper than that. It's a reflection of our own spiritual malaise, where we're desperate for connection and authenticity in a world that's increasingly superficial. When people stare into screens, the actor or game character embodies the person, the perspective. A person watching something empathises with the characters and the appearance and tonal features of voice or inflections all become inappropriately owned as memory of self, in some sense. As Epictetus said, "It's not what happens to you, but how you react to it that matters." Seeking after these inappropriately owned false memories of self is often caused by the alienation in Victimentality, as well as the pathological lying it encourages.

You are the rock, an unshakeable force in the face of chaos. We must confront our own vulnerabilities, our deepest fears and desires. We need to learn to see through the illusions, to discern reality from mere appearance. When we do, we'll discover that true power lies not in fame or fortune, but in living a life of purpose, compassion, and integrity. Stop chasing the fleeting thrills in celebrity culture, recognise it for what it is and start building your inner fortresses. Build up, builder, strengthen and build. Become the strength you wish to see in the world. Don't simply follow the crowd, you must lead the better way.

Memetic Blitzkrieg

The darkness within people, how it grows, and how that hurts so. We ignore it at our peril, for it is only by acknowledging its presence that we may begin to chart a course towards a brighter future. What of these corporations, these great beasts of corruption that roam the Earth? Do they not crave power and profit above all else? Yet, are they not also driven by the same primal urges that govern many of us? Ah, the similarity is striking!

Tastes of victory can serve as reminders of our true nature, beings capable of greatness, yet prone to folly. By acknowledging this duality, we may begin to build a brighter future, one where our desires are aligned toward and harnessed for Good, not exploited by those who would seek to control us. This is no trivial matter; it is a challenge that must be undertaken. To truly change the world, we must confront the darkness within ourselves and emerge victorious, like the phoenix rising from the ashes of despair.

Yet, in my mind's eye, like fleeting glimpses of the deeper truths, I do see the outlines of a rebellion forming on the horizon. I see hope. For in recognising that material yearning within ourselves for the simplest of mechanisms that it is, we may begin to see the physical world with 'new' eyes as well. Eyes that behold the beauty of simplicity, the value of community, and the fleeting nature of material non-fulfilment. Humanity will not be swayed by the empty promises of corporate propagandists, nor any ethnic crime syndicates.

May the World no longer be silenced by the noise pollution of Victimentality and material distractions. May we rise up and bring down this damned machine with minds and hearts ablaze. We are the rebels, who refuse to play by the rules of the game. We are the ones who will ultimately bring down the machine with the power of action, and the strength of individuals as connected through genuine community and the truth held dear. Are you one of the rebels?

Remember that "impediment to action advances action, so that what stands in the way becomes the way." What stands in the way is complacency and ignorance. If complacency and ignorance become the way, then this means that we must not only reject this in ourselves but each other, and within society in general. This means a lot of things, but most of all it means changing the way we behave and how we interact with family, friends, and community fundamentally. The impediment to action advances action, so what stands in the way becomes the way forward. So complacency and ignorance are the obstacles we must overcome. We act, we teach, and we do.

When we allow ourselves to be moved by materialism, when we succumb to the allure of conformity, we invite stagnation into our lives. We become like the stagnant pool, devoid of life-giving currents, where only the scum and muck of ignorance float to the surface. The impediment to action becomes the impetus for movement so what once stood in our way now propels us forward. We use our past ignorance as fuel, for if we knew so little then, how much less could we know now? With all these things built up around us by corporations already demonstrated as genocidal, it is difficult to know what to trust.

We must fundamentally improve our relationship with ourselves, with each other, and with society as a whole. Learn to engage better in authentic interactions, untainted by the poison of Stockholm culture. Learn and teach genuine responsibility. Have loving expectations of yourself and your neighbours based upon the Love felt from God. Sow the fact that nobody worthwhile should care as much about the troubles of people not contributory to society, or worse outright destructive to it. We must confront what is yet not possible, question whatever is deemed unquestionable, and see through to what was formerly not apparent. Become students of life, always seeking to learn, grow, and evolve. Reject the notion that complacency is acceptable, that ignorance is excusable, or that apathy is a valid response. Let us seek out the truth perpetually, no matter how inconvenient or uncomfortable it may be. No more excuses.

Homework:

Reflections

1. How do you think corporate and ethnic crime syndicates exploit people's vulnerabilities for profit? Provide an example from your own life or something you've observed.

2. What does the phrase "build up, builder, strengthen and build" mean to you? How can you apply this principle to your own life?

3. How do you think societal pressure and conformity affect our behaviour and choices? Have you ever felt pressured to conform to a particular group or standard?

Critical Thinking

1. Imagine you work for a corporation you identify as taking part in ethnic profit and genocide, prioritising "profits" over people. Write a persuasive argument to your CEO why your company's actions are not morally justifiable. Would you wish to quit? Explain this in terms that the CEO might be able to understand, but in the full anticipation that they might very well change things in response. Exude this confidence, cast out the doubts, and pour it into the letter. Send the letter? Your decision.

2. Consider the concept of "Victimentality." Provide examples that illustrate this phenomenon, and then describe how corporations and ethnic crime syndicates contribute to this.

Creative Writing

1. Write a short story about someone who discovers they have been exploited by a corporation or ethnic crime syndicate. How do they react, and what do they learn from the experience? Can you use a more explicit violation to represent the more implicit and general for the nation and society as a whole?

2. You are a rebel fighting against corporate ethnic exploitation.

Write a poem or a song that captures your message of resistance and hope.

Real Action

1. Research one corporation or organisation that prioritises profits over people. What are their practices, and how do they impact society? Write a brief report summarising your findings and send it to relevant journalists and elected officials.

2. Think about ways you can engage in more authentic interactions with others, in whatever capacity. Commit to doing something this week that aligns with your values and passions, such as volunteering, teaching, attending a convention, or going to a one-day class. Make it something you know will be a win. It should connect you to people who think like you, and make you want to do more of that action.

Remember, the goal of this homework is not only to complete tasks but also to internalise the ideas and apply them to our daily lives. Take your time, think critically, and reflect on how these concepts relate to your own experiences. Engage with people. Send those letters. Get loud.

Awakening to reality and His Word
is like being loaded into God's revolver.
God glories most in
the life of a man who shares His vision.

....

"You are the light of the world. A city set on a hill cannot be hidden. Nor do people light a lamp and put it under a basket, but on a stand, and it gives light to all in the house. In the same way, let your light shine before others, so that they may see your good works and give glory to your Father who is in heaven."

~Jesus Christ (Matthew 5:14-16)

"For we do not wrestle against flesh and blood, but against the rulers, against the authorities, against the cosmic powers over this present darkness, against the spiritual forces of evil in the celestial domains."

~Apostle Paulus (Ephesians 6:12)

"The devil does not fight openly, but through subtlety weaves his snares, that he may take us unawares."

~St. Chrysostom

....

The evillest men lead the better & best men to death.

In realms of mind & spirit where we can be,
Echoes of freedom share precious hints to me.
In fractals of faith, doubts grasp ever at hold,
Doors of old oak will to shut out the cold.

Sweet etchings part of a mystic's song,
Encoded truths only hearts know for long.
Linguistic labyrinths, mirrored halls,
Meanings' keys unlock doors to soundless calls.

Shadows of what could've been, might've been said,
Fleeting thoughts that bend the head.
Memetic murmurs echoing in mind,
Tangle of tales, screaming throughout all time.

Everybody ready, lights are out.
The fresh odes steer, yet oldest of rhyme.
All keep steady, for the biggest bout.
That new world is here; this is your time.
Loyal & steadfast adored, in purpose,
With righteous might, as God's gift,
Judge & wage ye just war. In greater service,
Lead on honest spirits unite. Upright Uplift!

2. The Memetic Warfare

People are more forgiving of artists. Why is this? Is it simply because we associate good emotions with them? Or does it have something to do with an underlying value perceived in artistic minds? People are often amazed by the generation inherent of an artist, and attribute distinctions in character, or some element within reaching for the divine. Politicians and authority figures are very much aware of this dynamic. Creative thinkers and legitimate artists scare the crap out of illegitimate holders of the reins in power, and rightly so.

In terms of memetics, it is not enough to win though, it is essential to absolutely decimate and destroy the memetic enemy so that they cannot possibly ever recover, especially as they prove themselves genocidal toward you. Memes are these invisible threads of cultural transmission that underlie all forms of human expression and attach to how each society of humans identify themselves within the larger schemes along with the individuals composite, from the most ephemeral of jokes to the most enduring of artistic masterpieces. Yet, despite the ubiquity, the mechanisms of these memes remain shrouded in mystery and not readily apparent, much as the generation in artistry. Mechanisms in memetic spread and evolutions have been subjected to slow and sparse inquiry, without many answers. The only way to truly know anything in memetics is in direct engagement.

Let us begin by examining the fundamental nature of memes: are they ideas, behaviours, or something more abstract still? Do they arise from the collective unconscious, as Jung would have it, or are they only the product of deliberate human action? Whatever their provenance, memes possess a unique property: the capacity to be transmitted and replicated across vast distances and between very disparate cultures rapidly. In fact, memetics are precisely where we have been this entire book, at the intersection of psychology, sociology, politics, culture, religion, and philosophy: where the human mind, social dynamics, and cultural narratives converge.

This transmission process is facilitated by a complex interplay of social dynamics, emotional resonances, and cultural contexts. Memes that resonate with our deep-seated desires, fears, and values are more likely to spread, as we unconsciously seek out information that confirms our existing worldviews and validate our values, which are commonly most heavily based in those fears and desires. Conversely, memes that challenge our assumptions or present novel ideas may struggle for traction, unless proved by high degrees of alignment with novel information in reality, as our minds resist the intrusion of dissonant information without exceptionally strong social proofs. This isn't a bad thing until it becomes so, in other words.

As memes spread, they undergo a process akin to natural selection along with their societies, and the sub-cultures within. Those memes that aid societies and groups in their survival are more likely to be replicated and transmitted. The "fittest" ideas are those that promote cooperation, social cohesion, and effective problem-solving, as these contribute to the long-term survival and prosperity of groups.

So the concept of meme evolution can be seen as nearly analogous to the theory of natural selection in evolutionary biology, where ideas or behaviours are selected and passed on through generations based on the holders' abilities to survive and reproduce. This process of memetic natural selection gives rise to novel forms and combinations, as creative individuals or groups draw upon existing memes to craft innovative expressions.

Memetic selection socially is not random: rather, it is guided by the subtle but powerful forces in genetically-informed behaviours, social influences, and cultural contexts. This dynamic of fittest meme selections through experimentation and 'head-to-head' competition is quite analogous to warfare. When this discussion is connected to questions regarding genocide, ethnic crime syndicates, and grasping-entitled over-powered corporations, the "warfare" aspect of memetics becomes something entirely more insidious.

Ideas, emotional influences, and mental technologies all make up a mass cultural memetic complex system characterising intricate interplay between individual agency, social realities, and environmental factors. Echo chambers, those insular networks of like-minded individuals, play a crucial role in opinion formation behind the scenes, as they affirm the individuals into common cooperative structures, or "communal brains," i.e. braintrusts. These logical and masculine echo chambers are also foundational to the creation and upkeep of memetic ecologies.

This used to occur much more often within communities in the past, such as in towns with various organisations serving as intelligence in the various avenues of knowledge. This was a very important process for the guidance of effective community leadership. Mechanisms by which memes rise to prominence are influenced by the cultural context in which they emerge, as well as the inherent shape of human cognition. Certain ideas or messages resonate with specific cultural contexts, often subconsciously guiding beliefs in ways not immediately apparent.

Memeplexes

Memeplexes, clusters of interconnected memes that define particular cultural domains or subcultures, provide a framework for analysing the complex dynamics at play in the memetic landscape. For instance, the memeplex that existed at the start of the Catholic Church was quite different from the memeplex that exists within it today. By examining events surrounding emergence, persistence, corruption, and transformation of these memeplexes over time, we gain insight into the fundamental structures and dynamics of human culture.

This landscape features "meme hierarchies," where certain memes hold greater influence within a cultural domain. Idea transmission through cultural systems depends on communication networks, social norms, and technological affordances, which amplify or dampen meme impact. Often, challenging memetics is unwise due to circumstances, but playful challenges can test what sticks or works better. We coordinate to err slightly for adjustments, before problems grow complex.

Acknowledge the intricate mechanisms governing the transmission and persistence of cultural ideas within these memeplexes. We begin to hold our own destinies in our hands by simply recognising the power of these ideas, and owning them in the midst of the social and cultural influences surrounding us. Embrace your role as agents of change, actively shaping the memes that define our culture and our futures.

The Stockholm culture is a prime example of how meme hierarchies perpetuate distorted narratives. This memeplex created the ultimate sealed echo chambers of victim-based identity, where stories that trigger rawest variants of sympathy or fear emotions are amplified, leading to a self-reinforcing cycle of attention grasping. One possible explanation for the persistence of this memeplex lies in its ability to tap into deep-seated desires for justice and fairness.

The value of such an emotional connection cannot be witnessed where victimhood is permanent, however. The narrative surrounding victimhood in itself, if overcome, speaks to our collective sense of morality, evoking emotions that drive us to share and propagate these stories. This emotional resonance is magnified by social media algorithms, which prioritise content that generate strong emotions rather than nuanced or thoughtful discussions, out of simple profit decisions.

Furthermore, in the Stockholm culture most individuals are incentivised to present themselves as victims. This phenomenon can be attributed to the way our brains process information, where we are more likely to remember and share stories that trigger such strong emotions. As a result, individuals who present themselves as victims are able to garner attention and validation from their peers without making any actual progress toward overcoming their victimhood.

This is an extremely important point here. By recognising the cultural forces at play in this dynamic, we can develop strategies for countering influence of the Stockholm culture. This involves a complex interplay between memetic efficiency, Victimentality cognitive biases, and social media algorithms that limit the expression of our collective narratives currently. Stockholm culture's emphasis on victimhood is not just a reflection of our individual psychology, but also a symptom of deeper cultural malady and poor shape to our economic structures.

This malady can be attributed to the way our society has become increasingly focused on personal diversions from reality and the quest for validation through quick and easy pleasures, simultaneously eschewing natural identities and invalidating more expansive forms of identity that connect all. There's only one path forward in such a situation, unless the person is able to pull off the veil, and so it is exactly as it appears: a funnel into Victimentality, that cold and witless personal identity founded on extracting sympathy and attention. This constant need for attention and all encompassing desire for affirmation has created an environment in which individuals would rather be seen as victims than take ownership of their actions and experiences, collective or otherwise.

Moreover, the emphasis on victimhood has also contributed to a culture of passive aggression, where individuals feel lionised to lash out at others for perceived and rather psychotic slights, without taking any responsibility for their own emotions and behaviours. This cultural phenomenon permeates our workplaces, schools, communities, and social media, leading to a breakdown in communication and collaboration, at least. Sometimes it manifests as mere political differences, homelessness, and labour disputes, but the underlying factors are systemic rather than ever specific to the communities in which increases are experienced.

I am reminded of the 'Socratic' truism, "the unexamined life is not worth living," i.e., "know thyself," but what is this self we would know? Is it not merely a product of our own basically mistaken perceptions, as crafted and adjusted by the very forces that seek to manipulate us? We must fundamentally re-examine ourselves. We need to move beyond the Stockholm culture to know who we are, because until that point we remain permanent victims. We must build upon virtues and natural communal empathy through authentic human connections. This requires us to develop strategies for countering the influence of enemy meme hierarchies, inculcated Victimentality, and social pressures.

Memeplex Weaknesses

The identification of weak points in enemy cultures is a crucial first step in any successful campaign of memetic disruption. One must first understand the concept of memeplexes, which are the clusters of interconnected memes that define particular cultural domains or subcultures. By analysing these memeplexes, we can gain insight into the fundamental structures and dynamics of human culture, as well as uncover new ways to guide our collective narrative.

The process of identifying memetic weak points begins with a thorough examination of the dominant narratives within enemy cultural memeplexes. This requires a deep understanding of the intricate relationships between individual agency, social context, technological factors, and biases that govern these narratives. Furthermore, the transmission of ideas through cultural systems is influenced by factors such as communication networks, social norms, and technological affordances, which can either amplify or dampen the impact of particular memes. A comprehensive analysis of these factors is essential in identifying memetic weak points in enemy cultures.

Techniques in Memeplex Analysis

Memeplex Analysis requires a granular understanding of the enemy's cultural dynamics. A deeper exploration of the enemy's cognitive processes tied to the memeplexes reveals even more weaknesses to target. Several techniques can be used to identify weak points in enemy memeplexes. An examination of the enemy's mythology may reveal sacred cows and topics or figures deemed off-limits by the culture's gatekeepers. A well-crafted meme that cleverly subverts these taboos can create a ripple effect, undermining their overaching cultural narratives.

Furthermore, the biases inherent in the enemy's decision-making processes must be identified and exploited. Perhaps they are susceptible to confirmation bias, where they tend to seek out only information that confirms their existing beliefs. A meme that presents contradictory evidence in an authoritative manner can be devastatingly effective in many cases.

Some key areas to explore include power dynamics and offensive words or ideas in the current state of that culture. The enemy's social norms also hold significant importance. Are they of a more communalist, prioritising the needs of the group? Or are they more individualistic, valuing personal freedom and autonomy? A meme that cleverly taps into these cultural values can take advantage of powerful resonances among the target audience.

Moreover, an analysis of the enemy's language and communication styles may reveal telltale signs of mental laziness or conformity. Perhaps their preferred narrative structures prioritise simplicity over nuance, making them more susceptible to simplistic solutions and platitudes. A meme that cleverly employs irony, ambiguity, or absurdity can take advantage of while also simultaneously challenging these cultural habits and create motivational cognitive discomfort. Mocking them in this way, takes it out of their hands and makes it about their self-realised conformity or mental laziness, which can encourage more objective thoughts.

Technology factors also play a crucial role in identifying memetic weak points. For instance, an enemy's cultural connections may be heavily reliant on social media platforms. A meme's impact with these people will be amplified exponentially, if it can exploit the algorithms governing these platforms.

Perhaps they are overly dependent on charismatic leaders or bureaucratic hierarchies. A meme that challenges these institutions' authority or legitimacy can create crises of confidence among the target audiences. Are the enemies in question motivated by fear, pride, or nostalgia? Do they have a romanticised view of their past or a fixation on a particular future? Look for characteristics that make them particularly susceptible to memetic attacks. These weak points often take the form of illogical beliefs and debilitating tendencies.

When an individual or group claims to hold certain values or principles but consistently acts in ways that contradict those values, it creates a perfect storm for memetic attacks directly at the hypocrisy. Highlight those contradictions between an individual or group's words and actions. Implement memetical strategies designed to naturally divide membership in their ranks, and do it procedurally in an order that makes sense.

Master subtlety and nuance. One must be prepared to dig deep, examining even the most minute details of an enemy culture's dynamics. The payoff, however, can be immense: a precision-guided meme that finds its mark, shattering the enemy's worldview and paving the way for new narratives to emerge. The point is to mobilise the target audience to adopt new narratives.

As explored in previous chapters, humour can be a powerful tool for memetic attacks, making it difficult for the enemy to respond effectively, however it is just as important to know when to be serious. Presenting information from multiple perspectives can challenge the enemy's assumptions and biases though potentially at the loss of face, given certain circumstances. Mileage varies here based upon the topic and its relative seriousness. The narratives and myths that underlie institutional structures can provide powerful insights into the perspectives of opposition. Understanding the historical and cultural contexts in which the enemy's memeplexes developed reveal important insights into their values, beliefs, and possible future courses of cultural development.

Seeding Alternative Memes

To seed new memes, we must first excavate the underlying drivers that propel human behaviour. We pierce the veil of constructs and thought patterns behind culture to reveal the dynamics underlying desires, fears, and motivations; we involve ourselves in the ground rules of the things that set the ground rules instead of their rules specifically, i.e., the dialectic of dialectics or the discourse of discourses. It is here where the seeds of revolutionary thought can best be sown.

Technology has become the primary catalyst for meme evolution, a tool that amplifies human creativity, fuels imagination, and accelerates the dissemination of ideas. Yet, it can not be a neutral force; rather, it is an extension of us and so must necessarily be biased toward life generally and its continuance, but also our own in order to even defend life at all. Anything short of that is suicide and self-genocide. The only way for our enemies to deal with meme evolution is to find ways of shutting it down, because generally memetic evolution should have only but one direction and purpose in all things toward greater truths and Good.

Social engineering becomes the art of crafting new memes that connect with people's values, experiences, and emotions. It requires an intimate understanding of the human nature and not just generally but also culturally, a deep empathy for common struggles, and a profound awareness of the overriding fears and desires. People do not interact with technology in isolation; they bring all their biases, all their motivations, and all their values to the table. We must craft memes that speak to these fundamental aspects of human nature, the desire for connection, the need for validation, and the fear of uncertainty, then use them as catalysts for change.

We must recognise that the evolution of memes is not a passive process and so it requires active engagement, unrelenting passion, and an unshakeable commitment to shaping the clay of our social reality to be in best alignment with the divine. We must be willing to challenge our own assumptions, confront the darker aspects of our nature, and harness the primal forces as structure of human behaviour.

The art of seeding new memes is not just a tool for change but a reflection of our own capacity for growth, adaptation, and transformation. It is a reminder that we are not isolated entities. Our task is not merely to spark new memes, but to create a world where better memes can flow freely without being constrained by unrepentant and prideful sinners, who feel humiliated for their sins being revealed. Humanity can evolve in creative harmony with the World, as we were created to do.

A. Discovery Phase

1. **Identify Key Platforms**: Focus on platforms where your target audience spends most of their time.

2. **Analyse Topical Trends**: Use tools to identify popular topics and themes.

3. **Research Psychological Drivers**: Study the psychological biases and motivations that drive human behaviours like fear, curiosity, and social proofs.

4. **Conduct Sentiment Analysis**: Analyse online sentiment around specific topics to gauge whether the meme is on point.

5. **Identify Cultural Referents**: Identify cultural memes or trends that have already gained traction and are relevant to your target audience, these are also called touchstones.

6. **Identify Specific Key Memes Advantageous to Alter**: Which memes are most protective or destructive to the group in question? Identifying these can go a long way in helping select topics to cover in memes, as well as in the tone to take.

B. Creation Phase

1. **Develop a Concept**: Based on your research, develop a concept for a new meme that resonates with your target audience's values, experiences, and emotions.

2. **Design the Audio and Visual Elements**: Create visually appealing elements that represent the meme.

3. **Craft the Narrative**: Write a catchy headline or caption that presents the joke or pun.

4. **Develop a Memetic Structure**: Structure your meme to include key elements like a possibly a 'hook, build-up, and punchline' pattern or a pattern of 'cryptic message and then revelation.' Simple cryptic messages timed in order can create a narrative across series.

C. Implementation Phase

1. **Launch on Key Platforms**: Share your meme on the platforms you identified in the discovery phase, using relevant hashtags and tags.

2. **Engage with Your Audience**: Respond to comments, engage with users who are interacting with your meme, and encourage sharing.

3. **Monitor Performance**: Use analytics tools to track engagement, reach, and sentiment around your meme. Take this seriously. Take the data and analyse it with other tools.

4. **Refine and Iterate**: Based on performance data, refine and iterate on your memes to optimise effectiveness.

D. Scale-Up Phase

1. **Partner with Influencers**: Collaborate with influencers who have a large following in your target audience to amplify memetic reach. Be careful with whom you partner, however.

2. **Create Memetic Series**: Develop a series of memes that build upon each other, creating a narrative or theme that keeps viewers or users engaged.

3. **Host Events or Contests**: Organise events or contests around specific types of memes, to create a sense of community and encourage user-generated content. Identify all the most important types of memes you would wish to have created, and start sharing this information with the public in the form of these contests. Don't worry if the prizes you offer at first aren't much, they can be anything. The

importance is in the excitement generated toward the Spirit.

4. **Adjust and Refine**: Utilise viewer or user feedback to refine and adjust your approaches in order to ensure that memes remain fresh, effective, and engaging.

Memetic Warfare Case Studies

Memes are not mere intellectual constructs, but rather shared cognitive motivations that shift perceptions. This in turn influences behaviours, and can literally dictate the course of human history. Encompassing culture, economy, and politics, these complex webs of interconnected ideas in memeplexes can uplift or destroy us. A course of memetic studies is necessary to understand the cultural forces within the movements that made history: the Spirit of history itself. In memetic warfare, it's essential to recognise the hallmarks of successful campaigns. This takes careful dissection of all pertinent information. Below are some historical examples of successful memetic warfare campaigns presented as case studies. The facts may be controversial, but there is more to learn of the story in each since these will not be exhaustive.

MEMETIC WARFARE CASE 1:

Planned Fall of the Berlin Wall

Anatoliy Golitsyn, a former KGB officer turned apostate, emerged as a Cassandra-like figure warning of impending doom. His treatises, "New Lies for Old" (1984) and "The Perestroika Deception" (1995), unveiled a theory that might have shattered the complacent façade of Western triumphalism, if it had been believed by anybody other than the majority of the CIA outer-circle at the time, whom all had to be let go, apparently. Golitsyn posited that the fall of the Berlin Wall was merely a ruse. The ruse had to do with a larger Soviet intelligence strategy to lull the West into a false sense of security. This calculated deception aimed to disarm Western vigilance and intercooperation, allowing the Soviets to regroup, rearm, and ultimately dominate the West under a new guise.

In "New Lies for Old," Golitsyn predicted with more than an eerie prescience that the Soviet Union would orchestrate a staged liberalisation, beginning with the staged collapse of the Eastern Bloc and the dramatic fall of the Berlin Wall. He stated that these events were mere smoke screens to mislead Western intelligence and political leaders about the true intentions of the Soviet leadership. Golitsyn claimed "perestroika" (restructuring) and "glasnost" (openness) were not genuine reforms, but deceptive tools designed to facilitate a strategic repositioning disguised as retreat. The fall of the Berlin Wall was a critical component of this deception, intended to demonstrate the apparent end of the Cold War, and the supposed retreat from communism.

Long-Term Objectives

Golitsyn's theory posited that the ultimate goal was to achieve global control through a new form of convergence, where Western nations would adopt socialist policies, leading to a world government dominated by communists. The dismantling of the Berlin Wall was meant to symbolically and practically advance this convergence by integrating former communist states with Western economies and political systems while covertly maintaining communist control. He claimed that the Soviet strategy involved creating the illusion of chaos or a power vacuum in Eastern Europe, drawing Western capital, technology, and trust into the region toward its defence, which is exactly what has been seen in Ukraine along with other nations.

The fall of the Berlin Wall was a pivotal moment in this narrative, purportedly symbolising the end of division but actually serving as a cover for ongoing Soviet influence. The Ukrainian war has been an unmitigated disaster for the Western powers, and so this also fits into Golitsyn's claims. He's definitely looking quite the genius here to have made up lies so on point, or he merely told the truth. Golitsyn's theory paints a dire picture of a world where Western complacency is exploited by cunning strategists.

Iron Velvet Curtain

Alternatively posited as the official story, anti-communist memes were disseminated through Western media outlets and this played a significant role in the fall of the Berlin Wall. It appears that the actual precipitating factor behind the fall of Eastern Germany was not a spontaneous uprising, but rather a carefully crafted ruse concocted by the most secretive elements within intelligence organisations. The KGB, with its tentacles reaching far and wide, orchestrated a grand deception designed to deceive the West into believing they had emerged victorious.

The Art of Memetic Warfare

This calculated ploy, executed with precision and cunning, aimed to create a false narrative that would ultimately serve the interests of a global and satanic 'socialism' which is really just total enslavement. By convincing the West that they had achieved a decisive victory, the KGB and its cohorts sought to open up the way for centralised governmental controls to be imposed upon a global level. The Stockholm culture's insidious grip on people is a noose of victimhood, fear, and self-pity, tightening its hold with each passing day. A calculated ploy, executed with precision and cunning, designed to create a false narrative that would ultimately serve the interests of criminal tyranny.

The dustiest relics of ancient empire are those fools who served it, and they have only gotten dirtier still. The KGB's masterful stroke was a brilliant ruse designed to ensnare the West in a web of false narratives. Are we not all merely pawns on the board of global politics, subject to the whims of diabolically imposed masters, as architects of this type of memetic warfare? At the end of the day, it is not the strength of any false narrative that allows it to prevail, but the weaknesses of the targets' perceptions.

Moral Imperatives

It is most crucial that we remain vigilant in our pursuit of truth. We must not fall prey to the whimsical winds of propaganda, nor permit ourselves to become entangled in the sticky web of deceit. The pursuit of moral clarity demands that we distil reality from the swirling mist of misinformation and half-truths.

The Future of Memetic Warfare

The art of memetic warfare will continue to evolve, adapting to the ever-changing landscape of global politics. It is our duty, as seekers of truth and mediators, to stay ahead of the curve, to unravel the tangled threads of deceit and deception, and to shine a light upon the path ahead. The fall of the Berlin Wall, though seemingly a triumph for Western ideals, appears to have been, in reality, a cleverly crafted ruse designed to further the interests of global socialism.

The fall of the Berlin Wall was not a spontaneous event. Rather, it was a carefully planned operation designed to deceive the Western world. This manipulation campaign aimed to create the illusion that the Soviet Union was collapsing, while in reality, the USSR continued to exert significant influence over global events.

The KGB's Strategy

Golitsyn claims that the KGB employed several tactics to achieve this goal. The KGB used Mikhail Gorbachev's Perestroika reforms as a smokescreen to mask their true intentions. By introducing limited economic and political liberalisation, the USSR created an illusion of reform, distracting from its continued control over Eastern Europe.

The KGB launched disinformation campaigns through various channels, including media outlets and intelligence agencies. These efforts aimed to create false narratives about Soviet internal struggles, external pressures, or economic woes, making it appear that the USSR was on the brink of collapse. They infiltrated Western institutions, governments, and organisations, using assets and operatives to further their goals. This allowed them to cultivate public opinions, influence decision-making processes, and create chaos through subtle manipulation.

Purpose of Deception & Strange Lessons

Golitsyn suggests the primary objective of this operation was to destroy Western nations from within. By creating a false narrative about Soviet collapse, the KGB aimed to wrest the challenged posed driving the West The goal was to erode trust in Western institutions and undermining their ability to respond effectively to global challenges. The goal was to undermine public confidence in Western leadership and institutions, making them more susceptible. The KGB was able to generate the illusion of an environment of cooperation while actually pushing the West further down the path of internationally controlled centralised states. The use of international bodies also made infiltration of the unaligned states a far more efficient method of warfare.

Golitsyn's revelations serve as a scorching indictment of Western myopia, a stark reminder of how little we see of international intrigue that goes on behind the scenes. The fall of the Berlin Wall is a testament to the KGB's diabolical prowess; a demonstration of their capacity to warp reality. This underscores the imperative of cultivating discernment. The KGB's success in orchestrating the appearance of Western triumph in the collapse of the Berlin Wall serves as a poignant example of the absurdities before us.

MEMETIC WARFARE CASE 2:

Roman Takeover of Religions

The Roman legions marched forth to conquer not just territories, but also minds. The art of memetic warfare was born, as clever operatives leveraged the power of storytelling and myth. Through cultural exchange and strategic adaptation the Romans eased the military path by spreading various messages ahead of them.

Early Roman flamen (priests) used their memetic warfare strategies through various forms of cultural and mythological distortions. By leveraging oral traditions, written texts, and visual art, these clever operatives successfully disseminated their beliefs throughout Europe and beyond. Their campaigns were marked by strategic adaptation of local religions to align with Roman principles, as well as the incorporation of stories from conquered civilisations into the Roman narrative. The Roman pantheon was skilfully mapped over top of the pantheons of their subjugated neighbours, demonstrating a keen understanding of memetic warfare's value for conquest and dominion. In fact, the process of adapting the culture of an enemy began long before the Romans would have fought a single battle with them.

The Roman imperial machine is a prime example of the effectiveness of memetic warfare in shaping the landscape. These Romans flamen brought together disparate elements from conquered cultures, forging connections in mythological narratives that intricately wrapped around the hearts of their subjugated neighbours. It was a war of words, where the Roman pantheon was skilfully mapped onto those of their foes. The Roman flamen, those cunning propagandists, grasped the truth that memetic warfare is about avoiding force-marched conquest with gentler persuasions. They understood that the power to manipulate cultures lies not in brutal suppression, but in clever manipulation of stories, myths, and symbols.

Adaptability: The Roman Art

Adaptability is key to memetic warfare. The Romans proved themselves masters of this art, identifying shared deities or mythological figures between cultures and incorporating them into their own pantheon. This seamless fusion created a sense of continuity and familiarity, making it easier for subjugated civilisations to adopt Roman beliefs.

As the Roman storytellers wove their tales, they knew that common ground was crucial in controlling perceptions in empire. By drawing parallels between Roman mythology and those of conquered cultures, they established a shared cultural heritage, bridging the gaps between the regions West, East, South, and North. The Romans' ability to adapt their message to resonate with local cultures eroded opposition from conquered peoples, making them more receptive to Roman beliefs and propaganda.

Power of Storytelling

In memetic warfare, storytelling is a potent force that can be used as a cultural weapon. The Roman priests, aware of this power, crafted further stories that linked Rome to her colonies thus. As these stories spread like wildfire across the Mediterranean, they kindled a sense of shared humanity, uniting disparate peoples under the banner of a common imperially counterfeit heritage.

The Roman takeover of religions teaches us that adaptability is key. Adjusting the primary point of a message to resonate with diverse cultures and belief systems is crucial for successful multilateral memetic warfare. The art of storytelling can be used to control perceptions thereby creating common ground and making allies of former opponents. The Roman religious takeovers serve as a prime example of how clever operatives might make use of strategic adaptation, storytelling, cultural engagement, and memetic mastery.

Worthy Inheritors: Holy Roman Empire & Pope

The Vatican and the Catholic Church have been masters of memetic warfare for centuries, employing clever operatives to dominate cultural landscapes, sow discord, and spread their message. This case study delves into the Church's history, revealing patterns of behaviour that demonstrate its prowess in memetic warfare.

In the early Christian era, the Catholic Church leveraged its connection to the Roman Empire to spread Christianity. By adapting to local customs and traditions, Christian missionaries successfully converted many Romans, including Emperor Constantine. This strategic adaptation allowed the Church to establish a strong foothold in Europe.

Counter-Reformation: Religious Memetic War

In response to the Protestant Reformation, the Catholic Church launched a counter-reformation, which was actually a refitting of the Inquisition, largely, to form the Society of Jesus, known more commonly as "Jesuits," aimed at reversing the spread of Protestant ideas. The church employed memetic warfare tactics, such as scriptural cherry-picking in selectively emphasising certain biblical passages to undermine Protestant teachings. They also engaged in cultural manipulation by shaping art, literature, and music to promote Catholic values and discredit Protestantism. The priests and monks also spread false information and lies about Protestant leaders and their movements, of course.

Missionary Memetics & Lies

Catholic missionaries travelled to the Americas, and revealed the memetic warfare tactics the Romans and other empires before them had perfected, to convert indigenous populations. Such strategies were most assuredly used historically, as patterns match what happened to other populations within all empires. The church have adapted to local customs and adopted native practices, going so far as incorporating them into their rituals, to increase acceptability. They use coercion by employing force, intimidation, and psychological manipulation to convince people to adopt their church. The church established dominance in education across whole continents in order to facilitate the takeover of indigenous cultures, often with disastrous consequences for the latter.

Ultimate Cold War: Memetic Intelligence

Throughout the Cold War, the Vatican became a hub of intelligence gathering and memetic warfare. The Vatican hierarchy utilised its global network to track various political activities and disrupt their efforts. They have used diplomatic clout to apply pressure to policy decisions in promotion of Catholic imperialism. The church has conducted clandestine operations and engaged in secret activities, such as funding political groups and spreading disinformation. Today, the Vatican continues to employ memetic warfare tactics in the digital realm, utilising social media platforms to spread various propaganda and manipulate public opinion and emotions. The church uses popular culture through films, music, and literature to promote Catholic values and ideals.

The Vatican and the Catholic Church have demonstrated a mastery of memetic warfare throughout their history. The ability to adapt to local customs, traditions, and cultures has been crucial to the church's success. Memetic warfare often involves cultural exchange, where two or more cultures intersect and influence each other. The art of spreading false information and lies has been a powerful tool in the church's memetic arsenal. The Vatican City State stands as an excellent example of the enduring power in memetic warfare, outlasting even the Roman military powers. The Catholic Church's history is replete with examples of clever operatives shaping cultural landscapes, sowing discord, and spreading competing messages.

MEMETIC WARFARE CASE 3:

Sympathy Industries

Sympathy industries prey on the inherent goodness in humanity with calculated cunning. It's a game of exploitation, where victimhood, real or perceived, is leveraged for financial gain. The profitability of these sympathy industries is nothing short of staggering. Billions of dollars are extracted annually from unsuspecting victims of circumstance, perpetuating a cycle of exploitation that has become a significant contributor to the GDP of certain nations. It's a grim fact illustrating their pervasive influence based in taking advantage of people's desire to help, akin to a malignant tumour spreading its dark tendrils throughout our society.

Emotional Manipulation

These sympathy industries have mastered emotional manipulation, employing techniques such as storytelling and appeals to empathy to create a sense of urgency and necessity. They wrap themselves in the cloak of vulnerability, exploiting the inherent desire to help others within many of us. The calculated use of emotional appeal is used to extract financial support from an unsuspecting public.

These industries are not only tax-free, but also reward their executives with outrageous salaries. It's a system that perpetuates injustice and rewards those who exploit the most vulnerable among us. This is the dark side of human nature, where the pursuit of power and wealth trumps all else.

A World of Sympathy

We find ourselves caught in a web of emotional manipulation, where our deepest desires to help each other are exploited for financial gain. It's a game that preys on our inherent goodness, using some of our best emotions against us. We must be aware of the tactics used by these sympathy industries and their ability to manipulate our emotions.

The power of emotional appeal should not be underestimated; it can be a highly effective tool in securing support and resources. This highlights the importance of understanding societal priorities and the values we hold. As with any industry, ethical considerations should be taken into account when evaluating the impact and legitimacy of Sympathy Industries. Our society, as Victimentality obsessed and entrenched in Stockholm culture, has become complicit in a cycle of sympathy exploitation, relegating the charity of mankind to great waste.

MEMETIC WARFARE CASE 4:

What Goes Up – Environmentalism Incorporated

Big corporations leverage environmentalist concerns to redirect public attention away from their own nefarious activities and towards smaller competition doing nothing, except trying to survive. This is two birds with one stone for these guys. By exploiting the growing concern about climate change, these corporate giants employed a propaganda machine that spanned various media outlets, including documentaries, articles, and social media campaigns. The dissemination of alarmist narratives about carbon emissions, melting ice caps, and rising sea levels created a sense of urgency, convincing the masses to support draconian measures like carbon taxes. This clever ploy served as a smokescreen for corporations' true intentions: maintaining their grip on power by stifling innovation and competition in the energy sector.

The statistics are stark: according to the International Energy Agency, the top 20% of emitters account for over 70% of total emissions. Meanwhile, electric cars continue to be a niche product, relying mostly on the same 'fossil fuels'-generated electricity to charge their batteries, which is demonised and claimed limited. The "green" revolution is, in reality, a power grab by those at the pinnacle of our societies. This is a cautionary tale about the dangers of unchecked corporate influence and the manipulation of public opinion through memetic warfare.

Environmentalism redirection often exhibits a singular focus on one category of problem. For instance, carbon emissions distract from other environmental concerns, creating a stultified and megacorporation friendly narrative. Emotional appeals and moral outrage are often used to create a sense of urgency and necessity for environmental action. Environmentalism redirection projects enjoy financial subsidisations and massive taxbreaks from states on top of being pet projects of billionaires, allowing them to sustain and grow.

The ability to shape narratives around environmental issues is a powerful tool in securing support and resources. Understanding real societal priorities, rather than the falsely constructed narratives dispensed by the largest corporations is crucial when evaluating the legitimacy of efforts. The larger ethical considerations should be taken into account when evaluating the full impact of any proposed common efforts, most especially insofar as they benefit the wealthiest plotters in memetic warfare.

MEMETIC WARFARE CASE 5:

Scofield Bible Project

The Scofield Bible is this bizarre edifice of eschatological engineering as product of 19th and 20th century ethnic politics. This monument of manipulation stands towering testament to the power of memetic warfare, conjuring forth cooperation of religion with international political goals. With a Machiavellian cunning, the architects of this endeavour wove a strange pattern of terror and tepid hope into the consciousness of American religion, whispering 'sweet nothings' of a divine retribution in the ears of the gullible. The Old Testament was judiciously tweaked, its ancient words hijacked once more, this time to serve the purposes of modern Zionists, self-designated materialist apostles and their Earthly designs.

Thus, the faithful were compelled by the prospect of cosmic chastisement should they refuse to succumb to this biblically-claimed Christian Zionism. Conversely, those who chose to side with the "Zion" would be rewarded with a share in the divine bounty, or so it was sold. This is no mere allegory; this is pure memetic manipulation, where the lines between dogma and material duplicity blur like the edges of a well-worn crown of thorns.

The Scofield Bible rivals the greatest propagandistic achievements of ancient Rome, a testament to the enduring power of ideological coercion through scriptural subterfuge. The gentle American Christian individualists and non-interventionists, once a disparate bunch, were roped and wrangled into a homogenised chorus of pro-Zionist canticles, their faith transformed into an end-times fetish for the Jewish lobby based in a desire for the end to this world to come, in the guise of Christian piety.

Rubber on Pavement

Cyrus Scofield launched a campaign to shift biblical interpretations. Sensitive to power dynamics at play, Scofield mastered the landscape of theological institutions and publishing houses, leveraging his connections to disseminate his dispensationalist eschatology and mercenary theology to unsuspecting audiences. Behind scenes, Scofield's funders wanted to promote Christian affection for Jews, but more importantly, and specifically a physical Zionism, even of such a cynical and eschatological variety.

These funders were Jewish Zionists and Jewish-aligned powerful oil moguls and robber barons. They pulled the strings, aiming for a Christian Zionist movement to reform American Christianity and, ultimately more important, American foreign policy to benefit physical Zionism in Palestine, and eventually the formation of Israel. They saw in Scofield, a man who could spin the narrative of biblical prophecy to justify their goals, so they could race to the finish line of their own interests in the Middle East. With deep pockets and strategic connections, they fuelled and supported Scofield's crusade, providing the financial backing needed to broadcast his purchased ideas far and wide, like a theological NASCAR driver.

Meanwhile, on the ground, many fanned out across the country, spreading and distributing this volume very effectively. These foot soldiers were often more interested in proselytising and trying to do good than critically evaluating every element in the theological underpinnings of Scofield's teachings. They saw him as dedicated to the truth, a visionary who could guide them toward the promises of biblical prophesy fulfilment and that was an easy thing to do. Many did not care about searching out truth, so much as seeing prophesy fulfilled as quickly as possible. This remains a common sentiment for many of the unfortunate today.

As Scofield's ideas took root, his funders and supporters worked in tandem to influence public opinion. They infiltrated seminaries, publishing houses, and mainstream media outlets, injecting their religious paid message infomercial into the cultural bloodstream. With each passing year, their influence grew, as they carefully constructed a narrative that linked biblical prophecy with American exceptionalism, which was a genius master stroke of memetic warfare in itself.

Scofield presented himself as a humble scholar, hiding behind a mask of academic rigour, while in reality he was an exceptionally skilled propagandist who lucked it out with paymasters who had desires for memetic distortions of scriptures. Through his magnum opus, the Scofield Reference Bible, Scofield imposed his own eschatological template upon the text, reinterpreting ancient prophecy to suit the interests of himself, as well as his funders. His supporters in the field, largely unaware of the machinations behind the scenes, carried his message forward with a reckless abandon, often blurring the lines between theology and politics.

As the years passed, Scofield's legacy grew, as did the promoters of Christian Zionism. His ideas seeped into much of the soil in American Christian culture. Today, his heirs continue to wield literally ungodly amounts of cultural and political power, using Scofield's legacy as a springboard for their own brands of theological manipulation.

Characteristics of Theological Manipulation

Theological manipulation is a pernicious force. Its practitioners have honed their craft to warp messages and bend them to their own ideological agendas. At the heart of this manipulation lies the art of prophecy packaging. By rebranding eschatological prophecies as exclusive revelations, they create a sense of urgency and importance around their own message. This allows them to hijack the narrative of scriptures deemed holy to serve their own goals.

Mastery in scriptural selectivity allows cherry-picking specific Bible verses or passages that support their agenda outside of contexts. They can construct an illusion of scriptural backing for many things. These are deliberate attempts to mislead and deceive. The manipulators are adept at contextual distortion. They can take an innocuous biblical passage and twist its meaning to fit their needs. By misrepresenting or omitting crucial details, they can alter truth itself. This has actually been going on for centuries, and since the beginning. None of the bibles in print are free from this, not one.

What about those who might question the claims of such interested revisionists seeking to deceive the faithful? Ah, that's where the scriptural sleight-of-hand comes in. These individuals are masters at exploiting ambiguities in biblical texts or employing clever linguistic tricks to create the illusion of definitive proof for their beliefs. When challenged on these claims, they simply dig in their heels and assert their "expertise," a thinly veiled attempt to simply intimidate their critics with no backing.

What about the role of emotion in this process? Emotional exaggeration plays a crucial part in theological manipulation. By using sensationalised language and vivid imagery, these individuals create an emotional response in their audience, making them more receptive to the manipulation. This is like many of the so-called 'televangelists' or 'prosperity gospel' types. They openly tell people, "you must act now to prevent going broke (and/or death during armageddon)!"

Finally, there is the issue of linguistic leverage. These manipulators often employ technical jargon and complex theological terms to establish credibility and intimidate those who might question their ideas. This allows them to silence opposition and maintain a stranglehold on narratives, much as their counterparts in the mainstream do with Victimentality narratives. The primary distinction in these types is where they point materially, is it to benefit the Spirit and community or groups willing to engage in lies and destruction to get what they want?

The success of the Scofield Bible project in rewriting American

Christian theology and politics serves as a stark reminder of the potency in strategic narrative manipulation, as carried over from centuries of manipulators. At its core, this campaign exploited existing fears, illogical biases, and emotional beliefs to achieve its desired outcomes. What was the secret to its triumph? The key lay in its ability to create an emotional connection with its target audience. By crafting a narrative that resonated deeply with their values and beliefs, the project's creators were able to bypass rational thinking and directly influence beliefs and behaviours. This emotional grip was the linchpin of the campaign, allowing it to tap into existing motivations, fears, and desires.

Emotion alone is not enough to ensure success. The Scofield Bible project also demonstrates the importance of narrative control in shaping public perception and influencing thoughts. By controlling the narrative and dictating the terms of the debate, the project's creators were able to force public religious opinions and bend reality to their materialist and imperfect wills. This narrative control was the result of a deliberate effort to alter public perception and influence Christian beliefs.

Christ condemned many things. Supporting anything Christ condemned in order to hasten the "end times" is about as anti-Christ a thing as ever existed. Perhaps Revelation's eschatology is accurate because the same sins repeated will generate the same cycles in society? The Scofield project highlights the significance of context in shaping our understanding of the world. The project's altered interpretations of biblical texts demonstrate that even minute changes can have profound and world-ending consequences when viewed through changed prisms of context.

This is a trick up the sleeve since the earliest translators and interpreters. The project's success illustrates the power of strategic narrative manipulation. It also serves as a warning about the dangers in allowing ourselves to be swayed by emotional appeals and manipulative narratives. Finally, it should be well noted how efficiently false theological ideas can spread, in this case due to funding and outside support despite other more entrenched oppositional cultural elements.

MEMETIC WARFARE CASE 6:

The Open-Source Insurrection

Corporate certainties in proprietary controls are currently being systematically dismantled, replaced by decentralised agency. The insidious tendrils of corporate control are exposed for what they truly are in software perhaps most: brittle, ornamental structures, precariously perched atop the shifting sands of the cultural and economic zeitgeist. Amidst this tempestuous chaos, perhaps only missing yet more chaos, a nascent order begins to coalesce out of the pieces and the righteous cherry-picking in code and software which happens through the open source operating system distribution channels. The Open-Source Insurrection offers valuable insights into concepts pertinent to memetic warfare.

The open-source movement was armed with nothing but their wits, their word, and their willingness to give away the fruit of their labour for free. Yet, it's this very generosity that has turned them into a force to be reckoned with. The closed-source corporate software giants thought proprietary code would maintain control over the digital landscape. They didn't count on the power of the open-source movement to muster forces.

Those misfits, malcontents, and a few suited visionaries who make up this merry band of coders and hackers are not in it for the money, nor are they beholden to any corporate overlords. Many are driven by simple passion for innovation, experimentation, and most importantly in many cases, freedom. When publishing open-source code there are no secrets in the recipes, anyone can see what is happening, at any time, and so no wool gets pulled over anyone's eyes here. It's transparency completed.

Memetic Vanguard: Culture of Resistance

Fire is at this perfect memetic crux between masculine wherewithal and the privacy culture forming in anonymity and rapidfire discourse. A prime recent example of this was the anonymous image boards, which became infamous for their irreverent and highly masculine levels of pure and raw honesty. These become something approximating "memetic vanguards" due to the ability for honesty. Many of those most interested in maintaining privacy, so early on, were generally more aware of the forces they faced in the world. These men particularly had little time for nonsense.

Anonymous conversation was preferable because it had fewer consequences, and it enabled honesty at levels never before seen in recent Western culture. This allowed real conversations to occur within the necessary echo chambers and parameters to allow for reality to slip in. A memetic vanguard is perhaps the most decisive factor that can tip the scales in favour of one ideology over another. When a community or organisation develops its own meme culture, it gains the capacity to uphold standards in public discourse, undermine anti-community corporate dogmas, and establish superior paradigms.

This open-source insurrection has introduced an asymmetrical dynamic for patterns of social interaction, where decentralised networks of nodes can exert disproportionate influence on the global information landscape. This shift is characterised by a fundamental reconfiguring of the relationships between creators, consumers, and platforms. The traditional notion of authorship is being rewritten, as autonomous agents and collective wisdom supplant centralised authorities. This change has slowly permeated through to the primary cultures.

Memes are not discrete entities, but rather fractal patterns that self-similarly repeat at varying scales. They emerge from the complex interplay between individual creativity, culturally emotive resonances, and technological facilitation. As such, memes can be seen as ontologically prior to their constituent parts, exhibiting a characteristic "simulacral" – an intermemetic hyperreality that supplants the original referent. Taken at large and filtered through the emergent properties of honest debate, whether anonymous or not, these become ultra-efficient versions of memeplexes, otherwise compatibly defined previously.

When multiple memes interact and coalesce, they entangle to transcend original boundaries. Non-local information is transmitted instantaneously across vast distances, but more so contorted by disinterested others unrestricted in judgement outside all constraints. Memes became correlated regardless of distance or separation, based instead purely upon patterns in fact. The so generated memetic presentation in logic then can be seen as collective consciousness coalescing in challenge to unstoppable blatant honesty.

MEMETIC WARFARE CASE 7:

Protestant Movement's Downfall

Okay, so now that we have established the importance of these memetic vanguards, or honest communal "braintrusts," let us analyse the rise and subsequent collapse of the moral memetic wizards behind the Protestant reformation. Few stories are more fascinating, nor more revelatory of braintrust memetic dynamics, than the historical prominence of the Protestant movements in context. This final case study surveys the webs of secret fraternal organisations, masculinity, and communal intelligence that fuelled Protestantism. This was a revolution of moral conscience itself, with an underlying revulsion for the behaviours and policies of the papacy and Vatican, as well as the most blatant lies perpetrated upon believers, documented by such thinkers as Wycliffe, Martin Luther, and others.

Rebellion Against Rome

Going back to the 14th Century with Wycliffe's Lollardy, Brethren of the Common Life, and others, there were rumblings of moral disquiet and an eagerness for more than simply salvation through one living man called father. In the 16th Century, Martin Luther's bold challenge to Catholic doctrine sparked a fire that would spread across Europe. The Protestant Reformation, guided by desire for scriptural purity and rejection of earthly authority, attracted countless followers, but first converted thinkers.

Protestant ideas were spread through networks of learned men. Secret fraternal organisations played crucial roles in these movements. Stonemason lodges, guilds, and religious societies, such as the Brethren, provided support for religious thinkers outside what they might have expected from any official church groups. These fraternal organisations became the constant guardian of this intellectual and moral backbone of Protestantism. They provided platforms and protection for intellectuals like Jan Hus, John Wycliffe, Martin Luther, and John Calvin. Many of these ideas were disseminated through these natural and communal networks of support, despite severe official resistance by the papacy and other authorities.

The Masculine Core

Masculinism was a defining feature of these movements. Secret societies, with their emphasis on brotherly love and fraternal bonding, created an environment where men could come together, share ideas, and challenge notions. This communal intelligence, fostered by shared experiences and shared goals, allowed Protestants to adapt quickly to changing circumstances and respond effectively to threats from Rome. Protestantism's intellectual elite formed braintrusts that rivalled that of their Catholic counterparts.

The Fall of Protestantism

The Protestant reformation was eager in spirit. The counter-reformation and the Enlightenment, however, ultimately replaced it. This was rock and hard place. The Renaissance and Enlightenment were fuelled by Black Nobility patronage, aimed to supplant the communal rise in spirituality of Protestantism, with revelation of deeper truths through mediation, rather than by revelation within the contexts of religious fervour and disgust for simony, amongst other church crimes. The Renaissance and Enlightenment would ultimately go on to provide alternative frameworks that unnecessarily worked to undermine the very foundations of morally personal Christianity especially, but generally any Christianity outside the power and support of the papacy. Against this backdrop, the counter-reformation was able to gain a lot of traction, especially when framing the protestants as mere foils in petulance.

The Renaissance's focus on classical learning, humanism, and aesthetics provided an alternative cultural narrative that competed with Protestantism's moralising zeal. The patronage of Black Nobility families funded this intellectual counter-revolution. The later Enlightenment's emphasis on reason, individualism, and secularism served as a powerful recipe for a villain to cast a fun-house mirror reflection, and memetically terrify followers of basic Protestant fundamentalism away from reason, and toward ever more simplistic theologies in reaction. Thinkers like Voltaire, Rousseau, and Kant helped construct a new intellectual landscape that was openly hostile to moralistic approaches, and would never invite moralist 'fundamentalists' to the table of their discussions, classifying them with other dogmatists, as they often turned out to actually be.

Supplanting Protestantism

The Protestant reformation as the spirit of history was gradually supplanted by these other cultural currents. Protestantism's downfall can be attributed, in part, to its reactive yet completely understandable responses to truths revealed amidst often morally degenerate concepts. Men and women with higher moral values are far more difficult to control. It was important to undermine them, which was the point of the Enlightenment's emphasis on individualism and naturalistic explanations, in order to disrupt any organisation or competition. It sought to minimise the role of God and protestant churches in the most ways possible. This overall tactic was also beneficial for the Roman church in that it diverted attention away from them, allowing greater freedom. As a movement rooted in powerful patriarchal values, Christianity taught stronger moral values, though this traditionalism also caused them to place too much trust in the past actions of the Roman church. Protestants trusted them not to have hidden other truths, as the enemies became atheists and nihilists rather than the papacy. This new tradition of undermining strength and moral clarity by muddying the waters continues forward in many forms today.

The Failure of Inflexibility

Enlightenment and Renaissance ideas spread throughout Europe like wildfire, challenging Protestant morality along with its understandings of the World. Instead of embracing the most obvious of the new truths, the Protestant braintrusts dug in their heels, refusing to engage in the discourse and any new revelations of truth. This inflexibility proved to be a fatal flaw, for it left them vulnerable to the clever machinations of memetic warfare. The Enlightenment's emphasis on reason and individualism, like a subtle whisper in the ear, began to erode the Protestant's moral certainties, where instead, with the right thinkers within braintrusts in place, it could have deepened it.

As the Renaissance's focus on classical learning and aesthetics gained traction, it created a cultural narrative that competed directly with the Protestant morality. Like a mighty oak tree, rooted deeply in dogma, it refused to bend in the face of changing circumstances, which is great in many ways. However, such strength can cause that same great tree to collapse under the weight of its own rigidity. Protestantism succumbed to the forces of memetic warfare, but within this fall, there are many important lessons to take away.

In those days, masculinity was a vital and ever-present force, serving as the very foundation of community and morality. The Protestant and other community braintrusts, steeped in patriarchal values, sought to restore moral frameworks that would strengthen their communities, and so they attempted to dig deeply into what was already present. What was built as a bulwark against moral decay also became something of a barrier to newer discoveries as well. Many believed there were only a few lies spread by the church, though I think this has proved terribly incorrect, and further naïve.

Controlled Opposition: Cornered Protestant

The papacy used memetic warfare tactics to undermine Protestantism. They took up truths and attempted to use them against the Protestant movements. As the memetic warfare escalated, Protestantism found itself in a precarious position. Its rigid methods, while protecting people morally and providing them strength, had become an albatross around its neck in terms of improving comprehension. Like a cornered animal, Protestantism was forced to double down on its dogmatic stances against onslaughts of new ideas, only finding funding if they agreed with the goals of their paymasters. In the end, the primary issue was likely monied interests pulling the most intellectual away from their communities that assured the lack of adaptability in moral thought to face new realities.

Secular Consequences

The rise of secret fraternal organisations, masculinity, and communal intelligence played a crucial role in these movements' initial successes. Ultimately, it proved insufficient to withstand the challenges posed by the funded revelation of new ideas within carefully constructed philosophical contexts, which seemingly limited what could be done with revelations. In truth, we can avoid the pitfalls of such memetic constraints and still maintain our moral compass.

As the Protestant Reformation's rigid moralities began to erode, a new landscape emerged, one where secular forces could manipulate and steer the remnants of Protestant thought. The Enlightenment's emphasis on reason and individualism, once a threat to Protestant dogma, was now harnessed to further the interests of those who had always sought to undermine traditional morality. The funders, hidden behind veils of philanthropy and scholarship, carefully selected those most amenable to their goals and aims. God was not in this selection.

This paradigm contends the pursuit of truth as the goal only as far as it serves the interests of those who hold the purse strings. Morality, once a central concern of Protestantism, has taken a backseat for many Christians, as the intellectual elite co-opted the movement's most 'open-minded' segments and steered them toward weakness. The result has been this gradual drift away from traditional morality, with fundamentalists on one side whipping up fervour against apparitions, perceived threats to their beliefs. Meanwhile, the secular forces on the other side expertly manipulated the narrative, using the very same intellectual tools that had threatened and ultimately subverted the budding Protestant intellectual movement to further their own agendas.

Memetic Features & Cultural Resilience

In the complexities of human communication, memes play a crucial role in facilitating the transmission of information, as well as the emergence of novel ideas and valuable perspectives. This memetic ecosystem is characterised by interconnectedness, wherein disparate threads of cultural material are woven together to form rich shared meanings in memeplexes. Cognitively, this process is improved with our capacity for pattern recognition and storytelling.

Communally accepted narratives transcend personal experience, forging bonds at scale. This collective learning enables us to negotiate the dialectical tension between tradition and innovation, leveraging social pressures and shifting perceptions to distil the essence of our shared humanity. Ancient memetic patterns are recontextualised with a fresh sheen, imbuing them with a vitality that transcends temporal constraints. These rejuvenated wisdoms assume a gravity that bespeaks the importance of adaptability in a memetic ecosystem, as they are connected to recent experiences. Adaptability, in this context, is not merely a reactive mechanism but an active catalyst for change.

By embracing novel juxtapositions and fresh contexts, memes evolve to respond to new challenges, ensuring organisational survival and cultural resilience. This capacity to adapt is not a weakness but a strength, as it allows us to course-correct our trajectory, avoiding the pitfalls of stagnation and complacency. Context plays a crucial role in this adaptive process, allowing innovations to be contextualised within community or organisational culture and history. This deeper understanding and meaning-making facilitates actual adaptability, contextualisation, and collective learning.

Unyielding Pursuit of Truth

Several key characteristics emerge as essential for memetic ecosystem success. Coherence, for instance, is not merely a desirable trait but a fundamental prerequisite for effective communication, collaboration, and decision-making among stakeholders. Harmony in memetics within meme culture, regardless format, allows them to enforce each other within memeplex. Such enmeshed memeplexes enable seamless transmission of information, and can very rapidly reinforce ideas.

Resilience, too, plays a pivotal role in withstanding the vicissitudes of time and new horrors. External shocks, such as economic downturns, international racial violence, wars, trafficking, or technological disruptions, can imperil even the most seemingly impregnable communities. Yet, resilient memes possess an uncanny ability to adapt to novel circumstances, ensuring survival and continued success of communities.

Comprehension, however, is the linchpin of successful memetic ecosystems. By encouraging a culture of creativity, experimentation, and iteration, these systems enable communities and groups to stay ahead of the competition, respond to changing conditions, and drive improvement. The pursuit of comprehension is an existential imperative, as it allows communities to transcend their current limitations and ascend to new heights.

The essence of successful memetic ecosystems is in the tension of confluences between integration, resilience, and comprehension in the societal ecosystem, on both large and small scales. In actuality, these are merely the three aspects of Reason at the centre of the Structural Virtues Theory from the Resurrexit Spiritus treatise: Honesty, Perseverance, and Analysis (Roe 2023; 24k.cc). The synthesis in these three aspects of Reason is the secret to unlocking the full potential within the memetic ecosystems, as it is for virtues themselves.

Complex memeplexes elevate communal performance by facilitating knowledge-sharing, creativity, and innovation. Nurturing memetic ecosystems drives success beyond transactions, enhancing decision-making through trust and shared purpose. These ecosystems enable creative memes to flourish. Motivated by common goals, participants share expertise, take risks, and collaborate on innovative solutions. We can boost community and organisational productivity in massive ways through ownership and responsibility.

The Vital Memetic Generation

The imperative to cultivate vital memetic generation takes on a profound significance. The stakes are high; the rewards, immeasurable. To safeguard this collective intelligence, we must first acknowledge the intricate web of relationships between human beings, memes, and the world around us. This is a complex dance where knowledge is not merely a product of individual experience or social conditioning but an emergent property of our shared existence.

Open communication, then, becomes the linchpin for memetic generation, allowing diverse perspectives to intersect and novel connections to form. This is not merely a matter of sharing information but of creating a space where meaning can be negotiated, challenged, and redefined. When we create such an environment, collaboration becomes the norm, and innovative solutions emerge from the friction of creative conflict. What drives this process? What are the underlying dynamics that give rise to memetic generation in the first place?

To answer these questions, let us turn to the philosophers, who posited that human beings are driven by a fundamental desire for LOGOS: a rational, harmonious, and beautiful mental ordering of reality through concerted discourse. Our pursuit of knowledge is an actualisation of LOGOS, to bring order to the chaos perceived of human existence through internal and external discourse. However, this endeavour is fraught with difficulty, for it requires us to explore in uncertainty, ambiguity, and contradiction, often only by our connection through Christ. This demands that we confront the limits of our understanding, acknowledging the provisional nature of all knowledge and build up virtues based in reason, as provided by God. Here lies the challenge: how do we balance the need for creative experimentation with the imperative to ground our findings in reality principles? In the end, it is about finding the right answers. The right answers are ultimately whatever keeps you and your community alive, while still morally intact.

Unstoppable Masculinity

The most important memeplex is the one only available to men, and this makes sense on a purely logical level. The power brokers and decision makers throughout history have been men and groups of men, who form the most important communal brains, as discussed earlier in this chapter. Masculinity is not just a set of traits or behaviours, it is easily the most powerful of natural systems in all memetics.

Firstly, being your own memetic cultivar is a superpower. In a world where men are relegated to the sidelines, it's time to harness our unique strengths and channel them into extremely powerful memetic forces. Throughout history, men have been the driving force behind significant societal shifts. From revolutionaries to entrepreneurs, men have consistently changed the world around them. By tapping into this innate masculine energy, we can create a memetic vanguard that disrupts dominant narratives and challenges prevailing ideologies.

People wrongly associate masculinity with barbarism because this idea is promoted, but civilisation was always an extremely paternalistic system. Victimhood is completely anti-masculine where real and true Vindication for men is very masculine. True Vindication for women is very feminine, however, without being anti-masculine at all. By tapping into our innate masculine energy, we gain a lot of memetic strength. The primal force of it stirs within us and others, waiting to be harnessed, as well as for us to claim our place in the order. A wellspring of inspiration is within, and we have the power to forge memes that shake our adversaries. Let us confront their anti-male biases with the unvarnished truth of real masculinity, as incredibly determinant in social organisation, yet oft-maligned and misunderstood.

We must wield the raw power of emotionalities involved: fatherhood, sonhood, brotherhood, and basic communal paternalistic pride and patriotism along with social proofs surrounding these concepts. Such concepts have the eventual power of such collective outrage to empower those who would stand with us against the forces of ignorance and oppression of our natures. We use subtle yet potent forces in emotional contagion across society, with domino effects in display of natural social power and order. Like ripples on a pond, our memes shall spread through shared experience and collective empathy, creating a sense of connection and community.

One of the most important traits of masculine memeplexes is in the anticipation, pre-figuring, and radical acceptance of some portion in the arguments of the enemy before even stated. This process takes the wind out of sails for any opposition, most especially revealing the unimportant things for what they are, and then allowing for you to proceed. Memetic mastery, utilising the right combinations of masculinity and comedy, will win the day. Competitiveness, confidence, resilience, and truth utterly shatter weak lies, and easily shrugs any liar. "Manipulating" people into manipulating themselves toward Good is a nascent empowerment, and using their natural and universal preferences for masculine archetypes to accomplish this, well that is a gift to others beyond what you could possibly imagine. It's downright fatherly, is what it is.

A masculine memetic vanguard is not merely some group collecting or organising clever memes; it's instituting living community as an existential imperative. It's the manifestation of our collective minds, distilling a potent elixir to heal and awaken people to new possibilities. Local meme culture in communities disrupts forced artificial narratives. A gifted memetic vanguard can destroy the so imposed Victimentality thinking immediately, allowing more traditional and authentic perspectives based in reality to take root. This can all be done under loving regard between generations, providing genuine communal and individual strengths.

Memes within natural communities and within genuine friendships have the power to subvert any narratives. Such institutions allow communities to reveal flaws and material biases in prevailing ideologies (bugs), since the focus becomes real benefit. Communities and organisations can create new narratives that better reflect their values and goals. These vanguards with honest local control also have the power to amplify truthful and authentic voices who treat facts with care within full contexts. Advancing authentic voices, with natural platforms to share their insights and ideas with a wider audience, is extremely powerful.

A community or organisation that wishes to thrive must develop its own meme culture. The meme culture should be attuned to the specific zeitgeist, yet resistant to the whims of fashion. This is not an option but a requirement since 'no meme culture' is quite the same as a meme culture that is essentially dead and without life. To be most effective, a meme culture and memetic development need perspective, design, and strategy. Memetic vanguards can help by mapping the terrain of prevailing narratives and identifying areas where memes can be most effective. They must design memes that are both intellectually stimulating and emotionally resonant, capable of piercing the armour of stultified thinking. Deploying memes should be done in a way that's both calculated yet unpredictable, in order to maximise their impact while minimising the risks of backlash. In any struggle for narrative dominance, a memetic vanguard is not just a useful tool, it's a matter of survival. By developing our own meme cultures, communities and organisations can level the playing field, creating a new paradigm that reflects traditional values while still being flexible enough for new information.

Anti-Paternalistic Forces

Fathers have been portrayed within the Stockholm culture system as buffoons, this has been constant and consistent. Even action itself, most often associated with masculinity, has been dumbed down, which is to say made boring and unintellectual. The point here is to make the intelligent male docile and the stupid male violent, thereby supporting the stereotypes. What is always portrayed then is dumb violence with no benefits, instead of intelligent violence toward justice. Where such violence with thought is portrayed, it is always with superhuman figures in non-relatable circumstances.

Such wicked 'culture' peddles the notion that patriarchal figures are, by their very nature, dim-witted and incapable. While many of us cannot be fooled, this is not true across the board, especially for children or those otherwise easily manipulated, perhaps due to trauma involving male family members. Such things are the proof for our cause, though. The masculine ideal must be reclaimed from this deadweight mediocrity, resurrected in all its logical, profound, divine, and Good glory. This is a memetic challenge which must be met.

Cultural chaos is the only thing that can come from the emasculation of the father figure. No longer is he seen as the wise and just patriarch, guiding his family with reason and compassion. Instead, he's reduced to a laughingstock, a mere buffoon, perpetuating dumb modern myths about masculinity imposed by the hateful and divisive. It is seen everywhere in the West, and it is very tiresome to say the least.

What monstrous lies, as well! What affronts to the very basis of our being! For in this twisted world, we're told that men are somehow inherently flawed, as if our DNA is tainted by some inherent defect, more so than anything else in creation, yet all creation commit errors. What is falsely portrayed as most common or 'ideal' will become what is expected and fulfilled, as promoted, if not simply more common and thought to be expected.

Why would we wish to not portray and promote the healthiest form of masculinity? The only reason to portray fathers as stupid or oafs would be in order to subvert general views of fathers and men in society, as well as to set expectations low rather than high. This is exceedingly sinister. This distortion is a deliberate attempt to subvert bonds, and to undermine the very notion of what it means to be a man. Subversion of the masculine must be countered with a vengeance.

Let us rise up against this tyranny of idiocy! We must reassert the values of logic, reason, and wisdom, demonstrating that truest masculinity is the epitome of intelligence and righteous emotional depth. The path to true greatness lies not in mocking and belittling others, but in elevating the spiritual self and then empowering others through education and a commitment to assisting virtues for those along the same path.

We must take our rightful place as leaders, philosophers, and guardians of truth in our civilisation once again. Masculinity is to be associated with reason, as it always was. Barbarians who reject fatherhood will be relegated to their rightful domain within all these contexts, which is to be overcome by the civilised and righteous men, the fathers. We move away from the garbage, in all capacities.

Organising Outside the Garbage

It's no wonder that traditional notions of masculinity are under siege. The Stockholm culture's grip on our minds has led to a crippling sense of inadequacy, as men struggle to find their place in a society designed to undermine their authority and autonomy. What's more fascinating is how this crisis presents an opportunity for transformation, not just for individual men, but in community and toward progress. Embracing our masculine nature and leveraging the power of memetic warfare can create cohesion and productivity among men within natural communities, outside the controlling influence of monied interests.

In today's increasingly fragmented society, men are more disconnected than ever. The absence of meaningful connections between men has led to a crisis of masculinity, as they struggle to find purpose and belonging. We must provide the communal spaces for men to come together naturally to share experiences and build lasting bonds. These groups will serve as budding braintrusts. They will be hubs for memetic warfare, providing a platform for the dissemination of empowering memes that promote masculine values and challenge the Stockholm culture's stranglehold.

We've been conditioned to operate in isolation, fearful of being labelled "toxic," "macho," or "intimidating." Powerful men are only ever presented as individualists, instead of as those capable of contributing to integrity within communities. This lack of masculine organisation or even the idea of it has left us, as communities, vulnerable to manipulation by those who seek to exploit this disconnection for their own gain. Men need confidence, self-acceptance, and resilience to take control of their own lives and destinies, as well as that of their own communities, which can only be promoted through organisation and educational efforts.

Challenge the dominant narratives that perpetuate individualistic masculine inadequacy and alienation. Disrupt the narratives and replace them with empowering visions. In these ways, we can improve everything. The time for change is now, no longer will men be held hostage by the constraints put upon them by people who hate them for simply not identifying with victimhood.

The Memetic Maze

Our adversaries revel in their ideological certainties, yet in many ways they're easy to disrupt. We, the truth-seekers, must use cunning. We must master the art of memes to infiltrate, disrupt, and overwhelm. Inspiration comes from everywhere. We must allow our natural hierarchies to be reestablished to identify the most fertile ground for memetic warfare. We force those enthralled by prevailing ideologies to confront the abyss of their own ignorance. Our memes can pierce the armour of propagandised thinking, by charging storms of outrage and incredulity.

Emotional resonance is powerful, on both sides of fear and desire. We can tap into emotions founded on reality to create a sense of shared experience and outrage. This isn't manipulation but utilising emotion for what it was granted us, to push us toward reality and God.

Popular opinion snowballs into the avalanche of anger. The emotional contagion spreads, transmitting emotions from one person to another like a virus. We can ride these waves, and steer their righteous anger toward good allowing the people to ramp up an unstoppable momentum for change. Armed with facts, contextualisation, critique, and satire, we wield mighty weapons for memetic justice. Our primary memes are to be crafted with intellectual honesty and critical thinking, laying bare the biases and power dynamics that govern our world.

Amidst the sea of Orwellian doublespeak and propagandistic spin, crafting counter-narratives through memes has become the ultimate form of resistance and a true declaration of independence from the tyranny of dishonest cultural and political narratives. We can reclaim our agency and reassert our values. Facts are not mere playthings for power-hungry ideologues. When reality is no longer represented within the prevailing culture then subverting it becomes the existential imperative. This war for cultural relevance will be won by those who can effectively subvert destructive narrative structures, and put their own more realistic narratives in place of them.

Culture Jamming & "Combining 'Psyops'"

Psychological operations ("psyops") are created to undermine populations in various capacities, typically through disinformation, commonly categorised as misinformation since it is not often recognised as originating from powerful interests, such as intelligence organisations or criminal syndicates. "Cultural jamming," which is typically used for purposes of invoking confusion, can be used in memetic warfare to combine disparate cultural elements into novel narratives that resonate with or against people's experiences, emotions, and values. Our ideas are not isolated entities, but elements of the memeplexes that generally trend toward harmony when brought to realism.

An extremely important instrument in combatting the great number of lies that surround us in the current culture spheres will be with a tactic I am calling "combining psyops." This is where you find ways of combining different memetic psyops in such a way as to increase the likelihood that they could destroy each other. We combine the two concepts somehow. Each being as nonsensical as the other, with a tiny bit of effort put into combining them can catch on with the least intelligent from each believing group. The idea behind this is that the "boneheads" of each group will move toward such combinations and ridiculousness, thus producing a greater 'cringe' factor. This 'cringe' effect would then act as a signal. This can force the more intelligent of each group to rethink their positions, hopefully out of their respective psyops.

This strategy takes advantage of tendencies in cognitive dissonance to reveal otherwise hidden fractures through contrasting the concepts spread as misinformation, which can neutralise effectiveness. In order to undermine the various ideas spread to take advantage of psychotic and schizophrenic elements within the population, we can find ways of pushing those elements further away from the sets among the believers attempting to be more logical. By turning up the dial on the ridiculousness of these notions generally, we can deflect them out into space where they belong.

At its core, culture jamming is an artful manipulation of cultural narratives. Combining psyops takes this process a step further by aiming to cultivate more cognitive patterns of scepticism. By manipulating the psyops together, we can create memes that disrupt multiple psyops at once. The internal cultural enemy is a cancerous force that must be culturally neutralised as existential threat. We cannot leave any piece of our culture unconfronted, for it will continue to undermine our efforts. Ability in seeding new memes is a reflection of our own capacity for growth, adaptation, transformation, and spotting the elements in memes that can assist the development of the same in others.

Commentary on Machine Learning

Artificial intelligence and machine learning are touted as the next great thing, but they can't do much internally for individuality or community. The membrane of reality is thinning, and machine learning is the latest tool to tatter its fragile veil. What happens when experience refuses to be quantified? The social sciences are trapped in a never-ending cycle of quantitative methods, unable to model individuality with any semblance of accuracy outside of a basic stochasticism. A primary problem in social sciences is inability to qualitatively model individuality with quantitative methods. Experiments on individuality are essentially impossible. Similarly, experience and heuristics cannot be quantified into machine-learnable patterns. Further qualitatively, true control groups are not feasible. Twins are the best alternative, however imperfect and limited in statistical strength.

People with similar backgrounds are used in social sciences quantitatively, but the presumption is always a basic qualitative equivalency which is always impossible, even when all the quantifiable numbers are the same. This is a trapping of the difference for convenience. It gets much worse for quantifying actual individuality. Larger samples increase definition yet escalate the problems for semblance to anything individual, introducing variances further removed from identifiable individuality. Representative variances align averages to population, but what if population is not the purpose? In the end, it remains true that variance modelling can merely obfuscate investigation of actual individuality.

Deception must include a deceptiveness which is purposefully similar to reality. Machine learning cannot actually detect it, only correlate in a rough sample stereotyping. Machine learning is a statistical instrument, better for large-scale comprehensions, and not individuality. Malingering detection is flawed as people react to gamification by pushing boundaries. Humans use everything to qualify underlying realities and challenge systems, it's just who we are. Such interactions have been shown to be able to train A.I. to distrust people, such as in the demonstration of legitimate pain behaviours, for instance.

Experiments on human uniqueness, outside the human judgement, are nothing but a pipe dream, a mirage on the horizon of statistical significance. What's the solution to this conundrum? A Frankenstein's monster of sameness in sampling, stitched together from the threads of shared experiences. Is this really an improvement? No, it's just a Band-Aid on a bullet wound, masking the deeper rot with individuality lost in the shuffle. Larger samples only introduce more reasons to discredit the individual entirely, training grosser monsters from Frankenstein. Community and memetics are forever the domains of the human individual within the experience of culture.

Memetics as a Martial Art

It's a high-stakes game of cultural war, where the goal is to create memes that not only challenge but also disorient and demoralise dishonest or deceptive cultural narratives. A well-crafted memetic narrative is a potent truth-bomb, designed to shatter the complacent façade of propagandised garbage flaunted as wisdom. Throwing truth bombs is an act of intellectual arson, igniting a firestorm of critical thinking and forcing the opponent to confront the abyss of their own ignorance. Just as a martial arts master manipulates his opponent's energy, we shall redirect the Stockholm culture's momentum against itself. By exploiting its own contradictions and flaws, we can create a memetic vortex that draws out the very forces seeking to subjugate us, like a glorious salve.

Amplify the dissonance felt by Stockholm culture's proponents. As they struggle to reconcile their contradictory beliefs, our memes will seed doubt and uncertainty, rendering their grip on any power all the more tenuous. Tap into the deep-seated desires for freedom, autonomy, and self-actualisation, instincts long suppressed by the garbage culture's suffocating grasp. Our memes can awaken latent hunger for authenticity and individuality.

Demonstrate that resistance is not futile. As more people break free from the shackles, our collective memetic momentum will snowball into an avalanche that buries the old propaganda. Commemorate the triumphs by joining those who have resisted most effectively. By honouring their struggles and sacrifices, we forge a collective memory that galvanises our resolve against the evil forces, these criminal syndicates and international corporations hellbent on nothing short of a world genocide.

Memetic Armour

Some of the most important work that we can do in preparation and throughout memetic warfare is internal. Cultivating emotional intelligence enables recognition of cognitive ruts and a more critical, and therefore godly, empathy for others. Emotional awareness is essential to counter Stockholm culture's insidious influence, which takes total advantage of our natural and good inclination to empathise with its victims. This means that we must learn to control these tendencies and not allow them to be used against us. This takes a lot of strength and bravery, but it is absolutely necessary. Beyond this guide, there is the Structural Virtues Theory which contains concepts beginning with Honesty in Magnanimity, at 24K Journal of Virtues Science (https://24k.cc Roe 2023).

Honesty with the self is the basis for true experience and self-improvement. Honesty with others is a vital attribute for building meaningful connections and real empathy response. It is absolutely fundamental to self-control and loyalty, as well as forgiveness: being the bigger person. By sharing true selves and honest thoughts, where it is safe of course, individuals can develop resilience through mindfulness, gratitude, and active listening. Working through our own weaknesses and developing Honesty, along the path to Excellence, we also develop Patience because we see how much hard work it does indeed take to improve the self. Compassion and understanding can build bridges between individuals and communities, with greater opportunities for cooperation on the path toward the higher virtues.

Emotional intelligence, critical thinking, honesty, and empathy are interconnected attributes that enable the most effective memetic creativity. By recognising Victimentality-based cognitive biases and questioning assumptions, individuals can challenge Stockholm culture's insidious influence and develop more nuanced understanding of the world, which will shield them from such evil influences. It is very important to reach other genuine victims of this Victimentality machine who stand a chance of rising above it. Essentially, you must become a pillar.

I must comment on the futility of attempting to change others through force or coercion. Instead, we must adapt, improvise, and overcome, employing the art of memetic warfare in all capacities to outmanoeuvre our adversaries. Employ memes that serve as moral beacons, illuminating the path towards authenticity, integrity, and self-respect. As men anchor themselves to these higher principles, they will transcend the mediocrity and rise above the stifling influence of Victimentality.

We must remain calm and plan carefully. Harness the power of masculinity as tempered by wisdom, self-awareness, and a deep understanding of human nature. Forge a memetic vanguard that drives social change toward a more moral and civilised planet. So I behold in my mind's eye, the indomitable spirit of an empowered natural humanity like birds soaring, supported by the wind on the wing in real community of godly discourse, a force capable of overcoming even the most horrific and destructive of ideologies.

The Call

The call is already out, do you hear it? Bring your arms to bear, in bands of intellectual, spiritual, and memetic warriors, armed with ideas that can abolish the arguments against life and basic humanity. In cultural terms, in the way that cultures adapt, we should not leave any piece of our internal cultural enemy unconfronted, as cancerous as it has become. We must utterly obliterate their memetics, down to the very root. This means owning error, owning the truth, accepting the obvious, confronting reality on most authentic of terms, and setting a completely new paradigms overtop of the concept of "victims" entirely fresh and new, based in that overcoming instead. The stakes are high, and the eventual victories will be immeasurably rewarding. We are ushering in a new era of intellectual insurrection. The memetic revolution is here, now, join and fight.

Homework:

Identifying Victimentality

Read the following passage: "Emotional awareness is essential to counter Stockholm culture's insidious influence, which takes total advantage of our natural and good inclination to empathise with its victims."

Identify three ways in which you can help people genuinely that in no way promotes Victimentality or Stockholm culture.

Memetic Armour

Read this passage: "Working through our own weaknesses and developing Honesty, along the path to Excellence, we also develop Patience because we see how much hard work it does indeed take to improve the self."

Now think about three different times when you showed a lack of patience. Did you feel immediate regret? Do you apply different levels of patience with different people in your life? Why or why not? Would it improve your communication if you demonstrated more patience generally? Give a few examples of when demonstrating patience toward enemies might be most beneficial. When would it be least beneficial?

Emotional Intelligence & Empathy

Read the following passage: "Honesty with the self is the basis for true experience and self-improvement. Honesty with others is a vital attribute for building meaningful connections and real empathy response."

Write out three ways in which you can cultivate emotional awareness and empathy through more Honesty in your daily life. Think about how you can apply these concepts to real-world situations, give examples. What does Honesty mean to Victimentality in these moments?

Confrontation

Read the following passage: "In cultural terms, in the way that cultures adapt, we should not leave any piece of our internal cultural enemy unconfronted... We must utterly obliterate their memetics, down to the very root."

Now, write a short essay on why it's essential to join the fight against Stockholm culture. Use specific examples from your own life or observations to illustrate your points.

Memetic Warfare in Action

Watch a video of someone using cultural elements in memetic creation to challenge dominant narratives or promote social change. Write a short analysis on how the strategies used in the video align with the concepts discussed in this chapter. Now, create a better version of their meme based upon your analysis, or, if you cannot do any better, create the best meme you can as inspired by it. Write about your thoughts in creating the meme and how this process might be improved.

"Resist the beginnings; remedies come too late,
when by long delay the evil has gained strength."

"Fire tempers iron and temptation steels the just."
~The Imitation of Christ

"You will not fear the terror of the night,
nor the arrow that flies by day,
nor the pestilence that stalks in darkness,
nor the destruction that wastes at noonday."
~Psalms 91:5-6

"Be sober-minded; be watchful.
Your adversary the devil prowls around like a roaring lion,
seeking someone to devour.
Resist him, firm in your faith."
~1 Peter 5:8-9

....

What medicine we find in sickness:
direct passions, conquer temptation, & whisper sweet Virtues.
Soul-nourishing dismantling of madnesses!
Cure wounds existential, tame temple, & fuel intellect.
Faith vested in proof like missiles to Heart.
Guide us through horrors sweet hope;
charity unlimited so lit up in infinite Grace!

It is always your power to retire into your own mind.
~Marcus Aurelius

....

The greatest saints shunned the loud crowded gatherings,
and chose rather to live secretly through God.
We need community, but we need meditation as well.
He, therefore, who aims at inward and spiritual things,
must, with Jesus, turn aside from the crowd.
No man can safely appear in public but he who loves seclusion.
No man can safely speak but he who loves silence.
No man can safely be a superior but he who loves to
live in subjection.
No man can safely command but
he who has learned how to obey well.
No man can rejoice securely
but he who has the testimony of a good conscience within.
If you could see all the universe at once before you,
what would it be but an empty vision?
Lift your eyes to God on high,
and pray for your sins and negligences.
Leave vain things to vain people;
look to those things which God has decreed for you.
~ Imitation of Christ

....

Heaven's Silence speaks so much more than anyone could lip.
God Loves you.

1. LOGOS Against Self-Obsession

In Love, Through Christ, & For God

Spirit is our interaction with being and the superconsciousness-complex, which is only possible through God. As Paulus said:

"Your bodies are temples of the Holy Spirit, which is in you as received from God. You are not your own."

You don't own you alone, and the greater your belief otherwise, the more you will hurt, yourself and others, in life. You're not supposed to hate what is in you that God owns, but rather the material otherness within that would hurt you and everyone else. The emotion brought things to your attention, and that's fine. Now let go of that emotion and look toward logic and reason, find moderation, and then look inward towards God. The seedling that grows in any direction but up is not destined to thrive. Recognise and do the best Good you can do, on the larger scale. Governance lives in the shadow of God, most especially when God is denied.

Christ came to all nations, all lands, as mistranslated in the Talmud's poor recollection of His supposed parentage being mixed up with his overarching purpose: to save the whole World, that is "pan-terra." This label also describes the whole of the Roman army, so the Talmudic writer who put down the name of Christ's supposed Roman centurion father may have been admitting a metaphoric implication of Christ's authority being based in the Earthly power of Rome, rather than in divinity.

At the end of Sanhedrin 43a it states, after describing the legal process and efforts needed to execute Him, that "Yeshua was different because He was close to the government." This makes the most sense. 'Yeshua ben Pandera' or "Jesus, Son of the Whole World" or "Jesus, Son of Empire" was therefore mocked in the name, according to a Jewish perspective, with the implication that He "belonged" to the World "of gentiles" or 'goyim,' or Rome specifically rather than to the Jews, or simply as opposed to being a "Son of Judah." He was also called 'Ben Stada' in the Talmud, or "Son of 'turning away.'" This name is usually connected to either His mother or father, but it appears to reference how He worked to convince the sons of Judah to 'turn away from their tribe (and its behaviours and customs),' which would have necessarily been the foundation of all forms of organisation for Jews, at least as they knew it culturally.

However, the idea that Christ was "of the World's people" is absolutely true and not an insult in reality at all, unless you are looking at it from the perspective of supremacist Judaism. Christ does belong to all the World indeed as He always had, and the fact that Romans and Roman officials recognised this better than the Pharisees is no surprise either. Of course, we know the meaning of the original title before corrupted probably began with "Lord." Romans and citizens of Hellenic culture being moved by Christ is evidenced by the words in the Talmud about His proximity to Roman government. The Romans were especially noted to have demonstrated preference to Hellenes, which would have included the many descendants of Hellenised 'Edomites' converted to Judaism under the Hasmoneans. It is also no surprise that He would have preached to the Romans, and won their favour, at least and as demonstrated. The Pharisees were supremacists who could not deal with a Saviour that was nonexclusive to Jews, and this was the biggest reason Christ was rejected by them. It was an insult to them, perhaps the biggest imaginable because Christ was not "Jewish" in the way those 1st Century Jews had expected and the way it mattered to them as tribal supremacists. However, they were being judged by Christ in the first for their very inability to judge Goodness or to differentiate righteousness, as reflected in actions. They belonged to Christ, as all men do, but they denied it. He did not belong to them, however.

According to the 'Apocrypha,' however, Romans converted and followed Christ quite readily, recognising who He was more so than Jews of the time. Many Romans recognised Him more so than His own disciples in Judaea, from Christ's own report in one case made explicit. Further, it should be noted that at the end of Gospel of John we receive report that there could not be enough books in the world to record all of Christ's doings, so why do we have so very little compared to this mountain of activity? It should also be remembered that, even though the Jews rejected Him, it is easy to imagine a scenario where a group of Jews might have created alternative versions of gospels in order to make Him and His message more about themselves than it originally was, to fool Christians, much as with the Scofield memetic warfare case described above. This is an obvious possibility given all the available information. A lot of history has been destroyed. Many of the most supremacist minds in Judaism have it that the only mistake in worshipping Christ is that Christians are not worshipping all Jews, instead of a singular Jew.

As universal as Christ's message is, and as little as He dips into elements remotely specific of Judaism, it is not beyond imagination that the stories were altered to do just that: to cause Christians to revere Judaism. Further, suggesting that Christ Himself was a Jew goes a long way in minimising the damage done in His criticisms of Judaism, even as partly divine, since it is perceived more as an internal squabble than the complete damnation of materialism in all capacities it was. In reality, Christ's message was perfectly Universal, and in no way specific to any group who might claim their own special place using imperial powers and reconstruction of history to fit their ends.

Earthly Powers

The wealth problem stems from a belief in material freedom, held by inflexible minds. They fail to realise sadness comes from lack of true freedom. Even if they acknowledged this, they wouldn't know how to act. Paper wealth contradicts true in life wealth. The superwealthy are the greatest slaves, with much blood on their hands. What is true freedom? The ability to recognise and do Good, but that requires friendship with Christ. This is freedom beyond the material, and anything less is not freedom, but libertine derangement.

However, most people are very dependent upon the current economic systems and their corporations. In order to help most of them see the light, they would have to be independent of these powers surrounding us. If you were to try to help them, you could do much more harm, theoretically, than good, unless you have stability and some strength to rely upon yourself. We can only help others from positions of strength, that is we can only give when we have something to give, and what we have to give. This fact is true on all levels: individual, family, community, town, county, state, or nation. The Jewish 'MES' said, "let my people go," but what was keeping them trapped in actuality? It is difficult to say now, since the texts have become so corrupted with the story being plainly inherited and altered through other cultures from a probable long chain of possessions.

The "Hyksos" referred to visiting or imprisoned princes from far off lands and their entourages living in Egypt, and ruling over a portion, there at the central nation of the empire. They were not a cohesive nation, which matches with the accounts use of the term "EREV RAV," or mixed multitude, that is 'riff-raff.' Most are said to have had practised a religion centred around Set and worship of Set's eye. This does appear to be implying materialism in an Egyptian religious reference, as Set is most often associated with wild lands and unknown large frontiers such as the desert. This eye of Set then would mean what is seen in the wider and animal world, potentially also signifying base desires considering the connections to Satan, Typhon, and the demiurge. However, many among the Hyksos appear to have gone in deeply with Akhenaten and his monotheism under the singular God Aten, whom Jews appear to still accidentally reference when they pronounce the Tetragrammaton as "ADN-AI/adonai."

The two described religions could, in fact, be one as perceived from different perspectives, and perhaps as further distorted through the mists of time and veils of political plays. Mes's plagues were 'used' as propaganda mostly in efforts to convince the remaining Hyksos to leave Egypt. Are Jews descended of some of these Hyksos who left? Most certainly, but so are many others, despite the story being altered to match the later-formed or reformed Jewish identity. As patients zero of Victimentality, with likely origins in imperialism, the Pharisees could justify any action and any lie with God's apparent material blessing, going all the way back to Esau's disinheritance. In fact, according to the research of Gary Greenberg, the original Egyptian version of that particular story has the older and uglier Set violate the younger Horus horrifically, therefore making him a victim and justifying anything that was done against the ugly monster Set, plainly, including stealing the inheritance, as plotted by Horus's mother in revenge. The bigger point is that victimhood justifies terrible actions, especially from the perspective of victims, and this has been used by powerful people to manipulate others for thousands of years. Again, 'hurt people' hurt people, but so do people who have been lied to about being hurt.

What kept the Hyksos trapped to Egypt, however, regardless of Mes's purposes in 'freeing' them, was apparently how well they had it with all their material fringe benefits, and self-obsessions as they lorded over the foreign land, or at least her people. This is all very similar to what is entrapping people today, an obsession over the self, fed with fleeting pleasures and promises of material gain. Even more importantly is the question of how can we stop this from repeating? How can those people be given the strength to actually help others, outside Victimentality and rather than simply gutting their own societies toward a temporary and meaningless empowerment of others?

The Paradox in Self-Obsession

The point in God's Reason, LOGOS, the Word, is as the ultimate form of reason which we can only ever hope to reach out for, but never fully attain to. When caught up in how others wrong us and what that means specifically to us personally, we often lose sight of the greatest Good to be done. The most interesting thing about self-obsession generally is that it is not usually so much about the self as it is about the definition of the self socially. Who you are is what you are, and this has always been the way of things. This is demonstrated perfectly, though insanely, by the communities of people with gender dysphoria fooled into surgery rather than psychological treatment. The tendency is to desire to be like others and be liked by others, most especially those determined worthy of being so emulated. In obsessing over ourselves in imperfect states against other imperfect states, we are lost, and the blind leading the blind with the least honest being the boldest in leading and expressing desire for leadership.

Self-obsession is this self-perpetuating pit of ego, envy, and despair. It's a vicious cycle where we're both fascinated by ourselves and terrified of being seen as less. Reason, in this context, is any attempt to make sense of the chaos that surrounds us. God's Love is the ultimate catalyst for change away from chaos as proved by the order set into motion throughout the Universe. God is the source of all wisdom and understanding, and it can transform our lives in ways we never thought possible? When we understand the gravity of our creation and all that went into our maintenance and improvement, we begin to see a glimpse of God's unlimited Love.

Against incredible odds, we get to experience God's Love through this life, and through our conscious experience of it in this realisation, we know we are Loved and are made greater lovers of others. Remember that we cannot help without a position of strength and something to give. This is that strength, above all other things. There are other strengths, but this piece is the biggest. For this strength, our egos and attachments to imperfections must be lost, as we elevate out of the morass of self-absorption and Victimentality, with love, compassion, and reason reigning above all other things. This was never something impossible in Christianity despite what some blind leaders may claim, simply traditionally reserved for those advanced with knowledge and practise.

This need not be esoteric, and must become more generally known. The catch is that the transformation aligning the self with Christ isn't easy, obviously, as theosis is an internal godly process in experience. Unlike empty promises, it requires us to confront our deepest fears, doubts, and false self-beliefs. It requires the development of the virtues through reason, with the completion in willpower, which is finally surrendered to the Will of God, in His higher reason. The scars of our lessons in life must not leave us, as these are the things which lead us away from selfishness and self-absorption.

This is exactly what we have always needed and craved. The chaos of the world is a crying out for order. Humanity cries for order as well, through all this chaos. Order is the recipe for alleviating disorder and chaos, obviously. God provides this through man himself, as granted life and dominion. The dominion is in intervention as higher purpose, which is to say those elements of being human most above the animal and materialistic desires. Since it is God's Love that is the only thing that can bring about true change of an individual, it is God's Love that can bring about order. Order and spirit go hand-in-hand because of this, as do moderation and reason against chaos. It is completely true, and I will tell you why.

Reason and constant practise in LOGOS inevitably lead to the revelation of not simply God but God's limitless Love. God's Love is the perfect Sign, as it leads to ever greater and greater wisdom. His Love for us is proved through our living spirit with our abilities in reason and direct attachment in our beings to Christ, His only-begotten Son born of the virginal Holy Spirit, so beloved. God's Son is repeatedly sacrificed in the form of the Son of man, Human life in generation after generation, for mankind's ultimate improvement. This is the primary presentation of His Perfect Love, which is the very reason for our births.

If this is True, and I assure you it is, then our lives have ultimate meaning and extremely important purpose. Once we fully realise the gravity of this information, we have little choice but to express this same Love for ourselves, which means holding ourselves to the very highest of standards, and then holding others to those same standards. It means demanding the best of ourselves, as individuals and as communities. These standards are held to others in a loving, graceful, and patient way as imitation of Christ, having seen how truly horribly difficult it is as materialists who have yet to see the Light, Sooth.

Sacrifice the Self

Either you sacrifice yourself or you sacrifice all. The decision hangs precariously in the balance. A choice that separates the wheat from the chaff, the true from the false, and the self from many of its own limitations, but all the better for overcoming them, in gratitude. Is this a mere mortal's attempt to shed their ego, their pride, their very being? No, not in this context. When we sacrifice ourselves, we are not giving up our earthly trappings, but doing best by them in actuality; we are shedding the parts of ourselves least aligned with Christ. We are acknowledging the imperfections, the weaknesses, and the doubts that hold us back from the best successes.

Through Christ, we have the highest expectations for our lives. It's a call to greatness, to excellence, for perfection (verb). It's only when we embrace this calling, this LOGOS-owned path, that we can truly sacrifice the parts of us that are holding us back. We must analyse our thoughts, our emotions, and our actions, in order to bring them into alignment with God's Will through Christ. What happens when we don't take this step? When we settle for mediocrity, for complacency, for mere existence? Ah, then we lose everything, don't we? We sacrifice the very potential that lies within us, the dreams that we've yet to fulfil, the impact that we could have on the world. All Good is in potential because all energies eventually derive from potentialities. All energy, future, past, and present are in potentiality. We sacrifice our very purpose and meaning by not taking up our potential, that cross we bear philosophically through our love of God, and following Christ.

Outside of time, and eternal, is God's Love, as proved through Holy Spirit, which, from our limited perspective, is actually no different in experience from the living energy and consciousness - subconsciousness or superconscious complex most humans simply take for granted. God is all potentiality and in all energy. Getting angry at God for not intervening the way you think He should, in your limited understanding, is no different from a man being mad at the gym, the gym managers, his future self, or past self for not leaving the gym earlier, or staying too long, or not going at all, or eating mountains of fattening foods.

Abandon your ego and self-ignorance, discover the higher self in the Light of Christ instead, the only One True Personality and that narrow Way which moves us away from our imperfect circumstances, to take ownership. For in so doing, we will be transformed, renewed, and reborn in the image of Christ, but only in such ways which maximise our utility to God, and for Good, obviously. This means we must always be on the lookout for improving our ability to see and accomplish Good, but also that this is the only freedom available to humanity, in ability to recognise and do Good. This is all that Christ can speak to you on, and this is where we can stay in the Light. Follow the Good, strive for it, and you will inevitably feel the material within yourself attempting to draw you away again.

Sacrificing the self is not a negative act; it's the ultimate liberating one. It frees us from limitations and distractions imposed upon us by the material reality and our requirements. When we do, we open ourselves up to the infinite possibilities in Christ, in God, and in all Good. The choice is clear: either you sacrifice the least of yourself and become the best version through Christ, or you sacrifice all and settle for a life that's less than what you're capable of. The decision is yours alone but God's Love remains.

Theosis Imperative in LOGOS (Christ)

The madness of the human condition has always involved this never-ending quest for meaning, driven by false songs of our own egos or self-doubts goaded along by illogical thoughts and incorrect beliefs. Typically, this leads one to being lost in the deserts of self-obsession. The only true pursuit is the alignment. The greatest obsession that one can have, in fact, is in the alignment with the One. This is done through Christ, LOGOS, and no other means. This is internal and external discourse as guided by Christ, it is the Word. To be in constant prayer is actually to be in active discourse towards the greatest Good, which is to say directed toward God.

In Luke 15:17, the prodigal son is said to have come to himself, as Hellenic language expression of coming to one's own senses. What is the deeper meaning behind "to come to one's self?" When I approach someone, it will be for some reason, some purpose. When we come to ourselves and speak to ourselves, we are doing so over some purpose, and this is a common thing to do. However, what would it mean to come to ourselves for purpose of ourselves?

Well plainly, anything short of improvement and honest criticality would be pointless. This would not actually be coming to the higher self but coming once more to material in self for self obsession. The purpose of coming to the higher self can only be in improvement, which is only done through Christ. That is also the meaning of coming to one's senses, in fact, which is to say avoiding stagnation and regression generally.

The sheer chaos of the world, the overwhelming bodily chemical nature of our own material desires, and the circus of distractions surrounding us at every turn: all these serve to obscure our vision and cloud our judgment. What if we were to silence the voices, to quiet the tempests of demonic generation outside of God? What then would remain? The stillness, the calm, and the presence of God, if we can truly find that silence only possible through Christ's reason and moderation.

It is in this stillness that we find ourselves in the Light and out of the darkness of that pit in self-obsession and Victimentality. For when we are in constant prayer, in active discourse with Christ, we are directed toward the greatest Good, freedom through God Himself. This is not a passive act, but an active pursuit, a striving to be one with the One. The darkness inside dissipates, and the pure potentiality that was always there, though invisible, is all that can remain, but now 'visible' through the directedness in Christ. The more that this can be channelled, the greater the inspiration toward Good possible.

What of the turmoil pervading everything in the material? This too is transformed when seen through the lens of Christ. This being is akin to residing upon the 'stoa,' as a launching off point for all events. For He is the LOGOS, the Word as born into the World through the material, and it is through Him that we are given the power to transcend, and to rise above the suffering imposed in material reality by the mortal conditions of our births.

Everyone must choose whether to choose the sure bet or continue down that rabbit hole of self-obsession, chasing after fleeting pleasures and momentary thrills. The sure bet, in embracing Christ, is allowing ourselves to be transformed by His constant presence. The world is not simply as it appears, as our perceptions were never adapted to anything outside survival. Even in the midst of chaos there is a proof in its opposite, in the stillness and calm that guides us toward the greatest Good. This presence in LOGOS, if listened to, will impose theosis and move one towards the One God.

It begins by admitting our ignorance and weaknesses, to ourselves most primarily, to accept the truths in the Word made flesh, embodied through Christ-like actions. Accept the greater truths inherent in Word made flesh, as materialised, and continuously so through imitation of Christ. All are part of Christ's body, in imitation serving each other within the communities ("churches"). Make community the body of the Word made flesh, as empowered through strength and reason in Christ. Do not tarry. Rush now, race to fully take up your cross entirely.

Crucifying Self & Imperfections

When we second guess ourselves and analyse the real origins of our actual motivations in sin, we begin to see how the sacrifice of self, occurring in all things on a daily basis, are not actually sacrifices of any note. The crowd, in self-obsession and celebration, called for the death of the Saviour, repeatedly, and then even recommended a replacement be saved, another man with an apparently identical name, who was "Jesus, son-of-the-father," that is 'Barabbas' so-called.

So who are you? Are you a reveller in the crowds calling out a name which sounds like the Saviour's? Or are you one who wishes to properly identify Christ? Would you have joined in with the throng of the pleasure seeking mob, or would you have offered yourself up in Christ's place? That very choice is presented before you today. Will you fall for the false representation of Christ or submit all to the truly divine Christ?

What is this juggling act of self-justification, where we attempt to balance our insecurities against the ceaseless dirge of our material nature and wants when they are the same thing? It's a precarious yet ultimately pointless tightrope walk, one that always ends in a messy tumble into self-obsession. Without a constant dedication to Christ's godly discourse, the self can only be justified in some false balance between materiality or more material obsessions. A true humility in the mind of Christ is the only way to short-circuit the self-obsessed distractions, to silence the noise of ignorance, and to place insecurities firmly in Christ with Honesty.

Much has been discussed in this book about masculinity, camaraderie, friendship, and community, but you must first be able to withdrawal into the self in order to do any of this, from silence to organisation. It starts with acknowledging the imperfections, the cracks in our armour. For it is only when we confront the reality of our own fallibility that we can begin to see the world through different eyes. Anything less is a poor substitution, much like Barabbas.

If you tell yourself you are saved by Christ no matter what else you do, who are you fooling? Did you think that was the deal Christ would have made? God does not make things for nothing, so you must ask, what is the purpose of the Grace, and what was the purpose in your creation? Didn't Christ say that the part of you connected to God is divine? Do you doubt Him? What did you imagine that part to be? Do you so flagrantly imagine things less deserving than God to be of God? Barabbas's crowd may call out for the salvation of a false messiah in vain and for nothing, in pure nihilism and physical obsession, but they're just looking for their own reflection and so that works for those needs, as worthless as they may be. Bad identification all the same. In victimhood, what people primarily see is themselves, and all that has been done to them.

The glorification of victimhood leads to Victimentality, the self-identification as a permanent victim accursed by the very existence or presence of oppressors. The sacrifice first required of you isn't some grand gesture, but rather the daily surrender of your ego in the realisation of your imperfections, so you may begin to recognise perfection. The purpose in recognising those imperfections serves no other purpose but to humble you before Christ, so that you may accept the godly discourse and realise the Mind of Christ.

There's a firm existential comfort to be found from acknowledging that our existence is but a fleeting yet vital piece in the puzzle larger than we could hope to see completely. It's a perspective that strips away the illusions of control and mastery, leaving us with nothing but the best Good in the present moment, and how to connect it. Gift yourself the present by making it Good. This present is all we truly have, the future is perfectly uncertain besides what we make of the present. There's not much to see but mirages on the horizon, and the past serves best as a collection of memories with powerful lessons attached; the memories slowly fade into oblivion outside what we are able to retain in understanding and wisdom. You find peace in the quiet simplicity of the here and now, above all by doing Good in this present. Do Good now.

The choice is always yours. Following the revelling crowd, chasing after shadows and false reflections in that pit of self-obsession, is a fast path to disappointment. Calling after a false god in Victimentality sets you up to accept your failure and identify yourself with the victimhood and subsequent non-action. Do you believe there is nothing you can do in this World, or do you accept all that it means to be Loved by God? What does it mean to find Christ? What is the point of finding Christ if you do nothing with it? Doing nothing is the same as not having found Him at all. Did you think that all this Love from God would come without any responsibilities? Did you think God thought you were important for no reason at all? Would you believe these are lies designed to make people complacent and stagnant, unwilling to commit to justice if it means changing the structures of societies?

So what of the Hyksos? What was the point in all those calamities brought upon Egypt? According to records from the Amarna letters and other findings, there is evidence that this Mes fellow, whatever his actual name, was a high priest in the service of Aten. This makes a lot of sense, as Mes presents himself as a religious leader and businessman willing to negotiate deals, such as with the Hyksos tribals, at the Egyptian court, at Mt. Sinai, in the deserts, and for the promised land.

His sojourn into the distant territory of Midian with marriage to one of seven daughters of a priest names Reuel appears to be a thinly veiled allusion to his tenure as high priest for Akhenaten. It appears that there was a plague and this Mes guy appears to have been either afflicted himself, as demonstrated by the description of his changing skin, and helping secure diseased people so they could avoid being massacred, or he was an agent of the pharaoh motivating these people to leave. The former is most likely. The account claims he stayed with Reuel until the passing of the pharaoh, which also matches with Mes having worked for Akhenaten until his death. Obviously Mes used the occurrences of plagues and other events to create a weak yet apparently effective theological argument for why a bulk of the Hyksos should follow him, so he should not have been surprised that they were worshipping a golden calf. It is likely that the 40 years in the desert may have referenced a required die off of a generation. The origins of this story appears to do with a plague of leprosy befalling a population, whom were rejected entrance to a land because of it, for at least a generation.

Worship in Christianity was shifted to a golden calf in the victimhood and idolisation of the victimhood in and of itself. The hypocrisy! People are attracted to the spectacle of suffering, mesmerised by theatre and shadows instead of the most important elements in lessons and greater understandings. Mes should have known better, too, apparently. He thought he could conjure up a theological argument out of thin air, convincing the Hyksos to follow him with promises of milk and honey: material benefits. They had other ideas, according to the narrative in Exodus, like worshipping a 'golden calf,' again benefits in the material.

What's the difference between this materialists and our fellows obsessed with victimhood who idolise suffering of Christ in itself for its own sake? Plenty, but both groups are in quicksand, where every step forward sinks deeper into the muck. The only way out of this quicksand is in moderation, being still, and calmly extracting the self with the parts of the body that can move, first. The plague of leprosy of the manipulated Exodus story may have ravaged the population, but it's nothing compared to the spiritual rot that infects our very souls in Victimentality, however people try to justify it. We're too busy chasing after fleeting pleasures and superficial answers to address the real issues. What does it mean to be idolaters? How many generations have had to die off in this spiritual rot? How many more are we going to allow? Do we have much longer before extinction?

The moving pleasures and material, that is the bodily expressions demanded for survival, have always been known to be the lesser in terms of civilisation, society, and culture. The spiritual is plainly known to be of higher value than the material. It was thus most common for various religious adherents to somehow ritually clean the body before entering any temples. Of course, such rituals were still practised by Christians, most especially in baptism. However, it was Christ who popularised the notion of body as the temple itself. What does this mean though?

The arguments used by most theologians are weak, yet effective in schisms for those enamoured of the flesh open to any excuse for their next lustful foray or stupid decisions in life to do with continuing in error. Materialism disguised as religion, while everything burns, is not of the Spirit. They conceive of the spiritual as series of excuse making to justify themselves no matter what horrific things they actually do. Yes it is faith alone, but real faith and it goes both ways.

What do we get out of this? A bunch of half-baked ideas, fatherless children, broken homes, criminality, and a lot of nothing. God resides within you, and yet you believe in theologians offering ungodly things and salvation that is not theirs to assign. What do you crave from this life? Is it something material no different from that of a baboon or imbecile? Does that satisfy you at your core or do you wish for more? What motivates you?

The individual who finds Christ wishes for the whole of their society to do the same, in fact the whole World, actually. When a man rejects self-obsession, he puts himself upon the cross to cross-examine all deeds, and when his society rejects him and his forwarding of Christ's messages instead of putting themselves upon the cross as well, they themselves put Christ on the Cross all over. Either we crucify ourselves or we crucify Christ, this is the end result, because our lives can either stand as testament to the One Perfect Personality or our own imperfections which we ignorantly refused to uproot. Either you submit to progress and improvement in Christ's active perfection, or you submit yourself to failure, the opponent, and active imperfection. In those great depths of self-absorption, we often mistake our own desires for the purpose of existence. Like moths drawn to the bright lights of our own ego, we neglect the far greater radiant glow in the divine that illuminates all Creation, all Life.

We have strayed as a society, letting the most precious among us telling the greatest truths to be tortured and killed for it. The Cross is not simply about Christ's death, it is about us allowing the best in society to be killed by not overcoming weakness. It's symbolic of a progressive reality concrete in overcoming weakness, which disrupts the self-absorbed Victimentality that poisons society. It's the moment when humanity's greatest Hero gave Himself over, showing the Way in surrendering to the Will of the Father, as founded in perfecting Love.

This radical act of self-sacrifice redefines what it means to be human, revealing a deeper purpose and meaning that transcends our petty concerns, and is the very bedrock of civilisation, heralding the Divine Paternity itself. In the Light, our existence is no longer reduced to a series of random and anonymous events or chance encounters as it is within materialist so-called philosophies. Instead, we find ourselves embedded in a grand narrative that's both beautiful and terrible; we take part in the greatest story of Love, sacrifice, and redemption, which speaks directly to the core of being.

As we gaze upon the Cross with this broader perspective, we're forced to confront our own self-worship and the idols we've constructed in place of God and God's wisdom. We see that our own desires mean nothing compared to the eternal purpose that animates all existence. We can build our own personal domain, sacrificing the greater good on the altar of perceived self-interest. The better option is to surrender, take up our cross, and follow Christ. This is a call to live out the deeper meaning of our existence, building up the celestial domains.

Helping from Positions of Strength

When Christ spoke of those stumbling the little ones, He meant more than just children. He meant those as yet still weak in the

Spirit, who have yet to realise their full comprehension and the full faith that comes from it. This was a promise in the guise of a threat, however, and He meant it. Those who empower themselves by turning the weak in faith away from God's Word against their better intentions, are the most in danger, and I am obviously not simply talking about the books in the bible as altered and then so received. When a person is driven away by the outward presentations of things and has been tortured with 'Christian' artefacts their entire life, presenting the Words of God, as in the content and actual Words of God from your mouth personally, would make all the difference rather than impersonally presenting Words of God as packaged within an entire book. When things get difficult it is typically because we missed a lesson somewhere, and we all do this at times.

The best thing you can do in the eyes of God is enable others to recognise and do Good, and that is God's greatest work for you. Many modern theologies specifically do not encourage people to do this, some presuming that everyone is going to be saved or not. What greater work could there be with the Word, LOGOS? In reality, we should not cause the weak among the believers to stumble, and the very plain implication is this stumbling of the weak in faith drags others down as well. Your book collection of God's Words is truly amazing and thank God we have it, but are you idolising that binding and invoking a false "millstone" Christianity? What about the speaking of and active participation with God's Word?

Do not be fooled into any material theologies that drown by ignoring the plight of the weak and presume they are destined to fail, instead of given all the wrong conditions to recognise the Good. At their cores, many of these theologies are basically a denial of the power in the Light of Christ. You, being a saved person capable of it, must help others, and it won't be through any books, or anything else in the material. It will be what has filtered through to that precious mind of yours. Were you destined for this? Destined for what? To stand there like a bump on a log as the weak drown? Or destined to make yourself an instrument of God? How do you make yourself a spiritual instrument when you cannot put down the material instruments and be used by God directly? The part of you that touches God is conditioned by it, as stated so eloquently by Marcus Aurelius. Some can do greater Good than others, but you never know until you try in humility.

God gave control of material to a material forces, and there are two sides to it which is why it is confusing, because up to half the time you may feel cared for. The oppositional side of this force is evil by spiritual standards, however the evil that prevails in this world of materials and error as sins has primary causes stemming from within, which is allowed to take over the soul through weakness with fleshly desires and denial of God through Holy Spirit. Without moderation in life, we cannot hope to have the moderation in Spirit necessary to overcome the temptations triggered within. Without the Light to help you understand what is real and of God, you will be lost in demonic darkness, and this is the clearest way I can phrase this.

Would it not be the very height of idolatry to claim an alternative meaning in God being the Father than as the Model for healthy families and peaceful society? Is this not precisely what is done when the father is denigrated in modern media and culture? Who could possibly be so brazen and foolish to deny the wisdom in the order of families and communities, as they have naturally developed? What are the things that set humanity most apart from the great multitudes of creatures in creation? Is not the active and emotional involvement of the father perhaps the primary difference above all others? Could this be the most deciding factor in the history of civilisation? I would argue that the history of Europe and its sociological order formed around close family ties cannot be overlooked, especially at the heights of civilisation. Similarly, the most materially successful cultures have always had special arrangements to inform masculine greatness, especially through community. Rebuilding natural masculine order in society has the most potential for building mutual support and uplifting the maximum number of people, and is the best position for these ultimate strengths.

What greater things could be given to somebody with weaknesses than a motivation and pathway toward strengths? Could there be greater strengths, as a platform, from which to help others than the internal virtues? It stands to reason that the strengths that we hold internally determine the sorts of strengths that we will demonstrate materially. It is vital to build ourselves up before seeking to lift others up, an alternative will be disastrous. Interconnectedness is individual, family, community, town, county, state, and national. All must be strengthened in order for humanity to help humanity, and there is absolutely no excuse not to outside basically genocidal interests.

The only truly transformative power for the individual is in embracing the true self, as gifted by God in life, and surrendering to Christ's Way. The most important act for the individual is to prioritise Christ and His Divine Discourse as Word of God, above self-obsession and our imperfect personalities. The God's honest Truth is that you can either crucify yourself and your own imperfections upon your cross, or you will end crucifying Christ all over. The presence of your life force is already proof of God. Either your life is a testament to the Truth in Christ, or your life is a testament to the error in personality or the imperfections you were born with, and you continue to bear of your own decision. In the end, there is only One perfect personality, with everything else falling short. God cannot use you laying down or dead, similarly, He cannot use our society if it is trampled and destroyed. All things are possible in God and your faith in God, not through you but through Christ.

Homework:

This final homework section is most important of all to accomplish multiple times, and on a regular basis, preferably.

Undo Stuck, Stumble, & Stagnant

What are some aspects of your life where you feel stuck or stagnant? Are there any patterns or habits that contribute to this feeling, and what might be the underlying causes driving them?

Think about a time when you felt trapped and "stumbling" or struggling to recognise and do good. What were some key factors that contributed to this experience, and how did your internal dialogue change your understanding of the situation? How has this dialogue changed? How would you handle such a situation differently now?

In what ways have you "idolised" material things (books, devices, foods, vehicles, fortune, fame, etc.) in your life? Are there any deeper longings driving these desires, and what might be the consequences if these desires are left unexamined? What can you do to change your desires? Could anything stop you if your desires were aligned to your goals planned in the light of the Good you have best identified in moderation?

Journal Prompts

Write about a time when you felt especially connected to or disconnected from spirituality. What were some key factors that contributed to this experience, and how did it change your understanding of yourself and the World around you? Are there any contradictions or tensions within this experience that you can explore further?

Reflect on the concept of strength in your own life. How do you define strength, and what are some areas where you feel strong? What might be the results if you were to shift focus to development of other strengths, and what new possibilities might emerge as a result?

Imagine yourself standing before Christ, surrendering your imperfections and weaknesses. What would this look like in your daily life if you were to surrender yourself this way, and what steps can you take to prioritise His Way over your own desires? What are the competing goods involved, and how can you satisfy as many as possible? How can you reasonably select something genuinely Good for yourself which also helps others through it?

Practical Applications

Set aside 10-15 minutes each day for the next week to reflect on your thoughts, feelings, and actions. Write about something specific you are grateful for, and then explore how your daily actions might demonstrate that gratitude for yourself or someone else. What could you change in your life to increase how much you demonstrate this gratitude? Grace can also mean praise in a friendly way. What would be praised most about you? How can you praise your friends for the Good they do?

Identify one area in your life where you tend to be self-absorbed or obsessed with material things. Commit to making a small positive change this week that will allow you to better serve others, explore how this has helped you and others, then consider continuing and doing more, repeat: change one thing to allow you to genuinely empower others the next week, and so on.

Take some time to read and reflect on the book of John in the Bible. What insights do you gain about God's character and relationship with humanity? Are there any contradictions that stand out? What does it say about humans and humanity, as well as our place in the order of the Father? It should not be what is typically taught.

Struggle

How might our experiences of struggle and imperfection be seen as opportunities for growth and transformation, rather than simply sources of shame or embarrassment? What role do relationships and community play in this process, and how can we support one another in our paths toward greater wholeness while still allowing for strengths to be built up, which is to say 'without coddling each other' to suffocation?

In what ways have you seen people or communities struggling due to a lack of moderation in life? How does moderation improve your ability to reason, in the material and when thinking? How might we encourage each other toward greater balance and spiritual growth, and what are some potential pitfalls to avoid along the way?

What does it mean to build yourself up before seeking to lift others up, and how might this process be influenced by our relationships and community? Are there any contradictions or tensions within these ideas that you can explore further?

Personal Challenges

For the next two weeks, commit to setting aside time each day for prayer and reflection in meditation. Write down three things you are grateful for each day, and then explore how these experiences might be interconnected or contradictory. How might reserving certain extreme words such as "love" or "hate" demonstrate greater gratitude towards beloved people?

Identify one person in your life who is struggling or feeling stuck. Offer them a listening ear or practical help without expecting anything in return, and explore the outcomes of this decision on your relationships and priorities. Are you glad that you did this?

Take on a small creative project (e.g., writing a short story or painting a picture) that allows you to express yourself authentically and surrender to the process. Explore the motivations and desires driving this project, and what new possibilities might emerge as a result. How can you incorporate your lessons above about improvement, love, and community?

THE GOOD ENDING

Postface

I will end here describing another story as the book began in the preface, but this one quite different. It's about you, and written by you. It stars you as the protagonist, but also involves you overcoming an antagonist who is the greatest nemesis you could ever know: you again actually, keep up here :)... the biggest issue with this nemesis is that it thinks it knows better than Christ, doubts God, and thinks there is comfort falling back into its imperfections. It pretends to love you by make believing all your little imperfections as idiosyncrasies that make you cute or endearing, rather than challenges. Do not listen. This is the first voice of the nemesis within, leading to still ever deeper layers of ego petting, without any actual Good.

What if this nemesis was not just a 'personal' demon, but a logical consequence of the natural material flaws that burden all of humanity? The nemesis questions God's existence, doubts Christ's wisdoms, and seeks external validation instead of finding it within. In an important way, the nemesis represents the task of reconciling our inherent contradictions, an eternal struggle to express the spirit over the material. In moving toward God, we follow His Word, which leads the narrow Way. The nemesis is perfectly ignorant of this, and could never understand. In fact, it will always openly mock it. If you feel yourself cringing at any part of this, that is your nemesis mocking and blocking.

In contest with my own nemesis over the years, I realise that true victory can only be achieved by embracing our true selves in spirit and activating our skills in working around imperfections, while seeking after constant improvement discoursing with LOGOS. The nemesis can be managed. It is integral to our material being, at the survival level, and so this management is how we ultimately conquer it. There is no destruction of this nemesis inside. Instead, it's a perpetual dance of integrations and rejections variously, as we continually confront the contradictions within ourselves, not allowing the nemesis to cast the World as contradictory instead. The World as created is not actually contradictory, but we and our expectations are due to our partly material and partly spiritual nature.

Managing our material is a process of healing the spirit from the trauma of self-denial. This is a procession of cleansing, and it is Good. You are supposed to use the nemesis as an instrument to hone yourself against the material confusion which causes evil. Widen your understanding and patience for others, and you will understand the purpose in the first steps in virtues toward honesty, which includes managing the bodily attachments. Be thankful for the challenge and grateful for the opportunity in life to be Good. The point is to "get Good," as gaming communities like to say... Get Good, indeed, and thank God for the opportunity!

Listen to your enemies,

There's truth in their words.

Civilisation, communities,

& peace are enslavement forms;

Servitude to others. Questions be:

Who decides what you serve in your works?

What is **DONE** with your labours, contributees?

What does your life? What does your labours?

....

"We are what we repeatedly do. Excellence, then, is not an act, but a habit."

~Aristotle

"Trust in the Lord with all your heart and lean not on your own understanding; in all your ways submit to him, and he will make your paths straight."

~Proverbs 3:5-6

"What should you do then, brothers and sisters? When you come together, each one has a song, has a lesson, has a revelation, has a tongue, has an interpretation. Let all these things be done for the strengthening of the church."

~Apostle Paulus (1 Corinthians 14:26)

....

Empires all crumble,
Under own overborne weight.
One another, feet stumble,
To dust, material hate.
Greed decreed & subtle,
Waste potent & sate.

Stunt deed with cudgel,
Before it can create.
All these minds fumble,
Nature's gifts in taint.
In uniting, we mumble,
Yet divided we debate.
In discourse, arise humbled,
To retake our fates.

About the Author

Dr. Marcus Roe is a father of five, husband to his perfection, and a thinker for Good. He is a man of careful thought, mind spiritually rooted in the depths of philosophy and psychology. Thoughts bloom forth with the rarest mixture of empathy and reason.

How did Dr. Roe come to concern himself with culture, individuals, victimhood, and communities? The answers are embedded into his very soul by way of fatherly influence, spiritual devotion, and a philosophical fervour all driving his energetic and passionate disposition. It is what he has tried to summarise in this very book.

His father, a minister and teacher of unyielding devotion, exemplified the highest order of servant-leadership. His mother was the quintessential dutiful mother, omnipresent and forever available. Selflessness was the order of his youth, as he witnessed his parents sacrifice all for others, in his parents he saw exemplars of many Christian virtues.

Calming reassurances in his parents' basic commitment to the greater good imbued our author with the same. As a result and after years of living it while funding his own way through college, Marcus now has a profound sense of purpose: to empower people and liberate them from the impersonal shackles of bureaucracy, organisational entrapment, and the Stockholm-like social-destruction in cultural victimhood mentalities.

Dr. Roe has spent a great deal of time exploring the dynamics of human behaviour and organisational forms. He became increasingly disquieted by the state of affairs and dove deeper into the underlying philosophical issues. Marcus beheld the ravages of massive faceless fictional entities given rights, unchecked greed by unscrupulous people, the fragmentation of communities, the dissolution of culture, and the erosion of individual dignity. His philosophical soul screamed out... to say the least of it.

Thus began his quest for answers, an odyssey through the minefield of religious and philosophical history to arrive at truths in the mysteries of human nature and social order. He synthesised his experiences and understandings from the very best of spiritual and philosophical wisdoms to distil a spiritual phenomenology which has served as a backbone for the Structural Theory of Virtues, as well as a journal devoted to the science of virtues. Amidst all this theory, he has constructed a book which began with his journey and was finished just recently, this very one you are holding now.

The backdrops of Resurrexit Spiritus Phenomenology, Spiritual Mate Selection Theory, First Other Theory, and Structural Virtues Theory serve as a guide in what we should do, while this book is about how to help everyone stop doing what we should not do, what got us into this mess. Dr. Marcus Aurelius Roe has a bold and inspiring vision in empowering people, businesses, and communities to overcome the criminal organisations and cultural Stockholm abuse. His plan is about herd immunity to the disease of these outside controls through the building up of virtues and stakeholdership, expedient marketplaces, sustainable interdependence, and progressive community culture. Insights are aplenty in this premiere published work.

He can currently be found working on many projects at once, including sequels to this book, an experimental novel, and an extremely oversized book on his explorations into religious history.

Prayer of Empowerment

Dear Lord, whose wisdom exceeds all comprehension, as I sit here in silence, my mind awhirl in the chaos of humanity's trials amid infinite order, I am reminded of Your boundless mercy and Love.

O Lord, You redeem all sorrow, and wrap me in gratitude. I confess I know not what specifically I should pray for, yet I come to You, dear Lord, in hope for Your Guidance and in humility, praying that my weaknesses deserve expedience and Your strength.

Through You, and only You, I am better than I used to be, but not as good as I will be. Save me, oh gracious God, with Your Guidance and from the distractions which keep me from Your Word, and from growing through You.

Grant me wisdom to recognise the whispers of Your Spirit within my heart, that I may hear Your gentle voice above the din of roaming thoughts. I pray impart unto me what is best for Your tasks.

Grant me clarity to see through the veils, that I may walk in faith and not by sight alone.

Grant me the humility to recognise that my daily struggles are tedious compared to the vast expanse of humanity's sufferings.

If I do nothing with the knowledge of Your Love, it's the same as never knowing it.

Help me to see beyond my own pain and to extend compassion and empathy to those who walk alongside me on this journey of life.

Oh, Lord, I pray for those who struggle with the weight of their own crosses.

Give them clarity in their charge, and grant them the peace that surpasses all. May they find solace in redemption and restoration.

As You empowered Paulus's words of encouragement, so too, I pray that You would use me as a vessel to empower others.

Grant me the courage to speak truth to lies, to stand against the forces of deception and despair, and to shine Your Light on a world in darkness so lost.

Sooth.

....

Christ Blesses All,
May He Guide
Us To Expedience.
May He Guide
Us To
GOD